Foreword

Not too long ago, I had the pleasure of playing a week of bridge with Kit Woolsey.

Now anyone who has played with a variety of partners knows that their ability and experience do not necessarily contribute to being a good partner. In Kit's case, however, we had no such problems and our short-lived partnership was a pleasure.

But there has always been a question in my mind about Kit. Every now and then there would be a lull in the action and I would look up to find Kit in some sort of a trance, his head gently nodding, gently bobbing. Eventually, he would come out of it with some play or bid. In spite of the fact that he usually came up with the winning decision, I have often wondered what he was thinking about.

Now I know.

I've certainly played my share of matchpoints and I feel secure that I am familiar with most strategies. Nonetheless, as I read *Matchpoints* I discovered a number of concepts which I had not fully appreciated and I found another group of concepts which had not really been crystalized in my mind.

One topic which had particular appeal to me was a section on slam bidding. Kit offers a number of pertinent points, three of which stick out for special comment.

1. Even at matchpoints, it is not necessary to pig out in six notrump. Quite often six of a minor will prove to be a top or near so. If six clubs is cold and six notrump is only so-so, you will win whenever six notrump fails or when the field gets to game only.

2. If your sequence tells you that three notrump is the best contract and you are already at, say, five clubs before making this discovery, go ahead and bid six clubs. If the field is making +630 or +660, your +620 will be as worthless as −100. Bid six clubs and hope. Not good bridge, but practical matchpoints.

3. In this day of science and more science, I am quite pleased to see someone recommending a throwback to the days of brute blasting.

You hold:

	No one vul			
♠AQ9764	LHO	Partner	RHO	You
♡A6				1♠
◇6	2◇	3♠*	4◇	
♣AJ62				

*Limit raise

Kit suggests that you simply bid six spades. Perhaps you will make it. Perhaps the opponents will save.

Quite crude. I like it.

Other topics range from a discussion to the peculiar problems of matchpoints to ways of creating additional problems for your opponents.

Later, Kit discusses whether to bid game or a partscore and then which game or partscore to bid. Should you play in an obvious four-four fit or should you reject it for three notrump? When should you attempt a four-three fit? Why should your decision differ at matchpoints as opposed to IMP's?

And finally, having negotiated the auction, how should you play it or defend it? In other words, should you go for the overtrick or play safe for the contract? Should you risk an extra undertrick or should you quietly accept down one? Alternatively, should you go all out to defeat their contract or is it sufficient to hold them to the contract or simply limit the overtricks?

All in all, Kit has covered or touched on an enormous number of significant ideas; you will not find such a summary between the covers of any other book.

A word of warning. This is not a book for the casual reader. There are many interwoven concepts and less than a careful reading will not give the reader the full benefit. In fact, a cursory reading may be dangerous. Handle it with care, however, and it will be a rewarding effort.

Michael Lawrence

TABLE OF CONTENTS

Introduction

The majority of events at bridge tournaments are played at matchpoint scoring. Matchpoints is popular because it is only necessary to get a partner rather than a team, and there is enough luck so that a weaker player has a chance to win on a good day.

The average player who plays in a matchpoint event usually understands the basic differences between matchpoints and IMP's, such as the importance of overtricks, the −200 kiss of death score, and the necessity for competing in low-level part-score battles. This is satisfactory for getting reasonable results, but more is necessary to achieve maximum scores from the bidding and play. Winning matchpoint tactics are quite unique, and those players who understand these tactics have a distinct advantage over other players regardless of playing ability.

This book explains these winning tactics in terms the average player can understand. Expert matchpoint players have been using them for years, even though many of these experts don't fully understand the reasons why these actions are successful. Any player who understands and successfully applies the concepts in this book will significantly improve his results in pair games.

The book is divided into five sections. The first section is on general concepts, and explains the overall goals which a matchpoint player is trying to achieve with his choices of bids and plays. It forms the basis from which the rest of the book is built. The next three sections are on constructive bidding, competitive bidding, and defensive bidding. There is a fair amount of overlap between these sections; for example, a constructive auction may suddenly become competitive. The competitive bidding section is the most important, for as we shall see, it is in competitive auctions that most of the matchpoints are won and lost. The final section is on the play of the hand, and explains the thinking process declarer and defenders must go through at matchpoints. Throughout these chapters, the important concepts are explained and then illustrated with several examples, with each example fully analyzed. In this way, the reader is shown how to approach a bidding or play problem at matchpoints.

This book is not a presentation of a bidding system or

philosophy. While some parts of the book may not be applicable to certain bidding methods, for the most part the concepts can be used with any bidding system or style. Bidding systems are used to gather the information with which to make the final decision. The emphasis in this book is on making that final decision correctly and, equally important, making it difficult for your opponents to make the correct decision. No doubt several of my personal preferences will slip into the discussion, but the major points are valid regardless of what bidding system or style is in use. Bidding sequences will be assumed to be "Standard American" unless otherwise specified.

The concepts presented here are the result of years of analysis, and they have survived the test of many sessions of tournament play. In very bad fields, such as some club games, or in unusually strong fields, such as the finals of the Blue Ribbon Pairs, some of the ideas may need modification, but most of them are valid for any pair game. Nothing in this book is gospel, and several of the recommended bids are based on my assessment of a hand which may be quite different from yours. This is particularly true of the review problems at the end of each section. There is not necessarily a right or wrong answer to any bidding situation. Top players whose bidding judgment I have the greatest respect for disagree with me on several of the answers. Our thinking process for analyzing the situations is the same, but a different evaluation of the hand can lead to a different conclusion. Many of the decisions are quite close. It is not so much the answer you arrive at that is important; how you came to your final conclusion is what matters. Learning to think along the suggested lines will improve the results of any player, regardless of his skill level.

GENERAL CONCEPTS

GENERAL CONCEPTS

THE COST OF BEING WRONG

Bridge is a game of decisions. It differs from games such as chess in that the element of chance affects most of these decisions. In chess, the consequences of any decision can, in principle, be calculated to the last detail. There is no factor of the game that is hidden from the player.

In bridge, on the other hand, the location of the unseen cards is an unknown factor. Unless a player can find a line of play or defense which guarantees that the maximum number of tricks available will be taken regardless of the lie of the unseen cards, he has a probability of getting less than the best available score regardless of which play he chooses.

When a player makes a bid or play which produces less than the optimal result on the hand, he is said to have made a wrong decision. This does not mean the player actually made a mistake; only that his decision turned out wrong. If you take a finesse with QJ109 opposite Axxx you are certainly making the correct play, but if you lose to a singleton king you have made the wrong decision, for the alternative play of going up ace does a trick better. If you open 1 NT with ♠J1074, ♡QJ7, ◇AQ5, ♣KQJ and play it there going down one trick when 2♠ in the four-four fit is cold you made a wrong decision with your choice of opening bid, even though it is certainly the correct call. The alternative of opening one of a suit would have been the winning action this time. When we talk about a wrong decision, we mean a decision different from what you would have done had you been able to see all fifty-two cards.

The nature of bridge is such that in a given session any player will make several wrong decisions, simply because he can't see his opponents' cards. It would seem that the goal would be to make as few wrong decisions as possible. This would indicate that, for any decision, the bid or play which has the greatest chance of being right should be chosen. However, this is not always correct. The reason is that some wrong decisions are more costly than others.

Let's look at a simple illustration of this principle from rubber bridge:

NORTH

♠ 6 5 4
♡ A 8
◊ A K 8 5
♣ Q 8 4 2

SOUTH

♠ A 10 8
♡ K J 4
◊ Q 7 4
♣ A K 7 5

Both vulnerable.

NORTH	EAST	SOUTH	WEST
—	—	1 NT	Pass
3 NT	Pass	Pass	Pass

Opening Lead: King of spades

You duck the first trick, but win the spade continuation as East shows out, pitching a heart. When you try the minor suits they both split badly; West started with four diamonds and East with four clubs. West discards spades on the second and third rounds of clubs, and East pitches a heart on the third round of diamonds. Now you lead a heart to the ace and a heart from dummy. Do you finesse or not? This is a silly question. Nobody in their right mind would risk a game contract at rubber bridge for an overtrick. A count of West's hand shows he has six spades, four diamonds, one club, and therefore two hearts. If you finesse and lose to his doubleton queen you are down, while the king of hearts is your ninth trick.

The obvious play of guaranteeing the contract will be wrong 75% of the time, while the heart finesse will be wrong only 25% of the time. Since East started with six hearts and West only two, East is a three to one favorite to hold the queen of hearts. So why do we all choose the play that is likely to be wrong? Because the cost of being wrong by failing to take the finesse is a mere overtrick, while the cost of being wrong by losing to the doubleton queen is a game contract.

What we are trying to do when we play bridge (or any game of imperfect knowledge) is to minimize the expected or average *cost* of being wrong, rather than the likelihood of being wrong. To calculate the cost of being wrong for a particular action, determine the probability of its being wrong and multiply it by how much it would cost if the action were taken and, in fact, were wrong. This cost is the difference between the result of the action in question and the optimal possible result which would be achieved if the winning action were taken.

The cost of being wrong depends on the scoring of the game, which explains why one bid or play might be correct at matchpoints while an alternative action is superior at IMPs or rubber bridge. In the previous example we lose an overtrick worth 30 points if we play the king and are wrong, while we lose the contract, game bonus, and a penalty for a total loss of about 700 points if we finesse and are wrong. So the average costs of the two plays are:

The king: .75 X 30 points = 22½ points.
The jack: .25 X 700 points = 175 points.

This calculation shows what we all know—that the king is clearly the better play, even though it is more likely to be wrong.

This type of reasoning can be applied to everyday decisions in life, and people do go through this analysis even if they don't realize they are doing so. One good example is the decision of whether or not to buy health insurance. Obviously the decision not to buy is more likely to be correct than the decision to buy, since buying is right only if you have a serious illness that year. The cost of being wrong by not buying may be so high, even including possible bankruptcy, that most people choose to pay the

13

cost of buying even though they know that they are probably wrong. Another real life decision is whether or not to exceed the speed limit. Since you are wrong in speeding only when you are caught, which is not likely, and since the cost is only moderate, say $50, many people choose to speed rather than pay the small cost of not speeding (being a little late or driving more slowly than they like). If these same people were driving through a known speed trap, with increased likelihood of getting caught, or if the fine for speeding were very high, say $2,000, the increase in expected cost of being wrong by speeding would cause speeders to stay under the speed limit.

This approach of estimating expected cost can be very helpful when you are trying to find the best percentage play on a hand. For example:

NORTH

♠ Q 7 3
♡ K 2
♢ A Q 4
♣ A K 7 5 4

SOUTH

♠ A K J 4 2
♡ Q J 6
♢ J 8 3
♣ 9 3

East-West vulnerable.

NORTH	EAST	SOUTH	WEST
—	—	1 ♠	Pass
2 ♣	Pass	2 ♠	Pass
4 NT	Pass	5 ♢	Pass
6 ♠	Pass	Pass	Pass

Opening Lead: Ace of hearts.

West leads the ace of hearts and shifts to a diamond. This is clearly his best defense, for you are forced to decide whether or not to take the diamond finesse before testing the clubs to see if they split three-three. The probability of a three-three club split is 36%. We analyze the costs of the alternative plays as follows: If you take the diamond finesse, you will be wrong when East has the king of diamonds. If this occurs you will cost the contract 36% of the time; namely when the clubs split three-three. If you rise with the ace of diamonds, you will be wrong when West has the king of diamonds. If this occurs you will cost the contract 64% of the time; when clubs aren't three-three. Consequently, we must ask the question: is East a 64 to 36 or better favorite to hold the king of diamonds; if so, we play for the three-three club split, if not, we take the diamond finesse. This question is, unfortunately, not too easy to answer. West has an obvious diamond shift if he doesn't hold the king, but if he does he might be wary of the shift for fear that South holds: ♠AKJxx, ♡QJx, ◇Jx, ♣xxx and only the diamond shift allows the contract to be made, for declarer would have no choice but to finesse and later pitch his losing club on the good diamond. Your decision would be based on your table feel and your judgment of West as a tricky or straightforward player, but at least we know what probability figure to use after this judgment has been made. Note that if dummy has the ten of diamonds instead of a small diamond the diamond shift away from the king would be quite safe, so the finesse should be taken unless we judged that this particular opponent could not work out that the shift is safe.

Throughout the rest of this book, as we examine different situations and problems, keep in mind that our goal is to minimize the cost of being wrong. The payment is in matchpoints, so the question to be asked about a possible bid or play is: What is the probability of this bid or play being wrong, and how many matchpoints will it cost (compared to the winning action) if it is wrong? The product of these figures is the expected or average cost of being wrong for a given play, and we want to choose the action which has the smallest expected cost. The determination of these figures can be quite difficult. Proper hand evaluation is needed to estimate the likelihood of being wrong, and understanding matchpoint scoring and what the rest of the field is likely to do is necessary to determine the cost of the action if it is wrong. No matter what type of decision is under consideration minimizing this expected cost of being wrong is our ultimate goal, so this chapter really forms the basis for the rest of the book.

THE MATHEMATICS
OF MATCHPOINTS

Matchpoint scoring is very simple. A pair scores one matchpoint for every other pair holding the same cards whom they outscore on a board, and one-half matchpoint for every pair they tie. Every tournament player is familiar with the scoring. In the heat of battle, however, it is easy to forget what the goal is—to garner as many matchpoints as possible on each hand.

Let's see what this means when we have a decision to make. Since the scoring is in matchpoints, the cost of making a losing decision is also measured in matchpoints. Consequently, the expected cost of being wrong is the probability that the action is wrong times the number of matchpoints the decision costs when it is, in fact, the wrong decision. The matchpoint cost is the difference between the matchpoint score you will receive for your wrong decision and the score you would have received for the winning decision. This expected cost is what we are trying to minimize.

It is apparent that some wrong decisions are far more costly than others, and the cost is not necessarily related to total points scored on the board. If your opponents step out of line and go for a number on a mundane part-score hand and you subsequently misdefend, setting then only 800 instead of 1100, you have lost 300 points but probably zero matchpoints, since +800 is likely to be a top. On the other hand, if you misdefend a 3NT contract and allow your opponents to score 630 instead of 600 it is only 30 extra points, but it will cost several matchpoints if most of the field is in 4♠ for +620. One of the primary goals of this book is to enable the reader to recognize which decisions will cost a larger number of matchpoints when wrong, and which will cost only a few matchpoints.

How does one estimate the cost in matchpoints of a losing action? It isn't easy, but it can usually be done fairly accurately. Let's suppose that we are playing on a twelve top, which is common (a larger top will make the numbers bigger, but it won't af-

17

fect the results). This means that the board is played at twelve other tables against which we will be comparing our score. Suppose that on a hand we have a choice of two actions, A or B, and we choose A when B was the winner; i.e. B would have gotten us a better score. Our cost in matchpoints is as follows: For each table where the result falls in between the score from action A and the score from action B we cost ourselves one matchpoint, since we go from beating their score to losing to their score. For each table where the result is exactly either the score from action A or the score from action B we cost ourselves one-half matchpoint, since we have a tie instead of a win or a loss instead of a tie. For each table where the result falls outside the scores from actions A and B we cost ourselves zero matchpoints, since either both actions beat the other score or both actions lose to the other score. In the latter case, these tables are no longer in competition with us for this hand, as far as our choice of actions is concerned.

Let's look at several hands which show how this reasoning is put into practice:

NORTH

♠ Q 8 6 3 2
♡ Q J 10
◇ A 4
♣ K Q 4

SOUTH

♠ A J 10 9 5
♡ K 5
◇ K 6
♣ A 9 7 2

None vulnerable.

NORTH	EAST	SOUTH	WEST
—	—	1 ♠	Pass
3 NT*	Pass	4 ♣	Pass
4 ◇	Pass	4 ♠	Pass
5 ♣	Pass	5 ◇	Pass
5 ♠	Pass	Pass	Pass

*balanced forcing raise

Opening Lead: Ace of hearts.

A tough bidding decision by South at his final turn, but he chooses not to bid the slam knowing he is off the ace of hearts and deciding, reasonably enough, that slam is at best on a finesse. His analysis is correct; it is exactly on a finesse. It is not an unreasonable slam, and several other pairs figure to bid it. Let's estimate that at six of the other twelve tables the slam will be bid. How should we play the spade suit, assuming that East is a good enough player to duck smoothly with Kx of spades? Many players will say to themselves: "I will have a bad board if the king is onside, since other pairs will be in slam. Therefore, I must hope that the king is offside, so I will play the ace in case it is offside singleton."

Let's try our matchpoint cost analysis and see what we conclude. Our possible plays are the finesse or the drop, and the possible scores for these plays are +450 if wrong and +480 if right. It is clear that the pairs in slam will score either +980 or −50, which are well out of our range, so the cost of choosing the wrong play compared to them is zero. What about the other pairs who stop in game? They, too, will score +450 or +480. Since these match our "right" and "wrong" scores, we lose a half matchpoint to each of them if we take the losing action, whichever one we take. Consequently, the matchpoint cost of both the finesse and the drop if wrong is the same—three matchpoints. Therefore, we should take the play which is least likely to be wrong.

A full matchpoint chart might help emphasize this point. Suppose, again, that half of the field bids the slam, and suppose further that the whole field takes the finesse. Our matchpoints

are as follows:
If we take the finesse:

Finesse works: Three matchpoints
Singleton king offside: Nine matchpoints

If we play for the drop:

Finesse works: Zero matchpoints
Singleton king offside: Twelve matchpoints

This table confirms the previous analysis—we gain three matchpoints by playing for the drop and being right, but we lose three matchpoints by playing for the drop and being wrong.

E-W vul., South holds: ♠10, ♡J53, ◇AQ8743, ♣KJ9

NORTH	EAST	SOUTH	WEST
—	—	—	1 ♠
Pass	2 ♠	3 ◇	3 ♠
4 ◇	4 ♠	?	

Should you save? It would be hard to imagine partner having a 4 ◇ bid that won't provide eight tricks opposite this hand, so the save won't go for too much. The key question is: will they make it? This is not so clear. Most players will simply try to judge if 4 ♠ will make, and if they think it is more likely than not to make they will save. However, a matchpoint cost analysis shows that this is not the correct approach. It would be fine if we could be sure that every E-W pair will bid to 4 ♠, but this is not likely to be the case. Our opponents were sort of pushed to game (remember that everybody won't risk an overcall at the three-level on AQxxxx), so it seems reasonable to assume that at half the other tables game will not be bid—E-W will stop in a spade part-score or possibly sell to 4 ◇. We can assume that 5 ◇ doubled will go for −300 or −500, so our matchpoint costs are as follows:

If we pass and are wrong we cost ourselves one-half matchpoint for each of the six tables at which game is bid, since the score there is −620 (or −300 or −500 if the save is taken there). We cost nothing against the tables at which game isn't bid, since −170 is outside our possible range. Total cost: Three matchpoints.

If we save and are wrong we again lose one-half matchpoint for each table at which game is bid. In addition we now lose one full matchpoint for each table at which game is not bid, since − 140 is between − 300 (or − 500) and + 100, which are our potential scores. Consequently, the matchpoint cost of saving and being wrong is nine matchpoints. Therefore, we are risking nine matchpoints by saving, but only risking three matchpoints by passing. The save doesn't seem justified, for there must be better than one chance in four that they will go down. A typical layout might be:

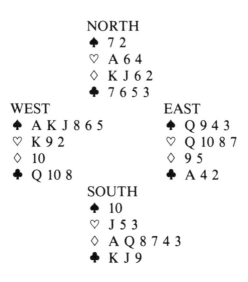

NORTH
♠ 7 2
♡ A 6 4
◊ K J 6 2
♣ 7 6 5 3

WEST
♠ A K J 8 6 5
♡ K 9 2
◊ 10
♣ Q 10 8

EAST
♠ Q 9 4 3
♡ Q 10 8 7
◊ 9 5
♣ A 4 2

SOUTH
♠ 10
♡ J 5 3
◊ A Q 8 7 4 3
♣ K J 9

West must guess the jack of hearts to make 4♠, while South will probably go down three in 5◊ doubled. A further argument against saving is that your overcall, which won't be made at all tables, will get partner off to what is likely to be the best lead for the defense. Consequently, even if 4♠ is cold, you have a chance to gain points from pairs who get off to an inferior lead which gives away an overtrick. You may be well ahead of the field simply by having gotten away with the overcall.

Both vul., South holds: ♠K4, ♡AQ82, ◇QJ74, ♣J109

NORTH	EAST	SOUTH	WEST
—	—	—	Pass
Pass	Pass	1 ◇	1 ♠
Double*	2 ♣	2 ♡	Pass
Pass	2 ♠	Pass	3 ♣
Pass	Pass	?	

*negative double

Now what? The obvious choices are 3♡, double, and pass. Apparently the opponents don't have an eight-card spade fit because they elected not to play in 2♠, and since both opponents are passed hands it is likely that other tables will not receive as much competition and will buy the hand for 2♡. A reasonable assessment of both contracts is that hearts will make eight or nine tricks, and 3♣ will make or go down one, with the probability of each result difficult to estimate accurately. If 3♣ is going down double is obviously the winning action, while if 3♣ is making either pass or 3♡ is better. So what is right?

Let's compare with the most likely result at other tables, 2♡ making either two or three. It is clear that pass is never the best action available; if 3♣ goes down double is the winner, while if 3♣ makes 3♡ should be tried. This does not necessarily mean that pass is not the percentage bid; all it means is that pass is never the double-dummy action. Let's first compare double with 3♡. Double is wrong when 3♣ makes. In this case it costs one-half matchpoint when 3♡ also makes, but nothing when 3♡ fails, since +110 is unattainable (remember, we are comparing with a table which bought the hand for 2♡, the most likely result). The 3♡ bid is wrong when 3♣ is going down. If this is the case it costs one-half matchpoint when 3♡ is making (we tie the +140 instead of beating it with +200), but costs a full matchpoint when 3♡ is going down (we get −100 instead of +200). Since both contracts figure to be close, double is clearly better than 3♡. What about pass vs. double? It is apparent that pass gains nothing over double even when it is right, since −110 will be almost as bad as −670, but pass loses heavily to double when it is wrong, because +110 (or +140) falls between +100 and +200. Consequently double is a standout, although this is far from obvious at first glance. The full hand was:

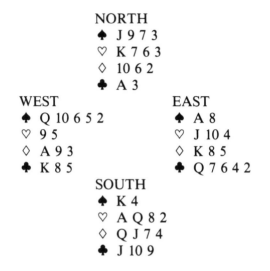

NORTH
♠ J 9 7 3
♡ K 7 6 3
◇ 10 6 2
♣ A 3

WEST
♠ Q 10 6 5 2
♡ 9 5
◇ A 9 3
♣ K 8 5

EAST
♠ A 8
♡ J 10 4
◇ K 8 5
♣ Q 7 6 4 2

SOUTH
♠ K 4
♡ A Q 8 2
◇ Q J 7 4
♣ J 10 9

3♣ doubled goes down one trick after a struggle, while hearts makes nine tricks due to the favorable lie of the E-W hands. Few pairs competed as vigorously as this E-W pair, so the swing between double and pass was almost an entire board.

NORTH
♠ 7
♡ K 7 4 2
◇ 9 5
♣ A Q 9 8 7 4

SOUTH
♠ A J 5
♡ A 10 5
◇ Q 7 6
♣ K J 3 2

Both vulnerable.

NORTH	EAST	SOUTH	WEST
—	—	1 NT	Pass
2 ♠*	Pass	2 NT**	Pass
3 ♡	Pass	3 ♠	Pass
3 NT	Pass	Pass	Pass

*transfer to clubs
**accepting if invitational

Opening Lead: Four of diamonds.

East plays the ten of diamonds on the opening lead and you grab your queen. How nice, a favorable lead for a change! You start to run your clubs, and East discards the king (!) of diamonds on the third club. Not a favorable lead, but a clear blunder by East at trick one. On the last three clubs West pitches the three of hearts, six of hearts, and jack of hearts. This can't really be happening (but it actually did happen—I could never have made up a story like this). Now you can guarantee eleven tricks by cashing the king of hearts and, when West shows out as expected, taking the marked heart finesse. Of course you can garner in twelve tricks by taking the first round heart finesse. This play is virtually certain to succeed, for no player in his right mind would pitch like this from QJxx. So what should you do? Here is a case where you should make a play that is almost sure to be wrong, playing the king of hearts, because the cost of being wrong is probably zero. You have already been handed two tricks, and +660 just has to be a complete top, which it was in real life. The first round finesse will cost several matchpoints if it happens to be wrong, for the defense can now cash some of the tricks that were rightfully theirs. Incidentally, for those of you who are curious, the first round finesse would have won.

There is one situation where you may choose to take an action which doesn't minimize the expected matchpoint cost of being wrong. On the last round or two of a session you may determine that you must get a good score on a board in order to have a chance to achieve your goal for the session, whether it be qualifying for the finals or winning the event. In this case it may be correct to take an anti-percentage action, such as trying to drop the stiff king offside on the first hand in this chapter, since if the slam makes you will not get the necessary good score whatever you do. However, this is seldom a good policy. Even the best estimators are frequently one or two boards off in their estimates, simply due to the innate randomness of bridge players and matchpoints. Consequently, it is rare that you can determine exactly what score is necessary on a given board.

It may seem difficult to estimate accurately what the rest of the field will be doing on a hand, but it is often important to try to make that estimate. Any time you have what appears to be a close choice between two alternatives, consider the possible consequences of these alternatives and compare them with likely results at other tables. You may find that one alternative will cost far fewer matchpoints than the other if it is wrong, and this will guide you in making your choice.

TWO WAYS TO WIN

When you go to a horse race, you bet on a horse to win. If the horse wins the race you get paid, otherwise not. Wouldn't it be nice if, for the same price, you would also collect on your bet if a second horse in the race happened to win. Even if this second horse didn't have much of a chance, it would still improve your probability of cashing in your bet.

When an expert chooses a bid or play, he is always on the lookout for that second horse. His action will usually have a primary way to succeed, but if it fails he likes having another chance. Any action which has more than one way to win is usually a better bet than one which puts all the eggs in one basket.

A well known theme illustrating this is a play which combines two chances, even though each individual chance may not be as good as an alternative play which only gives one chance. For example, consider the following play problem at IMPs:

NORTH
♠ 8 6
♡ J 9 6 5
♢ K J 8 7 4
♣ 7 2

SOUTH
♠ A 2
♡ A 7 2
♢ A 5 2
♣ A K J 10 3

Both vulnerable.

NORTH	EAST	SOUTH	WEST
—	—	2 NT	Pass
3 ♣	Pass	3 ◇	Pass
3 NT	Pass	Pass	Pass

Opening Lead: Queen of spades.

Declarer has six top tricks, and he needs to produce three more tricks from the minor suits without losing the lead. Because there is only one entry to dummy the diamond suit offers better prospects than the club suit, since queen doubleton or tripleton onside is more likely with five cards outstanding than with six cards outstanding. However, the astute declarer who wants to bet on more than one horse will first try to drop the doubleton queen of diamonds, and if that doesn't work he will resort to the club finesse. The chance of the queen of diamonds dropping doubleton combined with bringing in the club suit, is better than betting everything on the diamond suit. The really careful declarer who likes to have as many horses running for him as possible will time the play as follows:

a. Cash the ace of diamonds. If the queen drops singleton he is up to seven tricks, and now has two entries to dummy to take two club finesses for his contract. If not:

b. Cash the ace of clubs. If the queen drops singleton he is up to eight tricks, and simply takes the percentage finesse in diamonds for the ninth trick. If not:

c. Lead a diamond to the king. If the queen comes down, claim. If not:

d. Take the club finesse, and hope for the best in that suit.

Few players realize that it is possible to bet on more than one horse in the bidding, even though they do it all the time. Even a lowly 1♠ opening bid on ♠AQJ53, ♡K98, ◇103, ♣K106 has several things going for it. The primary reason for opening is to start a constructive auction to get to the best contract. However, if it is the opponents' hand or a competitive auction, the 1♠ opening bid has the following horses in the running:

a. The auction starts at a level at which it may be inconvenient for the the opponents to bid constructively.

b. A good sacrifice might be reached.

c. Partner may get off to the best opening lead.

d. The 1♠ opening puts us in command in a competitive part-score fight.

Naturally a player does not bother to think about all these things when he picks up this hand, since the 1♠ opening is so automatic. Anyone can make automatic bids; it is the right decision on borderline hands which separates the winners from the losers. As we shall see later, the previously mentioned factors do come into play when deciding on a borderline action.

Let's consider some common bidding sequences which leave the bidder with two ways to win:

You open with a 3♡ preempt. Your main hope is that it is the opponents' hand (or that they think it is their hand), and that they get to a bad contract because the preempt robs them of the necessary room to investigate. It is not so good if your partner holds the strong hand, but you still might win if he is able to place the contract accurately with the help of the preempt. The bad case is when you are dropped in 3♡ or, still worse, doubled and left there. However, even if you go for a number you still have one last horse to root for — maybe the opponents have a game or slam which outscores the number they collect on defense. This explains why you should tend to preempt less with outside strength. That outside strength may be just enough to stop the opponents from making their game or slam, thus eliminating one of your horses from the race.

The opponents stop in 2♡, and you risk a 2♠ balance. Your main hope is to push them to 3♡, giving you a free shot at a plus score if only eight tricks are available. However even if they double you there is still the chance that 2♠ will make or, as a last resort, if you are not vulnerable you may get out for −100 when they can make their part-score. If you are vulnerable that last horse is eliminated from the race once they apply the ax.

You double the opponents' Stayman bid with KQ109x of clubs. Your main chance for gain is that they ignore you and bid on to their normal contract, and that your double gets partner off to the best lead. However, if they stop off to redouble 2♣, your strong club holding keeps open the additional possibility that they just might not make it. Weaken your club holding just a bit by making the nine of clubs a small club, and the chances

28

of beating them when they redouble diminish considerably.

It must be noted that your extra chance to win often depends on the opponents misjudging a competitive auction. Your opponents need not be weak players; strong players will often go wrong if they are presented with difficult bidding problems. The most difficult players to play against are those who consistently give their opponents problems which don't have clear-cut solutions. What these players are doing, in effect, is making bids which have two ways to win—whichever way their opponent goes he might be wrong. If a competitive bid leaves an opponent no choice then the bid can win only on its own merit; it doesn't have the additional chance of misjudgment by the opponents.

Let's now look at some actual examples of this concept. In each case, look for the action which gives you extra chances to win by giving the opponents problems.

N-S vul., South holds: ♠AQ8, ♡AQ10763, ◊7, ♣AJ5

NORTH	EAST	SOUTH	WEST
—	—	1 ♡	3 ◊
4 ♡	5 ◊	?	

What now? Clearly you aren't going to settle for a penalty against 5 ◊, since eleven tricks should be safe at hearts and you probably can't get them for 700. What about slam? Who knows? It might be cold if North has ♠KJxx, ♡KJxx, ◊xx, ♣Kxx or it might have no play if North has ♠KJxx, ♡KJxx, ◊x, ♣xxxx. If you don't know, neither do your opponents, and they certainly have a good save if your slam makes. Therefore, you should just bid 6♡. You have two ways to win. Your main bet is that slam will make, which it might very well. Even if the slam is going down, you always have the possibility that the opponents may misjudge and take a phantom save, and this second horse turns the borderline decision to bid the slam into a winning percentage action. Note that bidding this way doesn't make it easy for the opponents to decide, for you might choose the same action when you know slam is cold. The full hand is:

```
                    NORTH
                    ♠ K 9 6 2
                    ♡ K J 8 5
                    ◇ 2
                    ♣ Q 6 4 2
    WEST                            EAST
    ♠ J 3                           ♠ 10 7 5 4
    ♡ 9                             ♡ 4 2
    ◇ K Q J 9 8 4 3                 ◇ A 10 6 5
    ♣ 10 7 3                        ♣ K 9 8
                    SOUTH
                    ♠ A Q 8
                    ♡ A Q 10 7 6 3
                    ◇ 7
                    ♣ A J 5
```

It turns out that the slam goes down, but how would you like to be in East's shoes trying to determine that? In practice East took the phantom save, and N-S collected +900 and a well-deserved good board.

N-S vul., South holds: ♠52, ♡A1082, ◇QJ2, ♣QJ107

NORTH	EAST	SOUTH	WEST
—	1 ◇	Pass	1 ♠
Pass	2 ◇	Pass	3 ◇
Pass	3 NT	?	

Should South double? It looks close. The opponents are in a close contract, they are not getting a favorable split in their long suit, diamonds, South has a good opening lead, and any spade strength North has lies over the spade bidder. On the other hand, South doesn't have a long suit to run; he just has to hope the opponents don't have nine tricks. If the double is wrong it will cost one-half matchpoint to other tables in 3NT, if right it will gain one-half matchpoint from these same tables, and there will be no effect on the score against tables where game isn't bid. From this analysis it seems that South should double if he thinks 3NT is a favorite to go down, which makes his decision borderline. However, the double has another way to win. The opponents can't be sure that South doesn't have something like ♠xx, ♡Kxx, ◊QJx, ♣KQJ10x, so they might go wrong and run to 4◊ when 3NT is cold. This second horse makes the close double a percentage action. It might be argued that South would not double with the solid club suit for fear of driving the opponents out of 3NT, but if South is the type of player who will double with both the solid club suit and the actual hand the opponents won't know where they are. The full hand was:

                    NORTH
                    ♠ K Q 9 6 4
                    ♡ J 6 5
                    ◊ 6
                    ♣ 9 5 4 3
    WEST   EAST
    ♠ A 10 8 7   ♠ J 3
    ♡ 7 4 3   ♡ K Q 9
    ◊ K 7 3   ◊ A 10 9 8 5 4
    ♣ K 8 6   ♣ A 2
                    SOUTH
                    ♠ 5 2
                    ♡ A 10 8 2
                    ◊ Q J 2
                    ♣ Q J 10 7

As you can see, 3NT is cold. East was nervous about his club holding, however, and he ran to 4◊. This contract went down one, a huge victory for the double, which gained one-half matchpoint from the other tables in 3NT and a full matchpoint from tables stopping in two or three diamonds. The second horse paid off quite nicely.

N-S vul., South holds: ♠KJ3, ♡AQ103, ◊K105, ♣J85

NORTH	EAST	SOUTH	WEST
1 ♣	Pass	?	

A 2NT response by South, bypassing the heart suit, has a lot going for it. The hand is described fairly accurately in one bid, notrump is played from what is probably the right side, the heart suit is concealed from the opponents possibly resulting in a favorable opening lead, and the non-vulnerable opponents are frozen out of the auction. If N-S do not have a four-four heart fit, 2NT is almost certainly the winning response, so this is South's main bet if he makes the bid. However, the race is not necesarily lost if North has four hearts. While a four-four heart fit will probably produce an extra trick, South's hand is balanced enough that 3NT could still be the winning contract; for example, North might hold ♠Qxx, ♡KJxx, ◇AJ, ♣K10xx. The possibility of 3NT being right if North does have four hearts combined with the clear gain if he doesn't makes 2NT the winning action in my opinion. If South had one more diamond and one fewer club the likelihood of taking the same number of tricks at notrump as in a four-four heart fit would decrease considerably, so the 2NT response loses much of its appeal since the second way to win is very unlikely.

N-S vul., South holds: ♠AQJ53, ♡K84, ◇7, ♣Q852

NORTH	EAST	SOUTH	WEST
—	1 ◇	1 ♠	1 NT
2 ♠	Pass	Pass	3 ◇
Pass	Pass	?	

It might not be immediately obvious, but pass is the bid that has two ways to win. The problem with bidding 3 ♠ is that it puts all your eggs into one basket. West, with his probable trump trick and fair hand opposite his partner's opening bid is virtually certain to double you, and if you go down you are − 200 for a bottom. Are you willing to bet everything on 3 ♠ making knowing that the king of spades is offside? I'm not so sure that I am. Passing, on the other hand, has two things going for it. In addition to the possibility of 3 ♠ going for 200, you have the chance that the opponents may be in the wrong contract—notrump might score more. A look at the actual hand will show how right passing can be:

NORTH
- ♠ 10 9 8 7
- ♡ Q J 10
- ♢ A 5 4
- ♣ 9 6 4

WEST
- ♠ K 6 4
- ♡ 6 5 2
- ♢ K J 9 2
- ♣ K 7 3

EAST
- ♠ 2
- ♡ A 9 7 3
- ♢ Q 10 8 6 3
- ♣ A J 10

SOUTH
- ♠ A Q J 5 3
- ♡ K 8 4
- ♢ 7
- ♣ Q 8 5 2

As you can see, notrump scores +120 for E-W, while diamonds scores only +110. West certainly would have doubled 3 ♠, and this contract goes down 1, −200, the worst possible result. Selling to 3 ◊ was worth a well above average score to N-S.

LOADING THE DICE

All bridge players will occasionally make non-standard or un-orthodox bids. These range from mild deviations such as bypassing a four-card major when responding to partner's opening minor suit bid or opening 1NT with a five-card major, to outlandish bids such as a preempt on a jack-high suit, opening 1NT with a singleton, or an out and out psychic bid. While it is possible to win without ever taking such actions, offbeat bids should be part of a successful player's repertoire. The trick is to know when to use them. Many players simply make these bids when the mood strikes them or when their "table feel" tells them that the time is right. There is a much better approach, which can turn these bids into winning percentage actions.

All non-standard actions come under the more general category of "taking a position". A position could be defined as an action which will lead to an irrecoverably bad board if it turns out poorly. Examples of this are bidding a thin minor-suit slam which the field won't find, doubling the opponents at a low level in the hopes that the penalty is greater than an available sure game, or passing out an opening one-bid in the balancing seat with a fair hand. All these actions risk very bad boards if they are wrong; the justification for them can only be that we think they are more likely to be right than wrong. In other words, we are willing to shoot craps on a board if we think the dice are loaded in our favor.

Now, how can we load the dice in our favor on offbeat actions? The previous chapter gave us the clue. We saw the importance of a bid having two ways to win, so it is equally important that our bids don't give the opponents two ways to win. It is clear that an offbeat bid is in grave danger of getting killed in some way—otherwise, it would probably be the standard bid. The key to making these bids winning actions is to use them only when everything else about the hand is perfect for the bid. If anything else is the least bit wrong, wait for another time. You just can't afford to give the opponents a second way to win on your questionable actions. I call this the double-flaw principle. If a hand is doubly flawed for a bid, try to find some other call.

Next time you are considering opening 1NT with a five-card major, take another look at your hand. Do you have any worthless doubletons? If so, that is a second flaw, and the 1NT bid should not be made. Considering a shaky two-level overcall? Save it for when you are not vulnerable, and make sure that you want that suit led. It would be silly if you got away with the overcall, only to get partner off to the wrong lead. Pondering a really light preempt? Make sure that the vulnerability is favorable, and no queen-doubletons on the side, please. It would be a shame if the opponents doubled you and you got out for less than the value of their game, only to find that their game doesn't make because of that queen.

The following hand, which I held some time ago, is a perfect illustration of the double-flaw principle. It came up in an IMP match, but the principle remains the same. As South, non-vul. vs. vul, I held: ♠—, ♡3, ♢109862, ♣J1076542, and it was two passes to me. Bids such as 3♣ and 4♣ would probably be normal in this situation, but I decided to try something really outlandish—a psychic 1NT opening bid! There was the danger inherent in any psychic bid that partner might not read it in time, but the bid seemed to have everything else going for it. The opponents have at least a game, the vulnerability is right, partner is limited so he won't go leaping to a slam, and if worst comes to worst my runout might not be too expensive. However, there is a hidden second flaw in the hand. Do you see it?

The psyche worked as well as could be expected. West had a balanced 27 (!) count, and had no idea how to handle this situation. The bidding proceeded:

NORTH	EAST	SOUTH	WEST
Pass	Pass	1 NT	Double
2 ♡	Double	3 ♣	Double
Pass	Pass	Pass	

Down only two, −300, when the opponents were cold for a slam. So what happened? We lost nine IMPs on the hand! Our teammates bid to a very reasonable grand slam in spades, but it had no play because North held J109x in spades. The second flaw was the spade void, which was an indication that suits may not be splitting well for the opponents, so that what happened at the other table was not that unlikely. One could say that "the operation was successful but the patient died." This is what we are trying to avoid. If the operation is risky, it is important to be sure that the patient will live if the operation succeeds; otherwise, the risk of the operation is not worthwhile. A better hand for this particular psyche would have been something like ♠xx, ♡xx, ◇x, ♣J10xxxxxx. If I had held this hand, I could be fairly confident that my teammates could make whatever they bid.

Let's look at a few examples and see how the dice are loaded:

None vul., South holds: ♠A754, ♡K103, ◇93, ♣KQ106

NORTH	EAST	SOUTH	WEST
1 NT	Pass	?	

Is this the hand to bypass the possible four-four spade fit and go straight to 3NT? As we shall see later, the hand meets many of the requirements—extra strength, lack of intermediates in the trump suit, and a strong side four-card suit. But what about that diamond holding? A worthless doubleton is very dangerous, for a diamond ruff will produce an extra trick if North has diamond length, and if he doesn't the defenders may be able to run the suit. Change the hand to ♠A754, ♡K103, ◇Q9, ♣K1063 and that second flaw is taken care of, so 3NT figures to be the winning action.

None vul., South holds: ♠4, ♡84, ◇J1085, ♣KQ10952

NORTH	EAST	SOUTH	WEST
—	Pass	?	

Feel like trying a three-level preempt on a six-bagger? Vulnerability is probably O.K., suit is excellent, side four-card minor is not bad. Pity that we are in second position. Partner is as likely to hold the strong hand as West, and this flaw makes the 3♣ opening a losing action. In third seat it would be clear-cut, and in first seat it would be a winner more often than not, but not in second seat. With ♠4, ♡84, ◇J108, ♣KQ109532 it would be correct. The hand has no flaws at all, so a second seat preempt is called for.

None vul., South holds: ♠AQ1062, ♡KJ105, ◇963, ♣3

NORTH	EAST	SOUTH	WEST
—	—	?	

This hand is about one to one and one-half points below my normal minimum opening bid standards (if your standards differ substantially, add or subtract a jack to make the hand the same relative to your framework). Is a super-light first seat opening bid likely to be a winner? I believe it is. The suits are strong, the majors are held, there are no rebid problems, and the vulnerability is best for competitive action. You may get buried if partner with a twelve-count and no great fit drives to a no-play game, but you will come out ahead in most variations. Any small change in the hand, such as removing the ten of spades or reversing the major suits (causing rebid problems) would make the light opening bid a likely losing action, but this hand has no second flaw so the 1♠ opening bid is best.

Both vul, South holds: ♠K1053, ♡K, ◇AQ108, ♣KJ92

NORTH	EAST	SOUTH	WEST
—	—	?	

Is this the hand for the feared 1NT opening with the singleton? There are several good features. The hand is very notrump oriented, there are several tenaces, the stiff king is ideal, and the strength is just right. There are, however, two flaws. One is that there is no serious rebid problem if you open 1◇ and partner responds 1♡, so the clever 1NT opening isn't necessary. Also, if partner transfers to hearts how happy will you be? Consequently, you should wait for another time. I would certainly try it if the stiff king were in clubs, since both of these flaws would be eliminated, and probably try it if the stiff king were in spades (despite the risk of a transfer to spades) because the rebid problem after a 1♠ response to 1◇ is so severe.

37

None vul., South holds: ♠K852, ♡6, ◇QJ109764, ♣5

NORTH	EAST	SOUTH	WEST
—	—	?	

The diamond suit, vulnerability, and position are all perfect for a 3◇ bid; the only question mark is the side four-card major. If this were the only problem I would take my chances with the preempt, but it is worse than that. The side major is spades, which outranks the opponents' potential heart fit. We may need the spade suit to outbid them. If the hand were either ♠6, ♡K852, ◇QJ109764, ♣5 or ♠K852, ♡QJ109764, ◇6, ♣5 I would go ahead with the preempt. The danger of losing the best major suit fit still exists, but at least our preempt suit is as good as our side four-card major for competing with the opponents potential fit. The actual hand was:

```
                    NORTH
                    ♠ A J 9 7 6
                    ♡ 10 9
                    ◇ 8 3 2
                    ♣ K J 7
        WEST                    EAST
        ♠ 4                     ♠ Q 10 3
        ♡ K Q J 7 4 3 2         ♡ A 8 5
        ◇ A K                   ◇ 5
        ♣ A Q 8                 ♣ 10 9 6 4 3 2
                    SOUTH
                    ♠ K 8 5 2
                    ♡ 6
                    ◇ Q J 10 9 7 6 4
                    ♣ 5
```

4♠ is a good save over the E-W 4♡ contract, and would have been reached if South had passed and North had overcalled the 1♡ opening bid with 1♠. Unfortunately, after the preempt the bidding proceeded:

NORTH	EAST	SOUTH	WEST
—	—	3 ◊	4 ♡
4 ♠	Double	Pass	Pass
5 ◊	Pass	Pass	Double
Pass	Pass	Pass	

North tested the water with 4 ♠, but when he got doubled it seemed best to run to the safety of the diamond suit. As you can see, 5 ◊ doubled goes down one too many.

E-W vul., South holds: ♠ QJ10983, ♡ 7, ◊ 6532, ♣ 96

NORTH	EAST	SOUTH	WEST
Pass	1 ◊	?	

Any red-blooded bridge player would bid 2 ♠, but how many would try 3 ♠? Yet, except for the lack of a seventh spade, the hand and the conditions are perfect. Partner is a passed hand so the opponents surely have at least a game, the vulnerability is right, and South has no outside garbage. Sure, South might go for more than the value of a game, but the opponents don't know this. Even if 3 ♠ is set 700 there is still the chance that E-W have a slam. If E-W don't double the extra level of bidding consumed will hurt their constructive auction considerably, and this will more than compensate for the few times that South is caught and goes for too large a number. If the hand had any flaws, such as Qx of clubs or partner not being a passed hand, then the risk of the 3 ♠ bid would not be worthwhile.

REVIEW PROBLEMS

1. You must walk a half mile to and from work. The morning weather forecast predicts a 10% probability of thunderstorms that afternoon. Should you take an umbrella?

2. Both vul., South holds: ♠A6, ♡AK86, ◇AQJ7, ♣J87

NORTH	EAST	SOUTH	WEST
—	—	1 ◇	Pass
1 ♠	Pass	2 NT	Pass
3 ◇	Pass	3 ♡	Pass
4 ♡	Pass	?	

3. N-S vul., South holds: ♠QJ94, ♡A763, ◇QJ, ♣A86

NORTH	EAST	SOUTH	WEST
—	—	—	1 ◇
Pass	1 ♠	Pass	2 ♠
Pass	3 ♣	Pass	3 NT
Pass	4 ♠	?	

4. None vul., South holds: ♠103, ♡J109852, ◇A5, ♣AQ2

NORTH	EAST	SOUTH	WEST
—	—	—	1 ♠
Pass	2 ◇	?	

5. None vul., South holds: ♠AJ976, ♡KJ5, ◇85, ♣K53

NORTH	EAST	SOUTH	WEST
—	—	—	3 ◇
Pass	Pass	?	

6. None vul., South holds: ♠KQJ109, ♡10, ◇10753, ♣1043

As dealer, should South open with a weak 2 ♠ bid?

7. Both vul., South holds: ♠105, ♡A42, ♢AQ107, ♣KQ82

NORTH	EAST	SOUTH	WEST
—	—	1 ♢	1 ♠
3 ♢ *	Pass	?	

*limit raise

8. Both vul., South holds ♠K72, ♡A94, ♢J742, ♣952

NORTH	EAST	SOUTH	WEST
—	—	Pass	1 ♡
Pass	1 ♠	Pass	3 ♡
Pass	4 ♣	Pass	4 NT
Pass	5 ♢	Pass	6 NT
Pass	Pass	?	

9. E-W vul., South holds: ♠AJ93, ♡A3, ♢A42, ♣KQJ9

NORTH	EAST	SOUTH	WEST
—	—	1 ♣	Pass
1 ♡	Pass	?	

10.

NORTH
♠ A K J 9 8
♡ A 4
♢ A Q 10
♣ 9 4 2

SOUTH
♠ 2
♡ Q 7 5 2
♢ J 9 8 6 2
♣ A J 6

Both vul.

NORTH	EAST	SOUTH	WEST
1 ♠	Pass	1 NT	Pass
2 NT	Pass	Pass	Pass

Opening Lead: Jack of hearts.

Plan the play.

41

SOLUTIONS

1. The expected cost of being wrong by not taking the umbrella is .10 X cost of getting drenched. The expected cost of being wrong by taking the umbrella is .90 X cost of unnecessarily lugging an umbrella around. So it's up to you. If getting drenched is more than nine times as costly as the nuisance of carrying an umbrella which isn't needed you should take the umbrella; if not, leave it at home.

2. South has two main choices. He can pass the 4♡ bid and play the four-three fit, or he can move on to a possible slam starting with a 4♠ cue bid. The four-three heart fit looks like it will play pretty well, with the strong trump suit and the short hand able to take the ruffs. Some likely field contracts are 3NT and 5◊, and 4♡ figures to outscore both of them. Consequently, it may not be necessary to bid the slam even if it is there. If North holds the perfect hand such as ♠KQxxx, ♡Qxx, ◊Kxxx, ♣x then failing to bid the slam will cost only one-half matchpoint against only those pairs in 4♡ or 6♡; it will cost nothing against those in 3NT or 5◊ since the 4♡ contract will beat them anyway. On the other hand, if North has ♠KQxx, ♡Qxx, ◊Kxxx, ♣xx (his actual hand), 4♡ is the best contract; bidding 5◊ costs one-half matchpoint to almost every other table, and bidding 6◊ costs even more. Pass figures to be the winning action on balance.

3. Should South double? He figures to beat it, as his aces should cash and his trump holding will produce two tricks more often than not. The bidding indicates that 3NT is a possible contract, and South can tell by looking at his hand that 3NT is likely to score as many tricks as 4♠. If this is the case, South will lose a full matchpoint to each table in 3NT by doubling and being wrong. The double also risks a full matchpoint to tables not in game if it tells declarer how to play the hand to make the contract. Since the double gains only against other tables in 4♠ when it is right, and only gains one-half matchpoint from these

tables, it is wrong to double even though South is a favorite to set the contract. The full hand was:

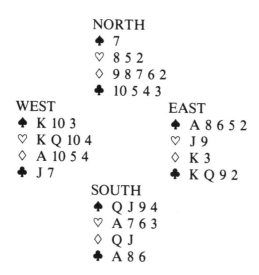

NORTH
♠ 7
♡ 8 5 2
♢ 9 8 7 6 2
♣ 10 5 4 3

WEST
♠ K 10 3
♡ K Q 10 4
♢ A 10 5 4
♣ J 7

EAST
♠ A 8 6 5 2
♡ J 9
♢ K 3
♣ K Q 9 2

SOUTH
♠ Q J 9 4
♡ A 7 6 3
♢ Q J
♣ A 8 6

With notrump easily taking ten tricks and the double guaranteeing that declarer played the spade suit correctly, the double was very costly.

4. To overcall or not to overcall, that is the question. It certainly is risky against a two over one response, but do the gains make it worthwhile? No, because South probably doesn't want a heart lead. West is likely to be declarer in spades or notrump, and South would prefer a natural club lead from his partner. This is a very serious flaw for the already risky overcall, so the overcall should be avoided.

5. This is a common type of problem. South can pass, bid 3 ♠, or double, and he is acting in the blind. Pass is the most committal action. It bets everything on the hand belonging to the opponents. The 3 ♠ call gets to spades or notrump when right, but eliminates the possibility of playing hearts or clubs, or defending. Double is the bid with the most horses in the running. Best would be if partner passed or bid spades, but if partner bids 3 ♡ or 4 ♣ South isn't dead yet, for these could well be winning contracts if North has a long suit and no spade support.

The double can work out badly when the hand belongs to E-W or when N-S miss a superior five-three spade fit, but it has more ways to win than the alternatives.

6. A weak two-bid on a five-bagger? This must be the hand for it. Excellent suit, nothing on the side, neither vul., first seat. The only flaw is the lack of a sixth spade, so South should try it.

7. South certainly has the strength to consider moving towards game, and five diamonds could be cold if North has, say, ♠xxx, ♡Kx, ◇KJxx, ♣Axxx. Consider what is likely to happen at other tables. Many if not most players holding the South hand will open 1NT. West will probably not risk entering at the two-level, and North will undoubtedly jump to 3NT with his presumed ten to twelve points and no four-card major. This is not likely to be a success due to West's spade suit. If 3NT is going down at other tables South gains nothing by bidding on if five diamonds makes, for both +150 and +600 beat −100. South does, however, risk one-half matchpoint against the 3NT bidders if he is wrong in bidding a minor suit game. Therefore, South should pass and guarantee his plus score.

8. Should South double for the spade lead? It's far from clear that a spade lead is a favorite to beat the contract, since East has only one ace. A matchpoint cost analysis shows that the double is a big winner. The reason is that the opponents are in their top spot, so South will be well below average if 6NT makes, and the spade lead has a good chance of being the difference between making and down one. If South doubles and is wrong he loses one-half matchpoint to other tables in 6NT, but loses nothing to tables in any other contract, including 6♡. On the other hand, if South fails to double and is wrong (i.e. the spade lead is the killer and North now leads something else), South again loses one-half matchpoint to other tables in 6NT, but costs a full matchpoint to tables in any other contract, of which there figure to be several. Consequently the double is by far the percentage bid, even if it succeeds somewhat less than half the time.

9. Time to bypass a four-card spade suit with a 2NT rebid?

Certainly a potential gain if North doesn't have four spades, as South would welcome a spade lead. But what if North does have four spades? Then 4♠ is almost certainly worth an extra trick over notrump, for South has strong spades and a weak diamond holding. Therefore, South's best rebid is 2♠. Put South's jack in diamonds rather than spades, giving him ♠A9xx, ♡Ax, ◊AJx, ♣KQJx and the 2NT bid is much better, since now notrump has a reasonable chance to be right even if N-S have a four-four spade fit. The difference can be seen by looking at both hands opposite something like ♠10xxx, ♡QJ9x, ◊10x, ♣Axx.

10. Both North and South bid very conservatively on this deal. There are many roads to 3NT, and they will be taken at most other tables. Consequently, South can assume that 3NT will be the normal contract, and he should plan his play accordingly. Overtricks are irrelevant, for scores at other tables must fall outside the range of +120 to +180. Undertricks might matter if 3NT goes down at some other tables. Therefore, South should play absolutely safe for his contract. This can be done by rising ace of hearts and playing on diamonds immediately, guaranteeing four diamonds, one heart, one club, and two spades for eight tricks. The danger in ducking the first trick is that East may shift to the ten of clubs and shut out declarer's diamond suit. The cost of being wrong by going up is only an overtrick or two, which as we have seen is of little value, but the cost of being wrong by ducking the first trick could be an undertrick or two, which might be meaningful if 3NT is being set at other tables. The full hand:

```
                    NORTH
                    ♠ A K J 9 8
                    ♡ A 4
                    ◇ A Q 10
                    ♣ 9 4 2
        WEST                    EAST
        ♠ 7 6 4                 ♠ Q 10 5 3
        ♡ J 10 9 8 3            ♡ K 6
        ◇ 5 3                   ◇ K 7 4
        ♣ Q 5 3                 ♣ K 10 8 7
                    SOUTH
                    ♠ 2
                    ♡ Q 7 5 2
                    ◇ J 9 8 6 2
                    ♣ A J 6
```

The ten of clubs shift is not that hard for East to find, after which East can defeat the contract by refusing to win the first round of diamonds.

CONSTRUCTIVE BIDDING

CONSTRUCTIVE BIDDING

THE BEST GAME

In this chapter, we shall examine situations where the only problem is which game to bid. Slam is out of the question, and the combined hands have enough strength that the entire field will certainly bid some game. In most cases there will be only two choices, usually a major suit or notrump, so matchpoint cost analysis won't tell us anything—you will simply lose one-half matchpoint to every table if you go wrong. Therefore, the goal is simply to be right more often than not.

THE FOUR-FOUR FIT

We all know that it is usually right to prefer a four-four major suit to notrump at matchpoints. The reason is that the major suit will produce an extra trick more often than not, and that extra trick translates into a better score. The winning player wants to do better than "usually"; he wants to be able to recognize hands on which the four-four fit will not produce that extra trick and head for 3NT when these hands occur.

There are three reasons why a four-four fit might produce an extra trick over notrump. They are:

1. A trump suit acts as a stopper so that the opponents can't run their long suit as they might in notrump.

2. If one player has a short suit, losers in that suit from the other hand can be ruffed. The beauty of a four-four fit is that the ruff can be taken in either hand, and the other hand still has the length to draw trumps. It may only take one such ruff to produce that extra trick.

3. A trump suit allows for more flexibility in the play, for such things as end-plays, establishing a long suit by ruffing, etc.

These are pretty powerful arguments for the four-four fit. If none of them produce the extra trick, however, then notrump with that extra ten points becomes the winner. It is clear that if one of the partnership's hands contains a singleton the four-four fit is virtually always right, just on the ruffing value alone, except in the rare case when the hand opposite the singleton is loaded with secondary values such as KQJ9 in the suit. The more interesting decisions occur when both hands are relatively balanced. There are four factors a player should consider when deciding whether or not to reject a four-four major suit fit. They are:

1. Strength. If the partnership has only 25-26 high card points the four-four fit is almost always right, whereas if the partnership has excess strength, say 29-30 high card points, then notrump has a good chance of producing the same number of tricks. There are two reasons for this. First, the extra strength may be sufficient to stop the opposition from running a suit

while declarer is busy setting up his winners. Second, the extra strength may produce the winner that makes it unnecessary to ruff a loser. For example:

NORTH
- ♠ K 10 6 5
- ♡ Q 7
- ◊ K J 7 4
- ♣ K J 2

SOUTH
- ♠ Q J 8 3
- ♣ K J 2
- ◊ A Q 8
- ♣ A 10 5

N-S vulnerable.

NORTH	EAST	SOUTH	WEST
—	—	1 NT	Pass
3 NT	Pass	Pass	Pass

There are eleven tricks available at notrump (three spades, two hearts, four diamonds, and two clubs). Two aces must be lost at spades, so notrump is the winner. However, a slight weakening of the hands changes the picture. For example, make South's ace of clubs the queen; now 4 ♠ is cold for ten tricks barring bad splits, while notrump makes only nine tricks after a heart lead, for declarer doesn't have time to knock out both black aces. Try making North's minor suit jacks small cards in the same suits. Spades still makes eleven tricks on reasonable splits, for North's losing club can be pitched on the long heart, but notrump now needs a three-three diamond split to make the same eleven tricks.

2. Holding in short suits. We have seen that the extra trick in the four-four fit often comes from a ruff. If the card being ruffed is a winner, no extra trick is gained. Aces and kings account for the first two rounds of a suit, but queens and jacks determine the fate of the rest of the suit. Therefore, if you have

51

a doubleton it is often necessary for the doubleton to include the queen or the jack for notrump to be the winner. For example, opposite a holding such as AJ10x, king-doubleton will produce no losers in a suit contract because the third round of the suit can be ruffed, while in notrump a finesse must be taken. Queen-doubleton opposite AJ10x, on the other hand, will lose either one trick or none at either notrump or a suit contract.

3. Holding in side four-card suits. Exactly the same theme applies as with doubletons, because the side suit may be ruffed out in partner's hand. If you have queens and jacks in the side suit you may be ruffing winners, but if the suit is empty the ruff may well be an extra trick. For example:

NORTH
♠ K 9 5 3
♡ A 10 2
♢ A 10 5 2
♣ Q 7

SOUTH
♠ A Q 8 4
♡ K 9 8 6
♢ K 4
♣ K J 3

Both vulnerable.

NORTH	EAST	SOUTH	WEST
—	—	1 NT	Pass
2 ♣	Pass	2 ♠	Pass
4 ♠	Pass	Pass	Pass

Despite the extra strength and the balanced nature of the North hand, his holdings in the red suits are a tip-off that a four-four spade fit is likely to produce an extra trick. The reason is that any shortness in these suits in partner's hand can be used to ruff third and fourth round losers. On this pair of hands notrump will make at most eleven tricks, possibly only ten, while spades is almost sure to make eleven tricks and may well make twelve with good splits, for North's third heart can be discarded on the long club. Change North's hand to: ♠K953, ♡AJ2, ◇QJ102, ♣Q7. Same strength, but the texture of the red suits now makes notrump a likely winner. Opposite the same South hand there are eleven tricks at both spades and notrump. With the second hand North should not bother with Stayman; he should just bid 3NT.

4. Trump holding. An eight-card fit will get a four-one split almost one-third of the time. If the trump suit has good intermediates, such as K10xx opposite QJxx, the bad split by itself won't cost a trump trick, but if the trump suit is empty such as Kxxx opposite Axxx, that four-one trump split will always cost the major suit player a trick. Consequently, the player rejecting the four-four fit should prefer to have a trump holding weak in intermediates. It's not that this helps notrump; what it does is give the notrumper an extra way to win when the suit player loses an extra trick due to a bad trump split. For example:

NORTH
♠ A 5 4 2
♡ K 9 7
◇ K J 10 6
♣ Q 3

SOUTH
♠ K 8 7 3
♡ A 5
◇ Q 8 4
♣ A K 8 4

N-S vulnerable.

NORTH	EAST	SOUTH	WEST
—	—	1 NT	Pass
3 NT	Pass	Pass	Pass

The North hand fits all the conditions for rejecting the four-four spade fit. Unfortunately South produces the wrong heart holding, and there are only ten tricks available in notrump after

53

a heart lead while spades easily makes eleven tricks on a three-two split. However, the notrumpers have an extra way to win even though they judged wrong—the spades might split four-one. Obviously you would prefer to be in 4♠ on the combined hands, but it is nice to know that you have that additional chance of a bad spade split if you opt for 3NT. If North's spade holding were QJ10x instead of Axxx, that extra way to win would go out the window.

At least three of the four conditions should be met in order to justify rejecting a four-four major suit fit, and meeting all four conditions is preferable. In close cases notrump should be preferred if a four-four fit is only a possibility and the search would lead to a more revealing auction, for you then gain by concealment when you don't have the four-four fit. In general, however, the four-four fit should be chosen.

Let's look at a few examples of this type of decision:

Both vul., South holds: ♠KJ63, ♡K2, ◇Q1062, ♣A32

NORTH	EAST	SOUTH	WEST
—	—	1 ◇	Pass
1 ♠	Pass	2 ♠	Pass
3 NT	Pass	?	

South should go to 4♠. His spade suit is strong (it contains the jack), and his heart holding doesn't include the queen or the jack, so the four-four fit figures to be better. The heart suit is of particular concern, for if North holds only four spades he doesn't have four hearts, or he would have responded 1♡ rather than 1♠. Consequently, there is a danger that the opponents may be able to set up their hearts at notrump.

N-S vul., South holds: ♠AJ, ♡A964, ◇K76, ♣QJ32

NORTH	EAST	SOUTH	WEST
1 ◇	Pass	?	

I consider bypassing the four-card heart suit and bidding 2NT a worthwhile gamble. The hand meets all the qualifications, so there is not likely to be an extra trick coming from a ruff. There is some danger that the spade suit may be inadequately stopped, but the extra strength may give South enough fast tricks anyway. In addition, the 2NT bid will be best when North doesn't have four hearts, for South protects his spade tenace and the N-S distribution isn't revealed to the opposition.

Both vul., South holds: ♠7632, ♡KQJ105, ◊KJ, ♣Q6

NORTH	EAST	SOUTH	WEST
1 NT	Pass	?	

South should see that a four-four spade fit is likely to be of little value, for his hearts don't need ruffs to become established and South has strength in his doubletons. A five-four or five-three heart fit, on the other hand, may produce an extra trick, since South may get to ruff a losing spade. Consequently, South should not bid Stayman but should instead try a straightforward 3♡ bid (or 2◊ if playing transfers), and leave the spade suit unmentioned.

THE FIVE-THREE FIT

Many of the same considerations are involved in deciding whether or not to bypass a five-three major suit fit to play notrump. The main difference is that a ruff is now of value only in the hand with the short trumps. Also, the hand with the three-card trump support might have a side suit such as AKxxx which can be established by ruffing without losing tricks in the suit, while in notrump a trick or two may have to be lost establishing the suit.

The hand with the three-card support is almost always better placed to make the final decision. If he is 4-3-3-3 notrump will probably produce the same number of tricks provided that the combined hands contain extra strength and that all suits are adequately stopped. If the hand with the three-card support has a doubleton, however, the five-three fit usually scores an extra trick. For notrump to be right the doubleton suit must be adequately stopped, yet have no valuable ruff in the short hand, and there must be no side suit that can be established by ruffing.

Both vul., South holds: ♠K5, ♡A7632, ◊Q73, ♣J84

NORTH	EAST	SOUTH	WEST
1 NT	Pass	?	

Despite the lack of intermediates in hearts and the scattered strength, South should transfer to hearts and then bid 3NT (or do whatever shows a five-card heart suit in the partnership methods). There is no extra strength, and the opening notrumper, who holds the potential three-card support, will be better placed to make the final decision.

N-S vul., South holds: ♠A93, ♡KQ5, ◊AJ7, ♣J1075

NORTH	EAST	SOUTH	WEST
1 ♠	Pass	?	

South should bid 2NT if it shows 13-15 balanced, or do whatever shows a balanced game-going hand in the partnership methods. He should be quite willing to bypass a five-three spade fit. He has extra strength, no ruffing values, and adequate stoppers opposite any doubletons. If North is distributional he will bid his second suit and South can get back to spades, but if North is relatively balanced notrump will probably be the winner.

None vul., South holds: ♠Q63, ♡J4, ◇AKJ, ♣KJ1062

NORTH	EAST	SOUTH	WEST
1 ♠	Pass	2 ♣	Pass
2 ♡	Pass	?	

Without the 2 ♡ bid South would probably opt to play in spades because of the heart weakness. After North bids 2 ♡ this is no longer as much of a problem, and with his super-strong diamond holding and extra strength South· has every reason to believe that notrump will take the same number of tricks as the major, so he should just bid 3NT and not bother supporting spades.

THE LONG SUIT

A common problem occurs when you have a long solid or semi-solid major suit but an otherwise relatively balanced hand and the partnership has all suits stopped. Should you gamble that notrump will produce the same number of tricks, or should you retreat to the safety of the suit? It is unlikely that dummy has any ruffing value, and usually there will not be a suit in dummy that can be advantageously established by ruffing. Timing is the key to the value of the trump suit. The trump suit serves as a stopper to fend off the enemy attack while you are busy setting up tricks in the other side suits. If there are no such tricks to be set up, then notrump will take the same number of tricks. What this means is that honor cards have their usual roles reversed. Aces, usually more desirable for suit play, are now preferred at notrump since they don't have to be set up. Kings and queens, usually indicative of a notrump hand, now point toward the suit contract since they require time to establish.

The following hand is a good illustration:

NORTH
♠ 3
♡ A 6 4
♢ A J 8 5 2
♣ J 9 5 3

SOUTH
♠ A K Q J 8 4 2
♡ 9 7
♢ 7
♣ A 7 6

E-W vulnerable.

NORTH	EAST	SOUTH	WEST
—	—	1 ♠	Pass
2 ♢	Pass	3 ♠	Pass
3 NT	Pass	?	

58

Since South's only side card is an ace, passing 3NT is a reasonable gamble, in the hope that there won't be any side tricks to be set up while the opponents are attacking their best suit. On the actual hand there are ten tricks available in either contract, and spades has little chance to score an extra trick. However, change South's hand to: ♠AKQJ842, ♡97, ◇7, ♣KQ7, and now a 4♠ call is more prudent. The clubs may have to be established, as in the actual hand, and there may not be time to do this at notrump.

E-W vul., South holds: ♠43, ♡QJ5, ◇A10653, ♣Q105

NORTH	EAST	SOUTH	WEST
1 ♠	Pass	1 NT	Pass
3 ♠	Pass	?	

I would take a shot at 3NT, since my slow tricks are in my short suits, the suits the opponents figure to lead. However with ♠43, ♡A65, ◇QJ653, ♣Q105 4♠ is preferable, since I may need time to establish diamonds. If you look at both hands opposite a typical 3♠ bid such as ♠KQJ10xx, ♡Kx, ◇Kx, ♣AJx it should be quite clear why notrump is more likely to be a winner on the first hand than on the second one.

This is a good place to clear up a misconception which exists in the minds of most bridge players about a difference between IMPs and matchpoints. I have often heard a player who is faced with a close choice of games say "At matchpoints I'd try 3NT and hope to take the same number of tricks, but at IMPs I'd play the safer major suit contract." This is backwards from the way one should think. On most hands, one should lean toward notrump more heavily at IMPs than at matchpoints.

The reason one prefers a suit contract to notrump is because of the possibility that the suit contract might produce more tricks. Suppose both contracts score the same number of tricks. Then notrump is superior at both forms of scoring. It is worth 10 more points for matchpoint purposes and might earn a game swing at IMPs if that number of tricks is nine. If the suit contract scores two more tricks than notrump it is better at both forms of scoring, for it is then worth 50 more points at matchpoints and a possible game swing at IMPs when the difference is ten tricks versus eight. If the suit contract takes exactly one more trick it is again better at matchpoints, since it scores 20 more points, but the difference is negligible at IMPs. Both contracts either make or go down, as the notrumpers are contracting for one less trick, and the one IMP swing for the overtrick is inconsequential. Thus, the major suit game needs to score two extra tricks to be superior to notrump at IMPs, while it needs to score only one extra trick to be superior at matchpoints, and notrump is superior at both forms of scoring if the contracts take the same number of tricks. Therefore, one should lean toward notrump more at IMPs than at matchpoints.

The following hand is an illustration of this principle:

NORTH
♠ 7
♡ A 9 8 6
♢ K 10 6 5 3
♣ J 9 7

SOUTH
♠ A K Q J 10 4
♡ 4 3
♢ A 7
♣ Q 10 6

Both vulnerable.

NORTH	EAST	SOUTH	WEST
—	—	1 ♠	Pass
1 NT	Pass	3 ♠	Pass
3 NT	Pass	?	

One would certainly want to be in 4 ♠ at matchpoints, since there are ten tricks available unless the opponents can negotiate a club ruff, while notrump will probably only make nine tricks if the defense leads or shifts to hearts, which they probably will. However at IMPs notrump is better, for 4 ♠ can go down on a club ruff while 3NT is cold. South has a very close decision on his final bid, and it might well be right to let the scoring be the deciding factor—bidding 3NT at IMPs and 4 ♠ at matchpoints.

If you think that the decision is not so close and that either 4♠ or 3NT is likely to be better at both forms of scoring I won't argue, but it would definitely be wrong to bid 4♠ at IMPs and pass 3NT at matchpoints, as many players do.

There is one type of hand which should play in notrump at matchpoints and a suit contract at IMPs. This is the hand which will certainly make game in the major suit simply because it is so strong, but where notrump might get buried by a wide open suit. For example:

Both vul., South holds: ♠K32, ♡A10532, ◇KJ5, ♣QJ

NORTH	EAST	SOUTH	WEST
1 NT	Pass	?	

In a matchpoint game the player holding the South hand decided not to try for slam (I agree), and to bypass a possible five-three heart fit by bidding Stayman and then jumping to 3NT when North didn't have four hearts. This didn't work too well, for North held ♠AQxx, ♡KQx, ◇AQxx, ♣xx and the defense ran the first five club tricks. I must confess that I wouldn't have done too well on the South hand either; in fact, I would have just bid 3NT and not even looked for a five-four heart fit, since I think it far more likely than not that notrump will score the same number of tricks. At IMPs, however, I would transfer the hand and then bid 3NT, for if North holds three hearts 4♡ must be virtually cold, so there is no reason to risk the opponents being able to run a suit.

SEVEN-CARD TRUMP FITS

Many of the same principles apply to choosing between a four-three major suit fit and notrump, although the arguments in favor of the suit contract must be stronger because of the shorter trump holding. Trump strength is of prime importance, particularly in the four-card holding. This is the big distinction between seven and eight-card trump fits. J9xx opposite Qxxx can be a quite satisfactory trump fit, but J9xx opposite Qxx can be a nightmare to play and should be avoided.

The main advantage of the four-three fit is the ability to score an extra trick by ruffing a loser in the short hand. Consequently, side-suit texture is very important in the hand with the four-card trump holding. A suit such as Axxx has several losers to be ruffed, while a suit such as QJxx is not so good because it is likely that only winners will be ruffed. Also, it is important that the four-card trump holding be strong. AKJx opposite Qxx is quite comfortable, since you can take a ruff in the short hand and then draw trumps, but Axxx opposite KQJ is not as good, for every ruff in the short hand may cost a trump trick.

A four-three fit is often chosen because one suit is inadequately stopped for notrump. It is important that the hand with the short trumps be able to take the ruffs in the weak suit. If the long hand is forced to take the taps, you are reduced to playing a three-three trump fit, and if the opponents' trumps don't split three-three the roof will cave in. For example:

NORTH
- ♠ K J 9
- ♡ 9 4
- ◇ K Q 5 3 2
- ♣ K J 9

SOUTH
- ♠ A Q 8 5
- ♡ 10 6
- ◇ A J 9 8
- ♣ Q 5 2

On these combined hands 4♠ is the only game with any play, and the chances are pretty good since the North hand with three trumps can take the force in hearts if necessary, so the game will go down only if the spades split five-one or the defenders can make declarer pull trumps before establishing a club trick by threatening a diamond ruff. However, change the hands to:

NORTH
♠ K J 9
♡ 9 6 4
◊ K Q 5 3
♣ K J 9

SOUTH
♠ A Q 8 5
♡ 10
◊ A J 9 8 2
♣ Q 5 2

Now 4♠, while not the worst contract ever reached, pretty much needs a three-three spade split, since the South hand is forced immediately in hearts. On this hand 5 ◊ is virtually cold, so it is a superior contract.

It is usually the hand with the four-card trump suit that is better placed to make the decision about a possible four-three fit. Consequently, it is generally correct to raise a major with three-card support if there is any ruffing value at all, and let partner carry the ball. For example:

None vul., South holds: ♠A4, ♡J73, ◊K10875, ♣KQ10

NORTH	EAST	SOUTH	WEST
—	—	1 ◊	Pass
1 ♡	Pass	?	

South should rebid 2♡, not 1NT. If North holds ♠97, ♡AQ104, ◊QJ6, ♣AJ64 he would simply raise 1NT to three, but after the 2♡ raise a likely bidding sequence might be:

NORTH	EAST	SOUTH	WEST
—	—	1 ◊	Pass
1 ♡	Pass	2 ♡	Pass
3 ♣	Pass	3 ◊	Pass
4 ♡	Pass	Pass	Pass

When South rebids 3 ◊ rather than 3NT North can diagnose the weakness in the spade suit, and he will bid 4 ♡ even though he knows it might be a four-three fit. On this pair of hands 3NT requires the hearts to behave to take even nine tricks, while 4 ♡ has chances even with the king of hearts offside or the hearts four-two, and will certainly make whenever 3NT does. However, if North instead holds: ♠KQ97, ♡AQ104, ◊QJ6, ♣64 the bidding would be:

NORTH	EAST	SOUTH	WEST
—	—	1 ◊	Pass
1 ♡	Pass	2 ♡	Pass
2 ♠	Pass	2 NT	Pass
3 NT	Pass	Pass	Pass

On this auction South will bid 2NT with only three hearts and the unbid suit, clubs, well under control. Now North has no reason to play the four-three fit, so he bids 3NT. Notrump will make at least as many tricks as hearts more often than not, since all suits are well stopped and there is no useful ruffing value in the short hand.

None vul., South holds: ♠7, ♡AK107, ◊8752, ♣K876

NORTH	EAST	SOUTH	WEST
—	—	Pass	Pass
1 ♠	Pass	?	

It seems at first glance that South's choices are the underbid of 1NT, the overbid of 2NT, and the mis-bid of 2♣. Careful reflection shows that 2♡ is likely to be the winning call, even though this promises five hearts. The hand is perfect for a potential four-three fit—strong trump holding, two side suits which can use some ruffs, and little danger of a force in the long

64

hand. I held this hand in the Life Master Pairs, tried a 2♡ response, and was raised to 4♡. The full hand is quite illuminating:

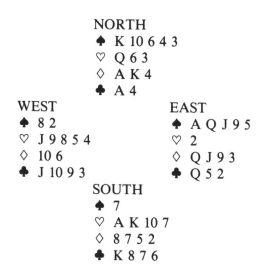

NORTH
♠ K 10 6 4 3
♡ Q 6 3
◇ A K 4
♣ A 4

WEST
♠ 8 2
♡ J 9 8 5 4
◇ 10 6
♣ J 10 9 3

EAST
♠ A Q J 9 5
♡ 2
◇ Q J 9 3
♣ Q 5 2

SOUTH
♠ 7
♡ A K 10 7
◇ 8 7 5 2
♣ K 8 7 6

West led the jack of clubs. I took two rounds of clubs ending in my hand, and led a spade to the king and East's ace. East returned a trump. I went up with the ace, ruffed a club, cashed two top diamonds, ruffed a spade, ruffed a club with the queen of hearts, and exited with a diamond. West was forced to ruff his partner's trick and give me the tenth trick with my ten of hearts, for 23 out of 25 matchpoints. Admittedly this was all a bit lucky, but considering that the four-three trump fit took ten tricks despite a five-one split while at notrump even eight tricks are far from certain, the hand illustrates how powerful a four-three fit can be if the right conditions are present.

Five-two trump fits usually will not produce a ruff in the short hand, the extra trick that is so valuable in a four-three fit. The five-card trump holding provides protection against an enemy suit being run. Therefore, the main reason for playing a five-two fit is to give yourself time to set up tricks while the trump suit serves as a stopper. The conditions which make a five-two major suit fit superior to notrump are:

1. A reasonably strong trump holding.
2. An unstopped or singly stopped side suit which the defense can run at notrump.

A five-two fit is often backed into, after all other possibilities have been explored and rejected. For example:

NORTH
♠ K 7
♡ A 10 8 7
◇ Q 10 9 8 3
♣ A 6

SOUTH
♠ A Q 8 5 4
♡ K 5
◇ K J 7 2
♣ 10 4

N-S vulnerable.

NORTH	EAST	SOUTH	WEST
—	—	1 ♠	Pass
2 ◇	Pass	3 ◇	Pass
3 ♡	Pass	4 ◇	Pass
4 ♠	Pass	Pass	Pass

After South's 3 ◇ bid North is concerned about the club situation, so he probes with a 3 ♡ call. If South had Kx of clubs and two small hearts he would bid 3NT, which would then be the right spot. However South has nothing in clubs, so notrump is out of the question. South's spades are too weak in intermediates to rebid, so he retreats to 4 ◇. North isn't willing to settle for a minor suit game yet, so he makes one more try for a better score with 4 ♠. South's spades are barely strong enough to play the five-two fit, so he passes. It should be noted that five diamonds is a much safer contract than 4 ♠; in fact, 6 ◇ will make if the spades split three-three. However, 4 ♠ will usually make, and will make five on a three-three spade fit, so it is the winning contract at matchpoints. If South's hand were

♠A10xxx, ♡KQ, ◇KJxx, ♣xx he should reject the five-two spade fit and move on to the safety of 5◇. The trump suit would be too weak to handle a five-two fit.

It should be noted that North's sequence on the previous hand (bidding diamonds, then hearts, then raising spades) should not be construed as showing a hand with a singleton club and slam interest. It is far more important to leave open all possibilities to arrive at the best game when the trump suit (or notrump) is in doubt. However, had South rebid 3NT instead of 4◇, then a 4♠ bid by North would show a stiff club and have slam implications. The logic is that if North was sure he wanted to play spades but had no slam interest he would have simply bid 3♠ over 3◇, and if the 3♡ call was a probe for the best game then North would have passed 3NT. The general principle is that any bid which can be interpreted as looking for the best game is of overriding importance. It is only when the trump suit is definitely established that slam tries can be made and understood.

MINOR SUIT GAMES

The lowly minor suit, at 20 points per trick, should be avoided if at all possible when choosing the best game. The usual reason for playing a minor suit game is that there is a suit inadequately stopped for notrump, and no major suit fit is strong enough to play, but the combined hands have enough strength to contract for eleven tricks. For example:

```
            NORTH
            ♠ K 9 6 4
            ♡ A Q 5 2
            ◇ J 5 2
            ♣ 4 2

            SOUTH
            ♠ A 7 5
            ♡ K 4
            ◇ A K Q 7 6 3
            ♣ 10 7
```

Both vulnerable.

NORTH	EAST	SOUTH	WEST
—	—	1 ◇	Pass
1 ♡	Pass	3 ◇	Pass
3 ♠	Pass	4 ◇	Pass
5 ◇	Pass	Pass	Pass

After South's 3 ◇ rebid, North probes for the best game with a 3 ♠ call. South doesn't have a club stopper for notrump, doesn't have a heart preference, and his spades are too weak to suggest a four-three spade game, so he must content himself with 4 ◇. North is too strong to pass, and the only game left open to him is 5 ◇, so he bids it. It should be noted that 3NT is down off the top with a club lead, 4 ♠ depends on a three-three spade split, and the winning contract of 4 ♡ (!), which depends only on a four-three heart split, is basically impossible to find, so 5 ◇ is a good contract and is likely to result in an above average score.

There is one type of hand which may belong in five of a minor even though all suits are adequately stopped. If both partners have singletons, and the suits opposite these singletons can't be easily established by force, then a five-four or even a four-four minor suit game may be the winner, even at matchpoints. The reason is that there just isn't any source of tricks at notrump, while in the minor suit contract declarer may combine a crossruff with setting up a long suit, and take several extra tricks. For example:

NORTH
♠ K Q 9 6 3
♡ 7
♢ A 7 4
♣ Q 10 8 2

SOUTH
♠ 2
♡ A J 8 6 5
♢ K 9 6
♣ A K 4 3

E-W vulnerable.

NORTH	EAST	SOUTH	WEST
—	—	1 ♡	Pass
1 ♠	Pass	2 ♣	Pass
3 ♣	Pass	3 ♢	Pass
3 ♠	Pass	3 NT	Pass
5 ♣	Pass	Pass	Pass

After North raises clubs, South can realize that this might be the type of hand that belongs in the minor, so instead of barging into 3NT he temporizes with 3 ♢. North rebids his fair spade suit, and now South suggests 3NT. North has help in diamonds, but he, too, can see that a trump suit may be very important because of his singleton heart. If South were sure of notrump he would have bid it immediately, therefore South must have a suit-oriented hand. Consequently, North makes the good decision to bid 5♣. The minor suit game will probably come to eleven tricks by attacking spades, but where are the tricks in notrump? If West doesn't have Axx in spades notrump will probably take only eight tricks, and if he does the club game could easily score twelve tricks, to beat 3NT just making, so 5♣ is a much better contract.

GAME OR PART-SCORE

Deciding whether or not to bid a close game can involve many factors. Usually the simple approach of bidding game only if you think it more likely to make than not will lead to the correct decision, since at matchpoints the object is to beat the other players holding your cards by any amount. At IMPs you like being in a 40% vulnerable game, since the cost of being wrong by bidding the game when it goes down is six IMPs, while the cost of not bidding game when it makes is ten IMPs. Therefore, the total cost of being wrong bidding the 40% game is 60% X 6 IMPs = 3.6 IMPs; for not bidding it the cost is 40% X 10 IMPs = 4.0 IMPs. At matchpoints, however, the cost is one-half matchpoint against every other pair whether you bid game or not, assuming no other result is possible, so you would prefer to stay out of a 40% game.

There are three different types of situations in which you may have to decide whether or not to bid a game. First, there may be no other possible contract—i.e. everybody in the room will be playing in spades, the only question is whether or not to bid the game. Secondly, there may be several different possible game or part-score contracts available for your side. Thirdly, there may be some possible opposing contracts to consider. There is some overlap among these three cases, but we will examine each one separately.

NO ALTERNATIVE CONTRACT

When there is no alternative denomination possible, the decision of whether or not to bid a game should, in theory, be based on your judgment as to whether game is a favorite to make. However, it is not necessarily that simple. If you find yourself in a contract which is different from the other tables, you may not get a chance to make the most of your superior declarer skills. We are all egotistical enough to believe that we play the dummy as well or better than the next guy. If we stop short of game and the rest of the field bids the game, all our skill in making overtricks won't help if the game makes.

For example:

E-W vul., South holds: ♠AKJ, ♡Q872, ◇KJ73, ♣QJ

NORTH	EAST	SOUTH	WEST
—	—	1 NT	Pass
2 NT	Pass	?	

Seventeen high card points, but what a terrible hand. Eleven of the points are stuffed into the short suits, there are no intermediates, and the hand contains only one ace. Despite this being a "maximum" 1NT opening in high cards, I would bet that 3NT will fail more often than not. However, I would still choose to bid the game. The reason is that the rest of the field will also bid it, since most of the other players just count points in notrump auctions.

Normally you should try to win a board in the bidding when the opportunity arises rather than make the "field bid" if you think your choice is better, since you must take advantage of superior bidding judgment. Also, it is usually not possible to determine that accurately what the field will do anyway. On this hand, however, it is clear that the rest of the room will be in 3NT, and the contract will certainly have some play even if it is not a favorite. If you pass 2NT you stake everything on your bidding judgment and the defense at the other tables. It won't make any difference how well you declare your hand. The hand is:

NORTH
- ♠ 9 5 3
- ♡ J 5 3
- ◇ A 10 9
- ♣ K 10 8 3

SOUTH
- ♠ A K J
- ♡ Q 8 7 2
- ◇ K J 7 3
- ♣ Q J

West leads the two of spades (fourth best), and you top East's six with your jack. You lead the queen of clubs, West plays the two, and East wins the ace and returns a spade. It appears as though West has four spades and three clubs. If he had four hearts he might have chosen a heart lead, while with four diamonds he would have preferred the spade lead since North didn't bid Stayman. Therefore West is more likely to have long diamonds than East, so you back this analysis by leading a diamond to the ten, which holds. You cross back with a club, lead a diamond to the nine, cash dummy's winners, and come back with a high spade to collect your king of diamonds for the tenth trick. Well played! West's hand was: ♠Q1042, ♡A4, ◇Q842, ♣752. With a normal opening lead, some help from the defense (East would have done better to duck the ace of clubs to foul up your entries), and sound reasoning you made one more trick than the rest of the field is likely to make. If you passed 2NT, however, your +180 will be a goose-egg, since everybody else will be in game (North certainly had the right tens and nines), and anybody can take nine tricks, so your good play was wasted. In this case, failing to bid 3NT costs a full matchpoint to those pairs who are +400, for you get +180 instead of +430. Had partner had the wrong hand and 3NT gone down you would only cost one-half matchpoint to the other tables by bidding the game, or possibly nothing if your skillful play gets you out for down one while the field is going down two.

A similar problem may exist when you stretch for a game that the field doesn't bid. If you are good enough to squeeze that extra trick out of the hand, it may not be necessary to bid the game to get a good score. +170 is as good as +620 if the rest of the room is +140. The danger in stretching too high is that the hand may break badly, and your extra trick may only mean one less undertrick. For example:

Both vul., South holds: ♠AKJ73, ♡63, ◇K1052, ♣K4

NORTH	EAST	SOUTH	WEST
—	—	1 ♠	Pass
2 ♠	Pass	?	

Is the South hand worth a game try? Perhaps it is (although personally I don't think so), but you can be pretty sure the point-counting field won't move toward game with only fourteen high card points and no great distribution. The combined hands are:

NORTH
♠ 10 8 6 4
♡ K Q 7
◇ 6 4 3
♣ A 9 3

SOUTH
♠ A K J 7 3
♡ 6 3
◇ K 10 5 2
♣ K 4

North will certainly accept if you invite, and while game is not hopeless you would rather not be there. The jack of hearts lead is covered by the queen and ace, and the heart return goes to dummy's king. You recognize the possibility of an end-play later in the hand, so you carefully ruff a heart before playing top spades. Unfortunately, East pitches a heart on the second spade. You continue with three rounds of clubs, ruffing the third, before exiting with a trump. East pitches his last heart on the spade, and West plays a fourth club which you ruff in dummy as East follows. Everybody is now down to nothing but diamonds, so you duck a diamond to West. This is a winning line of play, for West started with ♠Q92, ♡J102, ◇AQ9, ♣Q1065. Most other declarers will probably take only eight tricks, but your −100 still loses to their +110 even though you took an extra trick. Stretching to the game cost a full matchpoint against those declarers who stopped in 2♠ and made eight tricks, for you went from a potential +140 to −100. The overbid completely nullified your good play.

To summarize: If there is no other possible denomination and the question is simply whether or not to bid game, you should usually go with your judgment. In theory, you want to be in the game if it is better than even money, and stay out of the game if it is worse than even money. However, there may be some close decisions where your judgment is clearly contrary to what the field will be doing. In these cases it may be better to make the ''field bid'' if you fancy yourself a superior declarer.

OTHER CONTRACTS AVAILABLE

When there are several different contracts which might be reached at other tables, deciding whether or not to bid a game can get very tricky. No longer is it simply a question of deciding if game is a favorite to make. If the game you must bid is not likely to be the best game or if your part-score will probably outscore other part-scores, it is better to settle for the part-score. Conversely, if your part-score is probably inferior to other part-scores or if your game will definitely be the best result if it makes, it is better to stretch to the game. We shall examine several examples of these situations.

Both vul., South holds: ♠KJ76, ♡KQ975, ♢6, ♣K105

NORTH	EAST	SOUTH	WEST
—	—	—	3 ♣
3 ♢	Pass	3 ♡	Pass
4 ♢	Pass	?	

South had a difficult choice at his first turn. Perhaps 3NT is the better call, but 3♡ (forcing) leaves open the possibility of game in either major suit. Unfortunately North bid 4♢, the bid South least wanted to hear. South would like to go back and bid 3NT but that would be insufficient, so what should he do? 5♢ figures to be a favorite, but slam looks pretty unlikely. The problem is that if 5♢ makes 3NT will also make, probably with an overtrick or two. A large portion of the field figures to get to 3NT; either West won't make a vulnerable preempt or South will try 3NT rather than 3♡ at other tables. Consequently South will gain little by bidding 5♢, so his best bet is to pass and hope the cards lie badly so that no game makes. By passing, South gains one-half matchpoint from the 3NT players when he is right and nothing makes, while if South bids 5♢ he probably loses to the notrumpers even when he is right in bidding. The full hand:

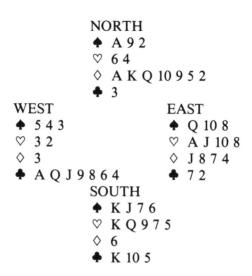

NORTH
♠ A 9 2
♡ 6 4
♢ A K Q 10 9 5 2
♣ 3

WEST
♠ 5 4 3
♡ 3 2
♢ 3
♣ A Q J 9 8 6 4

EAST
♠ Q 10 8
♡ A J 10 8
♢ J 8 7 4
♣ 7 2

SOUTH
♠ K J 7 6
♡ K Q 9 7 5
♢ 6
♣ K 10 5

Against 3NT West leads the queen of clubs, and the contract is doomed by the bad diamond split. The same bad split defeats 5♢, but if the diamonds behave 3NT will take at least 10 tricks, so pass is definitely the winning call.

E-W vul., South holds: ♠62, ♡AQJ5, ♢AQ83, ♣J32

NORTH	EAST	SOUTH	WEST
—	—	1 ♡	Pass
2 ♣	Pass	2 ♢	Pass
2 ♡	Pass	?	

South has somewhat more than a minimum opening bid and a mild fit for partner, so it seems as though he might move on toward a heart game in the four-three fit. However, it looks like he has already done well by opening the four-card major. Many pairs cannot find the four-three fit because system or personal preference will prevent them from opening 1♡, and the four-three fit seems right on this hand. Consequently, bidding 4♡ would be overkill. South should pass and take his good result for the best part-score, since he will probably beat the notrump and club part-scores. The combined hands are:

NORTH
- ♠ J 9
- ♡ K 6 2
- ◊ J 4 2
- ♣ A Q 10 7 6

SOUTH
- ♠ 6 2
- ♡ A Q J 5
- ◊ A Q 8 3
- ♣ J 3 2

4♡ is a very reasonable contract, which will probably make if either minor suit finesse succeeds and suits split normally. However, 2♡ making whatever it makes will outscore all other part-scores, and no other game is likely to make. Bidding 4♡ when it is wrong will cost a full matchpoint to tables in notrump or club part-scores, which are likely contracts, and 4♡ gains nothing against these results when it is right since +170 would still be a winner.

N-S vul., South holds: ♠7, ♡A104, ◊Q962, ♣Q10642

NORTH	EAST	SOUTH	WEST
—	—	—	3 ♡
3 ♠	Pass	?	

North can have a wide variety of hands for his overcall. On balance, I would guess that 3NT or 4♠ will fail more often than not. However, South should still bid 3NT. The reason is that there is no assurance that 3♠ is a decent contract, so South might as well go for all the marbles, even if it is slightly against the odds. Other tables may not face the preempt, and they will be able to stop low if they don't have a game, so it is best to shoot the works rather than languish in 3♠. If North has a distributional hand he may pull to 4♠ or best of all bid a minor.

The previous hand is an illustration of a very important principle in constructive bidding. The principle is: When you have a close decision between an overbid and an underbid, choose the bid that gets you to the proper denomination if the bid is successful. Usually this will mean probing on towards game in close situations to make sure you play in the right suit. Here is another example of this principle:

Both vul., South holds: ♠AK1062, ♡AQ85, ◊Q2, ♣K5

NORTH	EAST	SOUTH	WEST
—	—	1 ♠	Pass
1 NT	Pass	?	

On strength the hand is clearly worth a game invitation—a 2 ♡ call doesn't come close to doing justice to the hand. The hand is not, however, worth a game force. The value bid is, therefore, 2NT. The problem with a 2NT rebid is that the heart suit will probably be lost and the hand committed to notrump. It is better to make the slight overbid of 3 ♡. This may get you overboard on occasion when partner has a minimum, but at least you figure to land in the right denomination. If you overbid but play the right suit you may get lucky and make it, giving you a second chance to win, but if you bid 2NT and find partner with something like ♠x, ♡Kxxxx, ◊xxx, ♣QJxx nothing can save you—4 ♡ is cold and 2NT is probably down one.

Weaken the hand slightly to ♠AK1062, ♡AQ85, ◊72, ♣K5 and now the 3 ♡ rebid is simply too optimistic. A 2NT rebid still has the same problem, so it is best to make the mild underbid of 2 ♡. You may occasionally miss a good game, but you will never land in a ridiculous contract.

N-S vul., South holds: ♠Q10874, ♡Q985, ◊64, ♣107

NORTH	EAST	SOUTH	WEST
2 NT*	Pass	?	

*20-21 H.C.P.

Bid Stayman, followed by 3 ♠ over 3 ◊. The worst that can happen is that you get one trick too high, and maybe you'll get lucky and make it anyway. This is much less serious than missing the right major suit fit if you have one.

Both vul., South holds: ♠Q7, ♡AKJ964, ◊A83, ♣KQ

NORTH	EAST	SOUTH	WEST
—	—	1 ♡	Pass
1 ♠	Pass	?	

The hand is just about worth a game force, but which game? 4♡, 4♠, and 3NT are all candidates, so a jump to 3NT or 4♡ is unilateral and may shut out the winning contract. A phony 3◊ bid won't really solve the problem, and may lead to other complications. It is best to bid 3♡, a slight underbid. This leaves partner room to rebid his spades, bid 3NT, or raise to 4♡, thus maximizing your chances of getting to the best game. You may miss an odds-on game when partner passes on a minimum, but you still have a second way to win—that game you missed just might not make. Any time partner bids over 3♡ you will be pleased with your choice, for you are now more likely to get to the right game than if you had guessed yourself.

N-S vul., South holds: ♠KQ953, ♡93, ◊96, ♣K1032

NORTH	EAST	SOUTH	WEST
1 NT	Pass	2 ♡*	Pass
2 ♠	Pass	?	

*transfer

Even if 3♣ is a game force, it is a much better bid than 2NT. Now North can evaluate his hand intelligently, and get to 4♠ with ♠AJ, ♡xxx, ◊AKxx, ♣Axxx but play 3NT with ♠AJx, ♡KQ10x, ◊AQ10, ♣xxx. Over a 2NT rebid North can do little more than count his points and his spades to choose his bid. Getting to the right game on these hands can swing a full match-point against those in a part-score and one-half matchpoint against other pairs in game; stopping at 2NT or 3♠ can only gain one-half matchpoint from other tables if you are exactly right and neither game makes.

OPPONENTS IN THE AUCTION

When your opponents are in your constructive auction, there is another possibility to consider when deciding whether or not to bid a game. At other tables, players holding your cards may choose to defend, collecting a plus score that way. You must determine how large their score on defense is likely to be. If it figures to be only +50 or +100 you will be glad to settle for a part-score, while if it is likely to be higher you must bid the game to try and beat their score.

A common situation occurs when the opponents have a possible sacrifice against your game contract. For example:

N-S vul., South holds: ♠AQ10742, ♡A74, ◇9, ♣KJ5

NORTH	EAST	SOUTH	WEST
—	—	1 ♠	2 ◇
2 ♠	3 ◇	?	

Without the enemy competition this hand would only be worth a game try, since 4♠ figures to be an underdog if partner has a minimum. However, on the actual auction you should just go ahead and bid 4♠. This bid has two things going for it. First of all the opponents might take the 5◇ sacrifice, which you wouldn't mind at all since you are not that sure of making 4♠. Even if your opponents don't save, the save may be taken at other tables, and 5◇ doubled will probably go down two or three for +300 or +500 your way. If this is happening at other tables, you must try to get +620 to beat them. Failing to bid the game when it makes will cost a full matchpoint against tables at which the save is taken, while bidding the game and going down costs nothing against these tables. Of course at the time you bid 4♠ you don't know whether West has a save-oriented hand or not, but simply this possibility justifies the slight overbid.

Another time to stretch to a marginal game is when you have missed an opportunity to collect a number against an enemy overcall, and the opportunity may be taken at other tables. In this case you must bid the game and hope to outscore the result which could have been achieved on defense. For example:

Both vul., South holds: ♠92, ♡J7, ◇Q1097, ♣AQ1062

NORTH	EAST	SOUTH	WEST
1 ♠	2 ◇	Pass	Pass
2 ♡	Pass	?	

You are playing negative doubles, so you passed hoping partner could re-open with a double. Unfortunately, he chose 2♡. Perhaps his bid is reasonable, but many pairs play a re-opening double is almost automatic and will get a chance at 2◇ doubled. This will certainly go down at least one trick, for a minimum of +200. On value your hand is only worth a 2NT bid, for if partner has a distributional minimum game will not be a favorite. However, I would shoot the works with 3NT, since a part-score won't beat the number that may be collected at other tables. If you are wrong and game doesn't make you won't cost yourself anything against those tables in 2◇ doubled, but if you are wrong by failing to bid the game you cost yourself a full matchpoint against every +200 or +500 at other tables. It may seem as though the 3NT bid is in rage at partner's failure to re-open with a double (which it would be at IMPs or rubber bridge). At matchpoints it is so important to try to beat results at other tables that an "anti-percentage" call may be the winning bid if the "percentage" call won't get many matchpoints even if it is correct.

The time you should settle for a part-score is when you feel that at other tables players holding your cards may be selling out to enemy competition and only collecting +50 or +100. If this is the case, the part-score will be sufficient to garner the matchpoints, while stretching to game could cost points that were already locked up. For example:

None vul., South holds: ♠4, ♡K109832, ◇843, ♣KQ5

NORTH	EAST	SOUTH	WEST
1 ♣	1 ♠	2 ♡	2 ♠
3 ♡	Pass	?	

The 2 ♡ bid could have worked out very badly if partner didn't have heart support, but this time you are in luck. Partner clearly has a minimum or he would have bid a game himself, but even opposite a minimum opening bid with heart support game might be on—I would estimate it at about 50-50 from South's point of view. On this auction, however, it is clearly correct to pass 3 ♡. Many players will not risk the 2 ♡ call on your hand, and will sell to an undoubled spade part-score. +140 or +170 will beat these results just the same as +420 will, but −50 will lose to them if the spade part-score goes down. Consequently you gain nothing against these tables by bidding game even if you are right, but you lose a full matchpoint to those defending and beating a spade part-score if you are wrong in bidding a game. This is not one of those hands on which you have to worry about beating 4 ♠ saves at other tables, for East's pass of 3 ♡ indicates that the opponents simply do not have enough distribution to compete at that level, so 4 ♠ doesn't figure to be bid at other tables.

Let's carry this example further. Suppose West now competes to 3 ♠, and this is passed back around to you. It is now quite correct to bid 4 ♡, even after declining to do so earlier. You no longer have the good +140 or +170 available; now all you have is a small set of 3 ♠ (if it goes down at all!). Therefore it is now best to shoot out the 4 ♡ bid. This gains a full matchpoint from pairs who buy it for 3 ♡ when game makes, and then loses nothing to these pairs if game doesn't make, for you could never have beaten them once West bid 3 ♠. The full hand:

```
                    NORTH
                    ♠ 8 5 3
                    ♡ A J 4
                    ◇ Q J 7
                    ♣ A J 3 2
      WEST                      EAST
      ♠ K 10 6 2                ♠ A Q J 9 7
      ♡ Q 7 6                   ♡ 5
      ◇ K 6 2                   ◇ A 10 9 5
      ♣ 9 7 4                   ♣ 10 8 6
                    SOUTH
                    ♠ 4
                    ♡ K 10 9 8 3 2
                    ◇ 8 4 3
                    ♣ K Q 5
```

As you can see, 4♡ depends on guessing the heart queen, while
3♠ is down one. It is instructive to look at the results at all the
tables on this hand. They were:

N-S score	Matchpoints
+420	11½
+420	11½
+300	10
+170	9
+140	7
+140	7
+140	7
+100	5
+50	3
+50	3
+50	3
−50	½
−50	½

Looking at the matchpoints makes it clear that it is right to
buy the hand for 3♡ if possible, but push on to 4♡ if the opponents compete to 3♠. If you pass 3♡ and guess the heart
queen you cost yourself two and one-half matchpoints by failing
to bid game (from eleven and one-half to nine), but if you bid

on and misguess the queen the 4 ♡ call costs six and one-half matchpoints (from seven to one-half). If the opponents bid to 3 ♠, however, it is another story. If you bid on and misguess the queen the 4 ♡ call costs only two and one-half matchpoints (from three to one-half), while if you bid 4 ♡ and guess the queen you gain eight and one-half matchpoints from the bid (from three to eleven and one-half). The drastic change in the odds on the 4 ♡ call when the opponents bid 3 ♠ and when they don't is an illustrative example of the importance of matchpoint cost analysis in competitive auctions.

THE BEST PART-SCORE

When the most your side can make is a part-score, the opponents hold close to half the high-card strength. This means that at other tables the players holding your opponents' cards may be in the auction and might buy the contract. If this happens, any plus you earn for your part-score, particularly if it is greater than +100, will beat many pairs at other tables who defend and collect only small penalties. Furthermore, if the hand lies favorably for the opponents they may be able to make their part-score, so if you avoid going down more than −100 you may still get a reasonable board. It is important to understand that there may be competition at other tables even if your present opponents are silent. Others may take a more aggressive view with their cards.

If any plus score may be sufficient for a good board, it follows that you should aim for the safest plus score rather than the highest one in close situations. Minor suits, virtually ignored for game bidding, come into their own in constructive part-score auctions. For example:

N-S vul., South holds: ♠1094, ♡Q5, ◇AJ76, ♣J654

NORTH	EAST	SOUTH	WEST
1 ♡	Pass	1 NT	Pass
2 ◇	Pass	?	

Many players would bid 2 ♡ on the South hand, going after the higher scoring partial, but I think that they are wrong. Let's look at the combined hands and try to estimate some likely results:

NORTH
- ♠ Q 8
- ♡ A K 8 4 2
- ◇ Q 8 4 3
- ♣ K 8

SOUTH
- ♠ 10 9 4
- ♡ Q 5
- ◇ A J 7 6
- ♣ J 6 5 4

If everything works you might make + 140 in hearts, but if the hearts aren't three-three there is a reasonable chance that 2 ♡ will go down (losing two spades, two clubs, one diamond, and one heart), while 2 ◇ is safe against most distributions. If hearts make eight tricks and diamonds make nine tricks, not an unlikely result, it doesn't matter which contract you choose. This is a major difference between game and part-score bidding. In a game contract if the minor makes one extra trick over the major, the major still scores more. In low part-scores this is not true. The big swings on part-score hands occur when the opponents buy the contract at some other tables, which is not at all unlikely. Let's have a look at the full hand:

NORTH
- ♠ Q 8
- ♡ A K 8 4 2
- ◇ Q 8 4 3
- ♣ K 8

WEST
- ♠ K J 7 6
- ♡ J 10 7 6
- ◇ 9 2
- ♣ Q 9 2

EAST
- ♠ A 5 3 2
- ♡ 9 3
- ◇ K 10 5
- ♣ A 10 7 3

SOUTH
- ♠ 10 9 4
- ♡ Q 5
- ◇ A J 7 6
- ♣ J 6 5 4

This particular East chose not to bid, but it wouldn't be hard to imagine other Easts either making an initial takeout double or doubling 2 ◊. If this happens, E-W will probably buy the hand for 2 ♠ undoubled. At this contract they will probably lose two tricks in each red suit and one trick in each black suit for down one. 2 ◊ should make comfortably for N-S, but in 2 ♡ declarer has six losers. Consequently, bidding 2 ♡ rather than passing 2 ◊ costs a full matchpoint against tables in 2 ♠, while if 2 ♡ had made there would be no gain against these tables, since making two or three diamonds also beats those defending against a spade partial.

If the combined hands have near game strength (23 or 24 H.C.P.) then it becomes more important to strive for the higher scoring part-score. The riskier contract is more likely to make on sheer power, and the chance of enemy competition at other tables is decreased. In the previous example, make South's hand just a bit stronger, say ♠1094, ♡Q5, ◊AJ76, ♣Q654. Now you would want to be in hearts, for 2 ♡ is pretty secure and there is a reasonably good chance for nine tricks and + 140 which beats any possible result in diamonds. With this maximum notrump response South can recognize that this extra strength exists, so he should now bid 2 ♡. If South's hand is in the game zone, say ♠1094, ♡Q5, ◊AJ76, ♣A654, hearts is clearly superior to diamonds. Not only does 4 ♡ have a better chance to make than 5 ◊, but it scores more when it does make. If it appears that your side holds only a bare majority of the points, however, it is better to settle for the part-score that is most likely to make.

N-S vul., South holds: ♠53, ♡Q952, ◊KJ42, ♣876

NORTH	EAST	SOUTH	WEST
1 ◊	Pass	?	

South should raise to 2 ◊ rather than respond 1 ♡. In addition to the preemptive value of the raise, this hand is so weak that South should be content to play in the safer part-score if North is unable to take another bid. A four-three heart fit could be pretty scary, and the risk of missing a four-four heart fit is not very serious. If North has four hearts and a minimum opening bid there is a good chance that the opponents can make some spades, so any plus score should be an excellent result. If South's hand is stronger, say ♠K3, ♡Q952, ♢KJ42, ♣876 he should respond 1♡. The extra strength makes it worth going after a higher scoring part-score in hearts or notrump. The combined hands are:

NORTH
♠ Q 6 4
♡ K J 4
♢ A Q 6 5 3
♣ 9 3

SOUTH
♠ K 3
♡ Q 9 5 2
♢ K J 4 2
♣ 8 7 6

North will raise the 1♡ response to 2♡. This will probably make in spite of the flimsy trump holding, and if the hearts split three-three South may make +140 for a great score. However if South's king of spades were a small spade, as in the first hand, 2♡ would probably be a disaster, for the opponents could tap South in spades. Also other E-W pairs will be getting into the auction and making some spades. So N-S should be quite happy to buy the contract for 2♢ rather than risk some bad splits and −200 in 2♡.

Both vul., South holds: ♠J1062, ♡Q95, ♢J1087, ♣97

NORTH	EAST	SOUTH	WEST
1 NT	Pass	?	

2♣, Stayman, is South's percentage bid. If North has four spades it is great, if North has four hearts the four-three heart fit may well play better than 1NT, and if North responds 2♢ he is likely to have at least four diamonds, in which case 2♢ figures to be better than 1NT since South's hand is so weak. But with ♠J1062, ♡Q95, ♢J1087, ♣K7 South should pass 1NT. With the extra strength, it is better to go for the higher scoring notrump contract. Now, only spades is likely to be better than notrump. The four-three heart fit will probably not produce an extra trick, and notrump will almost certainly score better than a diamond part-score.

None vul., South holds: ♠ J52, ♡ A106, ◇ 543, ♣ J1062

NORTH	EAST	SOUTH	WEST
1 ♠	Pass	?	

South should raise to 2 ♠ rather than respond 1NT. In addition to the preemptive value of the 2 ♠ bid, spades will probably take one more trick than notrump if North has a minimum opening bid, and if North has a strong balanced hand there is still time to get to notrump if that is the right game. But if South had held ♠ J52, ♡ A106, ◇ QJ3, ♣ J1062 a 1NT response might be superior. The extra strength and stoppers in every suit make it likely that notrump will take as many tricks as spades if North has a balanced minimum, and if North is unbalanced he will take another call and South can get back to spades.

A four-four major suit fit is virtually always superior to no-trump at the part-score level. The most important requirement for notrump to be superior, excess strength, can't be met when there is not enough strength to make a game. For this reason, it is correct to probe for a four-four major suit fit even with a suitable notrump hand. For example:

Both vul., South holds: ♠ Q104, ♡ J973, ◇ K6, ♣ Q654

NORTH	EAST	SOUTH	WEST
1 ◇	Pass	?	

South should respond 1 ♡, not 1NT, despite the balanced nature of his hand. If North has four hearts and a minimum opening bid the four-four fit will probably take at least one more trick than notrump, and South can't afford to risk missing this fit if it exists. This is one of the major disadvantages of weak notrumps at matchpoints. A four-four major suit fit is often missed on a normal part-score hand.

The requirements for a four-three major suit fit to be superior to notrump at the part-score level are not nearly as strict as at the game level. All that is usually needed is a reasonable trump suit and any kind of potential ruffing value in the short hand. The reason is that it is not necessary to keep control of the hand at the part-score level. Declarer can often scramble home on a semi-crossruff for an extra trick. For example:

E-W vul., South holds: ♠A5, ♡K95, ◇AQ74, ♣J632

NORTH	EAST	SOUTH	WEST
—	—	1 ◇	Pass
1 ♡	Pass	?	

South should raise to 2♡ rather than rebid 1NT. If North has some non-descript minimum such as ♠Jxxx, ♡Axxx, ◇xx, ♣Kxx the four-three fit figures to bring in an extra trick over notrump one way or another, even though the trump suit is relatively weak, because declarer can score tricks with small trumps which wouldn't be available at notrump. The hand may be difficult to play, but it will be just as difficult to defend. If North happens to have five hearts the raise will almost certainly be right. An added bonus of raising on hands such as these is that responder won't feel compelled to rebid a five-card major for fear of missing a five-three fit, since he knows opener will raise on three-card support more often than not. If responder has a game-going hand with only four hearts, there is plenty of time to get to notrump if that is where the hand belongs.

There is one type of hand on which the four-three major suit fit should be avoided at the part-score level. When you have another suit that will produce tricks, it is better to play notrump so that suit can comfortably be run. For example:

Both vul., South holds: ♠K3, ♡Q98, ◇KQJ107, ♣K63

NORTH	EAST	SOUTH	WEST
—	—	1 ◇	Pass
1 ♡	Pass	?	

South should rebid 1NT, not 2♡. The diamonds will score in

notrump, but they may not be so valuable in a four-three heart fit because North won't be able to draw trumps conveniently and run the diamonds. If South had instead held ♠K3, ♡Q98, ◊A10765, ♣K63 a 2♡ bid would be preferable. The diamonds don't figure to run at notrump, so the ruffing value will probably produce the extra trick even if North has only four hearts.

PAVING THE WAY

This section will not be of much interest to some readers. Players who use methods which restrict choice of early actions such as five-card majors, forced response in any four-card major, required four-card support to raise a one-level response, etc., do not have the opportunity to make the types of decisions discussed in this chapter. These methods have their advantages, but they eliminate the option of using good judgment to make favorable delicate decisions early in the auction.

Players who play a free-wheeling style can base their initial actions on more than the number of cards in a suit. They can look at the quality of suits, the overall hand, and how the auction is likely to proceed to help them make their choice. Intelligent early decisions can shift the odds in favor of the player making the bid if he chooses wisely. We shall examine a few of these decisions in detail. Similar reasoning can be applied to all early decisions.

THE FOUR-CARD MAJOR OPENING

Many methods do not permit discretion in deciding whether or not to open a four-card major. Eastern Scientific and Precision forbid opening any four-card major, while Blue Team and Canape structures often compel a major suit opening on a 5432 suit. Let us suppose you play a natural style which allows leeway on this decision. What should the criteria be?

1. Trump strength. This is the most important consideration. Even if you play "four-card majors", partner will bid his hand as though you have five, since this is what you will have the great majority of the time you open a major. Therefore, you must be prepared to play a four-three fit, possibly at the game level, if partner has a good hand, three-card support, some distribution, so your trump suit had better be good enough to stand it. A hand such as ♠73, ♡AKQ4, ◇A972, ♣1092 is fine for a 1♡ opening bid, but something like ♠A3, ♡K864, ◇A972, ♣Q92 is better opened 1◇. The latter hand is not the type that you are anxious to play in a four-three heart fit. There is little danger that a four-four heart fit will be lost. If the opponents don't bid partner can certainly bid a four-card heart suit now or on the next round, and if the opponents enter the auction the negative double (which is used by almost all tournament players and can be considered "standard" today) will help to locate a four-four heart fit.

2. Side-suit texture. One of the advantages of playing a four-three major suit fit is the ability to ruff losers in the short hand. If the hand with the four-card major has 4-4-3-2 distribution (the most common distribution when considering whether or not to open a four-card major), the side four-card suit is the suit most likely to be ruffed in dummy. If this suit has late round losers we will be happy to ruff them, but if it is strong in intermediates the four-three fit is likely not to be of value. So with ♠J84, ♡AK106, ◇A763, ♣106 a 1♡ opening bid is right because the third and fourth rounds of diamonds may be ruffed in dummy, but ♠Q84, ♡AK106, ◇QJ63, ♣106 is better opened 1◇. The heart suit is strong, but the texture of the diamond suit suggests that a four-three heart fit will not take an ex-

tra trick over notrump.

3. Rebid considerations. In close decisions, the question of whether or not to open a four-card major is often decided by rebid considerations. Assume that partner will respond in your shortest suit. If you don't have a convenient rebid, it is time to reconsider your choice of opening bids.

None vul., South deals and holds:
♠AQJ5, ♡974, ◊94, ♣AJ54.

The black suits are quite satisfactory for opening the four-card major, but South should prefer a 1♣ opening bid. If South opens 1♠ and North responds 2◊, South will have a serious rebid problem. He can't very well rebid his four-card major, so he must rebid 2NT. Even if this shows a minimum opening bid, as it does with most players today, it is not really satisfactory due to the lack of a heart stopper. Also, there is virtually no chance to get to a club part-score after opening 1♠. A 1♣ opening bid does not suffer from any of these defects. South can easily rebid 1♠ over either red suit, and get both his suits in while staying at the one-level. The only things wrong with the 1♣ opening are the loss of the four-three spade fit when it is right (and it doesn't have to be right—another way for the 1♠ opening to lose), and the loss of the preemptive value of the 1♠ opening if the opponents are considering entering the auction. In my opinion, these defects don't compensate for the potential cost of the 1♠ opening when an awkward rebid causes problems.

A small change in the suits makes the four-card major opening bid much more attractive. With ♠AQJ5, ♡974, ◊AJ54, ♣94 a 1♠ opening bid is best. There are no rebid problems. 2◊ can be bid over 2♣, and 2♡ can be raised to three (since 2♡ shows a five-card suit over a 1♠ opening bid). It is the 1◊ opening which creates rebid problems after a 2♣ response. All the possible rebids (2◊, 2♠, or 2NT) have serious drawbacks. Consequently, a 1♠ opening is clear on this hand.

4. Looking ahead. If the decision on whether or not to open the four-card major is close, a look at how the auction might develop often provides the answer. Each situation must be analyzed individually. Here are a few examples.

Both vul., South deals and holds:
♠98, ♡AKJ6, ◇AKQ, ♣K832

Some players would open 2NT despite the worthless doubleton and the fact that the hand doesn't really evaluate to 20 points, but let's suppose that you reject the 2NT opening. Which is better, 1♣ or 1♡? If partner is so weak that he will pass either opening bid then you would rather play 1♡ than 1♣, while if he responds the 1♡ bid may work out well, since a four-three heart game could well be right. It could be argued that partner is more likely to keep the bidding open over 1♣ than over 1♡. This is true, but it is actually an argument in favor of the 1♡ opening. The reason you didn't open 2NT in the first place was so that you wouldn't get too high if partner had a bad hand. Suppose he holds something like ♠KJxx, ♡xxx, ◇Jxx, ♣xxx. He will certainly pass 1♡, but he might try 1♠ over a 1♣ opening bid, and now your 2NT rebid will put the contract at a dangerous level.

E-W vul., South deals and holds:
♠KQ107, ♡A983, ◇42, ♣KJ9

A 1♠ opening bid is best. The quality of suit clearly argues against a 1♡ opening bid. A 1♠ opening bid is O.K. as far as playing a four-three fit goes, but there is too great a danger of missing a four-four heart fit if partner responds 1NT. You don't dare rebid 2♡, for this could easily land you in a silly four-two spade fit. So the four-card major opening should be rejected on this hand. However, holding ♠A983, ♡KQ107, ◇42, ♣KJ9 a 1♡ opening bid is quite satisfactory. Now a four-four spade fit won't be missed because partner can respond 1♠, so all the lights are green for the four-card major opening.

None vul., South deals and holds:
♠4, ♡AQ106, ◇A10654, ♣KJ8.

Minimum opening bids with a singleton spade often present problems. Many four-card majorites would open 1♡, but I think they are wrong. Their argument is that if you open 1◇ and partner responds 1♠ you have no convenient rebid, while if you open 1 ♡ you can rebid 2 ◊ easily enough. This sounds convincing, but you might have second thoughts when partner takes a preference to 2 ♡ with ♠Kxxxx, ♡xx, ◊Qx, ♣Qxxx or ♠Kxxxx, ♡Kx, ◊xxx, ♣Qxx and the four-two fit is not the greatest contract in the world. It is true that opening 1 ◊ and rebidding 2 ◊ over 1 ♠ may not work out—partner might have to pass with ♠Kxxxx, ♡Kxxx, ◊x, ♣Qxx for example, and rebidding 1NT (my personal preference) has the disadvantage that partner will play you for a doubleton spade, so there are problems whatever you open. Suppose it is the opponents who bid spades. If you open 1 ◊ the four-heart fit can be recovered via the negative double, but if you open 1 ♡ the diamond suit may get lost forever, particularly if partner has three hearts. For example, suppose North has ♠Jxxx, ♡Jxx, ◊Kxxx, ♣Qx and the bidding goes:

NORTH	EAST	SOUTH	WEST
—	—	1 ♡	1 ♠
2 ♡	2 ♠	?	

You would like to be in 3 ◊, but you can't get there from here. 3 ◊ by you would be forcing, so you are stuck and must either sell to 2 ♠ or land in a very skinny 3 ♡ contract when 3 ◊ is clearly best. Had you opened 1 ◊ he would have raised to 2 ◊ on the actual hand, while had his red suits been reversed he would have made a negative double and you could then get to hearts. A 1 ◊ opening bid leaves you better placed in any competitive auction. The old philosophy of bidding your longest suit first has much to recommend it.

Interestingly enough, change the hand to ♠KJ8, ♡AQ106, ◊A10654, ♣4 and the 1 ♡ opening now has much more going for it. A 1 ♠ response suits you fine as you can raise, and the enemy is less likely to have a spade fit. If partner responds 1NT you can pass and have a reasonable chance of being right, while if partner responds 2 ♣ you are happier with your 2 ◊ rebid if you open 1 ♡ than if you open 1 ◊.

1NT WITH A FIVE-CARD MAJOR

Whether or not to open a strong notrump when holding a five-card major is often quite a problem. The main considerations are suit quality, rebid problems, and other flaws.

1. Suit quality. The main danger in opening 1NT with a five-card major is that you are very likely to miss a five-three major suit fit if you have one, for partner simply will not play you for a five-card major and most conventional methods over notrump openings do not allow the five-card major to be shown. Consequently, you should choose hands on which notrump has a good chance of being superior to the five-three fit. Such a hand is one which has a very weak trump suit. With ♠AQ10, ♡J6532, ◇KJ, ♣AJ2 a 1NT opening bid is surely best. If partner has some scattered collection such as ♠Kx, ♡Kxx, ◇A10xxx, ♣10xx, 3 NT is certainly better than 4♡, and if you take away one of his high cards 1NT is likely to take as many tricks as 2♡.

Another type of hand with which to consider opening 1NT is a hand with a very strong major and intermediates on the side. For example: ♠Q65, ♡AKQ74, ◇K93, ♣K2. A 1NT opening bid will probably work out well. Even if partner has three hearts there may not be any ruffing value opposite this hand. Your hearts are ready to run, and you can go right after your side tricks. Unless the opponents can establish a suit on the opening lead, notrump will probably take as many tricks as hearts.

The type of suit which calls for the suit opening bid rather than 1NT is one of intermediate strength. For example: ♠AQ4, ♡KJ1053, ◇K2, ♣QJ9. Despite the notrump orientation of the hand, a 1♡ opening bid is probably best. You can't afford to miss a five-three heart fit with this hand. The hearts are strong enough that you will be using the suit for tricks at notrump if you have a five-three heart fit, but weak enough that they will take time to establish. Consequently, the five-three fit is likely to produce an extra trick even if there is no ruffing value in dummy, simply because time will be required to establish tricks and the trump suit is needed as a stopper.

2. Rebid considerations. If you fail to open 1NT with a five-card major, you must consider your rebid problems after open-

ing the major. There are seldom any great problems with a spade suit, but the heart suit can present difficulties if partner responds 1♠. For example: ♠A9, ♡KJ1072, ◊KJ7, ♣A72. The hand isn't ideal for a 1NT opening bid, due to the intermediate strength of the heart suit. Nevertheless, 1NT is the best opening bid. The reason is that if you open 1♡ and partner responds 1♠ you are really stuck. 1NT is a clear underbid, 2NT is an equally large overbid, and two of a minor is likely to lead to a disastrous result, with partner possibly passing you out in a bad four-three or three-three fit. These problems are solved with a 1NT opening bid.

It must be noted that this hand is the worst sort of hand for a 1♡ bid. Any slight change makes the 1♡ opening more attractive. Weaken the hand a bit, and now the 1NT rebid is adequate, strengthen the hand a bit and a 2NT rebid isn't too much of a distortion, give South three spades and now it may be feasible to raise the 1♠ response to an appropriate level, particularly if you play Flannery and the 1♠ response implies a five-card suit.

3. Other flaws. When you open 1NT with a five-card major you risk a loss if partner has three of the major, so you would like to be pretty sure of showing a profit if he doesn't. Consequently, the hand should be perfect for notrump outside of the five-card major. This is another illustration of loading the dice in your favor. You don't want to give yourself two ways to lose. For example: ♠AKQ42, ♡87, ◊KJ7, ♣QJ2. South should open 1♠, not 1NT. The worthless doubleton in hearts is the second flaw. It would be sad if North had something like ♠Jx, ♡xx, ◊Axxx, ♣AKxxx. After a 1NT opening bid he would bid 3NT and the heart suit would be wide open. After a 1♠ opening, an intelligent auction might be:

NORTH	EAST	SOUTH	WEST
—	—	1 ♠	Pass
2 ♣	Pass	2 ♠	Pass
3 ◊	Pass	4 ♣	Pass
4 ♠	Pass	Pass	Pass

If you had opened 1NT you would have been right in that you didn't miss a five-three spade fit, but you would still come out a loser because of the second flaw, the worthless doubleton.

Both vul., South deals and holds:
♠K8, ♡J9642, ◇AQ108, ♣AQ.

South should open 1♡. The 5-4-2-2 distribution is too much of a flaw. Can't you just picture North holding something like ♠Q10xx, ♡x, ◇Kxxx, ♣Jxxx. You would certainly like to be in a diamond part-score, but it's tough to get there after a 1NT opening bid. Once again you got away with not opening the major (no five-three fit), but the second flaw (the four-card diamond suit) came back to haunt you. Avoid opening 1NT with a five-card major unless the hand is otherwise perfect for the action.

THE INITIAL RESPONSE

The proper choice of initial response is often the key to getting to the right contract. The main consideration is the rebid problem. You must think of partner's two or three most likely rebids, and anticipate how comfortable the auction will be after he makes them.

There are basically three types of hands to consider. These are minimum strength responses, game-invitational hands, and game forcing hands. We shall examine problems with all three types.

With a minimum strength response, directness is the key. Keep in mind that you will not bid again if partner makes a limited rebid, so you should hope that these bids will be the best contract. Also, you want to avoid complex auctions in which you have difficulty limiting your hand.

None vul., South holds: ♠KQ107, ♡73, ◇J10872, ♣32

NORTH	EAST	SOUTH	WEST
1 ♣	Pass	?	

A 1♠ response is better than 1◇. If partner raises to 2♠ you will be quite happy to play a possible four-three spade partial, and any non-forcing bid by partner can be easily passed. A 1◇ response loses the possibility of finding a four-three spade fit, and can lead to other complications. For example:

NORTH	EAST	SOUTH	WEST
1 ♣	Pass	1 ◇	Pass
1 ♠	Pass	?	

Should you raise to 2♠? If you do, partner will play you for a better hand, and bid a bad game with something like ♠Jxxx, ♡Ax, ◇Kx, ♣AKJxx. If you pass, however, you may find that partner has ♠AJxx, ♡xx, ◇x, ♣AKQxxx. He would have jumped to game over your 1♠ response, but was not strong enough to do more than bid 1♠ over a 1◇ response since a fit had not yet been found. Another problem with the 1 ◊ bid is that partner might hold ♠xxxx, ♡AQx, ◊Kxx, ♣KQx. A 1 ♠ rebid on this balanced hand is just too much of a distortion, so he will bid 1NT and the superior four-four spade fit will be lost. Also, if North rebids 1 ♡ you must now rebid 1 ♠. This might work out O.K., but it is better not to have to make two forcing bids on a six-count if it can easily be avoided.

Contrast with the following hand, same auction:

South holds ♠10874, ♡KJ9, ◊QJ62, ♣53.

Over the 1 ♣ opening bid, South should respond 1 ◊. All the arguments are in the other direction. South does not want to play a four-three spade fit, he can pass a 1 ♠ rebid secure that there is no game opposite a distributional black two-suiter, a 1 ♡ rebid can happily be passed, and missing a four-four spade fit if North has a balanced hand with bad spades might not be so bad. Players who use good judgment on hands like this will get better results than those who always bid up the line or always respond with any four-card major.

If you have a hand of intermediate strength, you are probably going to take another bid after partner rebids. The likely course of the auction must be examined carefully. For example:

N-S vul., South holds: ♠AQ8, ♡9752, ◊KQ85, ♣63

NORTH	EAST	SOUTH	WEST
1 ♣	Pass	?	

There is nothing particularly wrong with a 1 ◊ response, but 1 ♡ figures to make life easier for you and more difficult for the opponents. The point is that you plan to rebid 2NT over 2 ♡ or any other minimum rebid. This describes your hand accurately — game invitational, balanced, only four hearts, so there is little danger of getting stuck in a bad heart contract if partner has only three-card support. In addition, if partner doesn't have heart support your response may stop a heart lead against notrump, and this is likely to be the best lead for the defense. Another subtle problem with the 1 ◊ response is that if partner bids 1 ♡ it is not clear whether the hand is worth driving to game, but if the bidding goes:

NORTH	EAST	SOUTH	WEST
1 ♣	Pass	1 ♡	Pass
2 ♡	Pass	2 NT	

You have described your hand accurately, and partner has a good chance to make the right decision.

Both vul., South holds: ♠KJ4, ♡J74, ◊A532, ♣J53

NORTH	EAST	SOUTH	WEST
1 ♡	Pass	?	

The hand is just a bit weak for 2 ◊ followed by a heart raise. If partner has a 5-3-3-2 minimum either 1NT or 2♡ could be right—there are arguments both ways. The problems occur when partner doesn't have the balanced hand. Suppose you respond 1NT, and he rebids 2♣. What now? If you emerge from your shell with a 3 ♡ bid, it will be your luck to find partner with ♠xx, ♡Axxxx, ◊Qx, ♣AKxx and 3 ♡ will be in quite a bit of jeopardy. On the other hand, if you merely bid 2 ♡ partner will undoubtedly hold ♠Ax, ♡KQxxx, ◊xx, ♣AKxx and a good 4♡ game will be missed, for partner can't afford to bid again since your sequence doesn't promise three-card support. The solution to this dilemma is to bid 2 ♡ immediately. This doesn't show more strength than the 1NT response, but will be more encouraging to partner if he holds an intermediate hand with some distribution. He will pass with the first hand but make a game try with the second, and you will get to the right contract in both cases.

Conversely, suppose you had the same scattered strength but were weaker, say ♠KJ4, ♡J74, ◊J532, ♣J53. Now a 1NT response may turn out O.K. if partner passes, and will certainly be better if he has an unbalanced hand. You don't want him making a game try with a moderate hand, and the sequence:

NORTH	EAST	SOUTH	WEST
1 ♡	Pass	1 NT	Pass
2 ♣	Pass	2 ♡	

will slow him up, which is what you want.

With a game-going hand, you can assume that the only objective is to find the best game. Slam may be possible if partner has a strong opening bid, but that can be worried about later. The overwhelming majority of these hands will be game contracts. Since matchpoints is a game of frequency, finding the best game is more important. Consequently, you should look ahead so that the auction is likely to develop in such a way that one partner will be able to make the right decision. For example:

E-W vul., South holds: ♠AQ85, ♡A4, ◇83, ♣KJ962

NORTH	EAST	SOUTH	WEST
1 ♡	Pass	?	

South should respond 2♣ rather than 1♠. There are many possible game contracts, and you want to keep all avenues open. Over partner's likely 2◇ or 2♡ rebid you can now bid 2♠, establishing a game force at the two-level and giving the partnership maximum room to explore. The main difficulty with a 1♠ response is that the auction might go:

NORTH	EAST	SOUTH	WEST
1 ♡	Pass	1 ♠	Pass
2 ♠	Pass	3 ♣	Pass
3 ♠	Pass	?	

You knew you were probing for the best game when you rebid 3♣. Unfortunately, from partner's point of view 3♣ was a game try, so he signs off with a minimum (and possibly three-card spade support), and you have to guess what to do. Some hands he might hold for this auction are ♠KJx, ♡KJxxx, ◇Jx, ♣Axx (4♠ is best), ♠Jxx, ♡KQ10xx, ◇xx, ♣AKx (4♡ is best), or ♠Kxx, ♡Qxxxx, ◇KQ10, ♣Kx (now 3NT is the winner). After a 2♣ response you would have a good chance to get to the right contract opposite all of these hands.

Contrast this with a slightly weaker hand: ♠A1092, ♡A6, ◇86, ♣QJ873. With this hand, a 1♠ response is correct. Here you aren't strong enough to force to game, so the 2♣ bid can lead to problems. If partner rebids 2♡, what now? 2♠ may get you too high, and 2NT with no diamond stopper or 3♡ on a doubleton could easily lead to the wrong contract, particularly if partner holds something like ♠KJx, ♡Kxxxx, ◇xx, ♣AKx. After an initial 1♠ response, however, your rebid problems are all solved. Look at the possibilities:

1. North rebids 1NT. 2NT, or if forcing, 2♣, does justice to the hand. You almost certainly belong in notrump, and North can make a simple power evaluation.

2. North rebids 2♣. 3♣ by you is perfect. Some extra strength (you could have passed 2♣ with nothing) and club support. 3♣ will probably be the right contract if partner has a minimum, and you can't easily get there if you start with 2♣.

3. North rebids 2◇. 2NT is perfect. Unbid suit stopped, game invitational strength, and notrump is probably where you belong. No problem here.

4. North rebids 2♡. Now you can confidently raise to 3♡, since he has shown a six-card suit (with a five-card suit he must have some other bid available—work it out). So an invitational 3♡ bid is an accurate evaluation of the hand.

5. North rebids 2♠. Now your 3♣ bid is a game try, which is what you want it to be. If North has a minimum he will sign off at 3♠, which at least has a chance to be the winning contract, while if North has extra strength he will move toward the best game, so you may still get to 4♡ or 3NT if you belong there.

SLAM BIDDING

Slams play a very important role in IMP matches. Any time there is a slam in the air, there are always at least ten IMPs up for grabs if the slam is bid at one table and not bid at the other table. Good slam bidding mechanisms are very important to any partnership. That gadget that gets the partnership to a slightly safer six of a minor contract or keeps them out of an inferior slam because a critical weakness is diagnosed can swing many IMPs, and this large IMP swing justifies the caution and accurate methods even though opportunities to employ them may be infrequent.

At matchpoints, however, slam bidding takes a definite back seat to all other constructive or competitive bidding. Getting to the best game is at least as important as bidding a brilliant 60% slam in a four-four minor fit, since beating the field by 10 or 20 points is as big a win as a 750 point victory. Since slam decisions occur very infrequently relative to game and part-score decisions (perhaps 10% of all hands are in the slam zone), accurate slam bidding just isn't very important. Consequently, a player's first thoughts about a hand should be: how will we do in a constructive game auction or a competitive part-score battle, not how will a slam sequence work out. For example:

None vul., South holds: ♠AKQJ86, ♡74, ◇AQJ9, ♣4

NORTH	EAST	SOUTH	WEST
Pass	Pass	?	

South should simply open 4♠ at matchpoints. This is very likely to be the right contract opposite almost any North hand, and the bid puts tremendous pressure on the opponents. It is true that there may be a slam if North has the right hand. For example, as little as ♠xx, ♡Axxx, ◇K10xx, ♣xxx gives an excellent play for 6◇. For this reason, it is probably correct to open 1♠ or 2♣ (or 1♣ if a forcing club is your style) at IMPs. The swing of a missed slam is just too great to risk. At matchpoints, frequency is the name of the game. If you can shut the opponents out of a good save, or goad them into a bad one, or cause them to double you when you are cold, or escape a double when the hand belongs to the opponents, you will gain just as much as if you had reached a hard-to-bid slam by starting slowly, and one of these small gains is much more likely than getting to a good slam. At IMPs the gains from opening 4♠ when the opponents take the wrong action are usually only two to five IMPs as opposed to a double-figure swing for bidding a slam, but at matchpoints each swing is the same size.

WHICH SLAM TO BID

Slam bidding is one area where it is very important to try to determine what the field will be doing. If it is clear that the rest of the field will also get to slam, then it is very important to get to the highest scoring slam. If a substantial part of the field is likely to miss the slam, it is crucial to get to the safest slam. If you gamble 6NT and go down one when you are cold for six of a minor you cost yourself a full matchpoint to any table which stops in game, while if 6NT had made you gain nothing against these tables for playing notrump instead of the minor.

When the room is in slam, notrump is king. Six of a minor can never score more than 6NT, and six of a major only scores more if it makes seven. For example:

None vul., South holds: ♠76, ♡J95, ♢AQJ5, ♣KJ83

NORTH	EAST	SOUTH	WEST
2 NT*	Pass	?	

*21-22 H.C.P.

At IMPs you would haul out all your fancy slam bidding machinery over 2NT opening bids and attempt to find a four-four or five-four minor suit fit, for if such a fit exists it is probably safer than the notrump slam. At matchpoints you can throw your machinery out the window and bid a direct 6NT. Your hand is strong enough that the field will bid slam, and 6NT certainly figures to be a favorite even if it is not cold, so you must bid 6NT even if it is not aesthetically pleasing.

The combined hands:

NORTH
♠ A Q 10
♡ A K 2
♢ K 10 9 7
♣ A Q 4

SOUTH
♠ 7 6
♡ J 9 5
♢ A Q J 5
♣ K J 8 3

6♢ is virtually cold, while 6NT basically depends on one of two spade finesses or the queen of hearts dropping doubleton. At IMPs you would be pleased to arrive at 6♢, but at matchpoints it is essential to get to 6NT. It will make more often than not, and the occasional top you get for bidding 6♢ when 6NT goes down won't compensate for the more likely bottom you get when 6NT makes.

Weaken the South hand somewhat to make it:
♠76, ♡985, ♢AQJ5, ♣K983. Now it is far from clear that the field will bid a slam, so you should be happy to play a minor suit slam if you can locate a fit. Opposite the actual North hand 6♢ is a pretty good contract. If the diamonds split three-two it will make if clubs are three-three or if either spade honor is onside. 6NT is just fair—it needs both spade finesses or one spade finesse and a club split, with some outside squeeze possibilities. If the whole room bid a slam 6NT would not be bad, but since many pairs will stay out of slam 6♢ should be a reasonable result even if 6NT makes, and a top if 6NT goes down when 6♢ makes. Bidding 6NT and being wrong on this hand can be very costly, turning a near top into a near bottom, while getting to 6♢ and being wrong (i.e. 6NT also makes) will not cost nearly as much. The reason is that bidding 6NT as opposed to 6♢ risks a full matchpoint but gains nothing against those pairs who stop short of slam.

When it is clear that the field will bid a slam and you have a choice between a safe major suit slam and a good but not secure notrump slam, it is sometimes correct to choose the major suit slam even if 6NT is a favorite to make. The reason is that the major suit has an extra way to win—even if 6NT makes, the major may make seven and outscore notrump. This should only be done when you have all the aces, of course. If an ace is missing the major can't make seven, so you should bid 6NT if you think it more likely to make than not. For example:

Both vul., South holds: ♠A86, ♡AKQ3, ◇J73, ♣K62

NORTH	EAST	SOUTH	WEST
1 NT	Pass	2 ♣	Pass
2 ♡	Pass	?	

It would not have been unreasonable for South to have bid 6NT directly, as he certainly would have done had his four-card suit been a minor. South reasoned that if North had four hearts, a doubleton in the North hand might be valuable since South has no queens in his three-card suits, so a third round ruff could be worth an extra trick. Well, North came up with a four-card heart suit. What should South do? His percentage action is to bid 4 ♣ (Gerber) or use whatever his ace-asking mechanism is at this point. South isn't worried about being off two aces, which is virtually impossible opposite a strong notrump, and he isn't trying for a grand. There are North hands that will produce a good grand, but it would take better bidding methods than most of us have to determine if North has such a perfecto. What South is planning to do is to bid 6NT if he is off an ace, but 6 ♡ if he has all the aces. 6NT figures to be a favorite in any event, but 6 ♡ might make seven if North has the right hand and no aces are missing. The combined hands:

NORTH
- ♠ K 4
- ♡ J 9 8 5
- ◊ A K 8
- ♣ A J 10 5

SOUTH
- ♠ A 8 6
- ♡ A K Q 3
- ◊ J 7 3
- ♣ K 6 2

6NT depends on running four club tricks unless the diamond queen is nice enough to drop doubleton, but if four club tricks are available, 7 ♡ will make. However if North is missing an ace, he might hold ♠ Kx, ♡ Jxxx, ◊ AKQ, ♣ QJ10x. Now both 6 ♡ and 6NT are cold, so you would want to be in notrump.

TO BID A SLAM OR NOT

The problem of whether or not to bid a close slam is quite similar to that of bidding a close game. When there is only one possible denomination, you should usually bid it if you think it will make and not otherwise. Once again, really close decisions should be resolved in favor of making the "field bid" if possible. You can assume that most of the field will bid a "point-count" slam, but not one depending on distribution, so use this information to judge accordingly.

When alternative game contracts are possible, you must estimate how well your game contract will fare relative to other game contracts if you don't bid the slam. When the auction has forced you into a minor suit and you think that notrump will do well, it is better to shoot out a thin slam than to languish in five of a minor only to lose to the notrumpers. For example:

E-W vul., South holds: ♠ J7, ♡ 532, ◇ AQ962, ♣ AQ10

NORTH	EAST	SOUTH	WEST
1 ♠	Pass	2 ◇	Pass
2 ♡	Pass	3 NT	Pass
4 ◇	Pass	4 ♠	Pass
5 ♣	Pass	?	

Just what you didn't want to hear! You bid 4 ♠ in the hope that it might be the best game. Perhaps this wasn't too good a decision; signing off in 4NT might have been better. You were never really trying for slam, but things seem to have gotten out of hand. Now you know that partner is probably 5-4-4-0, but you seem to have the wrong cards for slam purposes. At IMPs you would just bid 5 ◇ and take your likely profit, but you can't afford to do that at matchpoints. One way or another, most of the field will get to 3NT. Perhaps they play 2 ◇ as a game force and don't have to use up bidding room with the 3NT bid as you did, perhaps some players with your hand will just respond 2NT over the 1 ♠ opening bid and the diamond fit won't be found, or perhaps any of a number of sequences, all of which end up in the most popular matchpoint contract. Unfortunately for you, it appears as though the field will be right. With your extra strength and powerful club holding, 3NT is likely to do very well. Your only hope for a decent board is to bid 6 ◇ and hope to get lucky, even though the slam figures to be an underdog. The combined hands:

NORTH
♠ A 9 5 4 2
♡ A Q 10 7
◇ K 8 7 3
♣ —

SOUTH
♠ J 7
♡ 5 3 2
◇ A Q 9 6 2
♣ A Q 10

6 ◇ is not a favorite to make, but it has reasonable plays. Stopping in 5 ◇ when 3NT makes ten tricks, as it will most of the time, will cost a full matchpoint against the notrumpers when slam makes (from +920 to +420 against their +430), while it costs nothing to bid 6 ◇ when the slam goes down, as you were dead anyway.

The converse applies when you believe you have reached a high-scoring game contract that the field is not likely to find. A good four-three major suit fit is a common example. When this happens, stopping in game will net you many matchpoints even if the slam makes. For example:

Both vul., South holds: ♠AQ10, ♡AQJ6, ◇AJ43, ♣62

NORTH	EAST	SOUTH	WEST
—	—	1 ♡	Pass
2 ◇	Pass	3 ◇*	Pass
3 ♡	Pass	3 ♠	Pass
4 ♣	Pass	4 ◇	Pass
4 ♡	Pass	?	

*extra strength

113

So far, the auction has worked out very well. Partner probably has the ace of clubs but not great club strength (since he didn't bid 3NT), only three hearts, and a fair but not particularly strong hand since he couldn't do more than bid 4♡ at his last turn. 6♢ certainly figures to have a reasonable play whatever he holds, and it might even be cold. However, you have only about 29-30 high card points between the combined hands and no great distribution, so most of the field will not get to slam. Most players cannot or will not open 1♡ on your hand, so the four-three heart fit will be lost at other tables. The most popular contract will be 3NT, with 5♢ being tried at a few tables. The four-three heart fit will probably outscore these other game contracts, so it is best to pass 4♡. Even if 6♢ makes, 4♡ should prove to be a winning matchpoint contract. The combined hands:

NORTH
♠ J 7 6
♡ K 3 2
♢ K 10 8 7 5
♣ A 8

SOUTH
♠ A Q 10
♡ A Q J 6
♢ A J 4 3
♣ 6 2

6♢ is a pretty good contract. If the diamonds come in it is cold, and if the diamonds don't behave it can still make if three rounds of hearts survive and the spade finesse works, so at IMPs you would like to be there. At matchpoints, however, 4♡ figures to be the winner. Notrump only does well when both spades and diamonds behave, while hearts can survive an unfavorable lie in either or both of these suits, particularly if the hearts are three-three. Consequently, 4♡ will score well on most lies of the cards, and it may be the best contract of all.

If your opponents might take a save against your slam, it is best to bid it even if you are not all that sure of making it.

N-S vul., South holds: ♠AQ9764, ♡A6, ◊6, ♣AJ62

NORTH	EAST	SOUTH	WEST
—	—	1 ♠	2 ◊
3 ♠*	4 ◊	?	

*limit raise

Who knows if slam will make. It probably depends a lot on
North's club holding. I would guess that slam is a slight underdog and that careful cue-bidding might give us a better idea, but
I would just go ahead and bid 6 ♠. Now the opponents have to
decide what to do. If they save I'm happy since I wasn't all that
sure of making and the slam may not be bid at other tables
anyway, while if they defend I may still make it. If I had held
♠AQ9764, ♡A6, ◊6, ♣AKJ2, I would expect 6♠ to make,
but seven to be off a trick somewhere. I would also expect most
of the field to bid the slam. Once again, I would leap to 6♠.
This time the opponents should take the save, but how can they
tell when I bid both hands the same way?

When you are bidding a slam, how you get there is often
more important than whether you get there. The opening lead,
vital at any contract, can be the whole difference in a slam
because the defense may not get a second chance. Overtricks are
also important, so a cashed or uncashed ace can mean a lot if
the rest of the field is also in slam. Consequently, it is often better to just blast away rather than conduct a careful scientific
auction. If you blast to a slam off two cashing tricks you may
still win if the defense doesn't cash them, but if your accurate
auction tells the opponents what to lead you not only lose to the
slam bidders who get away with it, but also to the pairs who stop
in game and don't get the best opening lead. Also, when the
slam is a good contract, a blasting auction may stop the lead to
hold in the overtrick. For example:

None vul., South holds: ♠KQ75, ♡AKQ108, ◊K9, ♣J5

NORTH	EAST	SOUTH	WEST
1 ♠	Pass	?	

No doubt you and your partner have careful methods to stay out of slam if partner holds ♠ AJxxx, ♡ xx, ◊ AQx, ♣ Qxx, and at IMPs these methods should definitely be employed. However, this is matchpoints! It is a fact of life that the field will be in slam on this hand unless they are off two aces. The practical player will simply bid Blackwood. If partner produces three aces, South should probably gamble out 7NT. This will make whenever the hearts produce five tricks, which is basically on a finesse at worst, and there may be other chances if North has extra strength. If partner has only two aces, South has several possible approaches. One is to take his chances with a 6NT bid, which is likely to work out but will look silly if North has a singleton small club. Another approach would be to try 5NT. I know this "promises" all the aces, but so what? There is no chance of North leaping to a grand on his solid suit when you hold the king and queen of that suit. If North shows a king we can now bid 6NT expecting to be a favorite, while if North has no king South can try 6 ♠ and hope for the best. Another approach is to bid 5NT, planning on bidding 6NT whether or not North has a king! This bluff may stop an opponent from making an aggressive lead from a king, since South "promised" all the aces, particularly after South bids 6NT when his partner doesn't have any kings. Any of these approaches are reasonable, and they are all better than bidding a mundane 6 ♠ after the two ace response and better than trying to bid the hand scientifically and winding up telling the opponents what to lead whether or not slam is reached. The point is that at matchpoints the extra ten points for notrump and the opening lead are so important that accuracy and scientific bidding in slam auctions is much less likely to be rewarded than at IMPs, where getting to the game or slam most likely to make has number one priority.

LOW-LEVEL INTERFERENCE

FREE BIDS

When the opponents enter your auction at a low level, it is extremely important to describe immediately any distributional features or trump support that you have even if this involves overbidding your values. The partner of an overcaller or takeout doubler may be waiting ready to throw a preemptive bid or raise at you, and if you don't get your suits bid now you will be forced to guess later at an uncomfortably high level. The concept of the "free bid" or "free raise" showing extra strength has been discarded by most good players. Today, a free bid, and especially a free raise, is often made on less strength than normal. For example:

None vul., South holds: ♠862, ♡K654, ♢83, ♣J1064

NORTH	EAST	SOUTH	WEST
1 ♡	2 ♢	?	

If East had passed, South would pass. If he raises, North may bid a game or make a game try which will get N-S overboard. If West reopens South can compete to 2 ♡, and North will carry the ball from there. However, East's overcall changes the picture. Passing is too dangerous, for West may raise to 3 ♢. Now what should South do if it comes around to him? If he tries 3 ♡ he may catch his partner with a balanced minimum, get doubled, and go for a number. On the other hand, if he sells to 3 ♢ it will be his luck to find North with ♠Ax, ♡AQxxxx, ♢xx, ♣K9x. If North has this hand E-W can almost certainly make 3 ♢, and 3 ♡ will go down at most one and might make, so N-S should compete to 3♡. Unfortunately, it is difficult for North to bid on his own over 3 ♢, for without heart support his hand could be a disaster at the three-level. The solution is for South to raise to 2 ♡ immediately. Now North can compete to 3 ♡ with the above hand but sell to 3 ♢ with a 5-3-3-2 minimum, and he will be right in both cases.

This illustrates an important principle of competitive bidding which will be discussed more in the next section. In a competitive auction, accuracy in game bidding is not nearly as important as in a totally constructive auction. A stretch to a marginal game has more than one way to win—it just might be the opponents' hand if the cards lie well for them, and you may steal the contract, often undoubled. In addition, you may induce a phantom sacrifice. The important point is to get your suits in fast when the competition starts.

Let's switch to opener's side and see how he should continue after an overcall and a raise. If the partner of the overcaller passes, his bidding is fairly normal. So if with none vul. the auction goes:

NORTH	EAST	SOUTH	WEST
—	—	1 ♡	2 ◇
2 ♡	Pass	?	

a. ♠432, ♡AQ865, ◇96, ♣AK8. South should pass and subsequently sell out if the enemy competes, since he has no extra strength or distribution.

b. ♠742, ♡AKJ76, ◇5, ♣AQJ8. South should bid 3♣, his normal game try.

c. ♠K9, ♡AKQ963, ◇9, ♣AQ108. South should just bid 4♡. This has the effect of putting pressure on West if he has a distributional hand—he is forced to guess at a high level whether or not to save.

d. ♠104, ♡AKQ92, ◇KQ2, ♣A75. South should bid 2NT, an accurate value bid.

e. ♠A5, ♡AQ9854, ◇94, ♣K63. South should pass. He will compete to 3♡ if West bids again, but South shouldn't bid 3♡ now when there is a good chance of buying the hand at 2♡. If the overcall had been in spades there would be more reason to bid 3♡, for it would be more likely that West would bid again.

Now, let's look at the same hands if East raises the overcall. The bidding has gone:

NORTH	EAST	SOUTH	WEST
—	—	1 ♡	2 ◇
2 ♡	3 ◇	?	

a. ♠432, ♡AQ865, ♢96, ♣AK8. South should pass. A balanced minimum is not the right hand with which to compete. If North has extra defense he may double, if he has extra offense (in particular a fourth trump) he will compete to 3♡, but if North has a normal minimum raise N-S are better off selling to 3♢, which they might beat, than competing to 3♡ which almost certainly won't make and might get doubled.

b. ♠742, ♡AKJ76, ♢5, ♣AQJ8. South should bid 4♡. Who knows? It might make, it might be the opponents' hand, or they might be goaded into a phantom sacrifice. Let them guess what to do.

c. ♠K9, ♡AKQ963, ♢9, ♣AQ108. South should bid 4♣. This is not a slam try, as it would be if East had passed. South is concerned about competition above 4♡, so he is describing a game-going hand with club length and strength to his partner, in the hope that North will know what to do if the opponents take a sacrifice.

d. ♠104, ♡AKQ92, ♢KQ2, ♣A75. South should double. This is basically a penalty double, although South is unlikely to have a real diamond stack after the suit has been bid and raised The double shows a strong balanced hand. North will usually pass with an average flattish raise, but bid three or four hearts with a more offensively oriented hand.

e. ♠A5, ♡ AQ9854, ♢94, ♣K63. South should bid 3♡. With the sixth trump, competing is a must. It is not clear who can make what, but 3♡ figures to be right regardless.

It should be noted that some bids change in meaning in the face of competition. For example:

Both vul., South holds: ♠8, ♡AQ874, ♢Q4, ♣AJ872

NORTH	EAST	SOUTH	WEST
—	—	1 ♡	1 ♠
2 ♡	2 ♠	?	

South should bid 3♣. This is not a game try, as it would be if RHO had remained silent. South is simply showing his values so that North may be able to make an intelligent decision if the enemy competes to 3♠. North should jump to game only with a perfect fitting maximum. The 3♣ bid does not create a force—the partnership can sell to 3 ♠ if there is nothing more to be said. Let's look at some North hands after the auction:

NORTH	EAST	SOUTH	WEST
—	—	1 ♡	1 ♠
2 ♡	2 ♠	3 ♣	3 ♠
?			

a. ♠K42, ♡J105, ◇876, ♣K1093. North will sell to 3 ♠. He doesn't have the offensive strength to compete to 4 ♡, and the club bid warns him that the enemy hands are likely to fit well, so the best bet is to sell and hope to beat it. Even if E-W score up +140 N-S may not get a bad board, for some N-S pairs may do worse by taking action over 3 ♠.

b. ♠K42, ♡J105, ◇K1093, ♣654. North should double 3 ♠. There are no guarantees with this double, but South's 3 ♣ bid indicates that North's diamond cards are likely to produce tricks on defense, since South figures to be short in diamonds. A "matchpoint double", protecting the potential +140 N-S might make in hearts, is clearly called for.

c. ♠742, ♡K532, ◇K876, ♣K3. North should try 4 ♡. This is the type of perfect hand on which N-S figure to have a good play for game even if South just has a distributional minimum.

An obvious question is: What should South do if he has a game try in clubs? The answer is: just bid a game and hope for the best. Maybe it will make, or maybe the opponents will do the wrong thing (sacrificing or selling) when they had a better auction available. There are several ways for this kind of bid to win, so the game try is not so important.

When you have a suit to show, it is better to show it right away than to risk getting frozen out of the auction, even if you must overbid somewhat. For example:

N-S vul., South holds: ♠93, ♡75, ◇KJ10652, ♣KJ6

NORTH	EAST	SOUTH	WEST
1 ♡	1 ♠	?	

Without the overcall, even the most liberal two over one bidders would probably agree that this hand isn't worth a 2 ◇ bid; 1NT is the correct response. The overcall changes matters considerably. A 1NT response is no longer feasible, since South has no spade stopper. If South passes, West may raise to 2♠ or even 3♠. When this comes back to South, he will be playing guessing games. It makes much more sense to bid 2◊ immediately, even if the point count is not there.

The importance of bidding your suits or raising partner when the opponents step into the auction is so great that some bids which would be forcing without the competition should no longer be forcing. For example:

N-S vul., South holds: ♠83, ♡AQ764, ◊AJ85, ♣J3

NORTH	EAST	SOUTH	WEST
—	—	1 ♡	Pass
2 ◊	2 ♠	?	

If East had passed, in most partnerships South should rebid 2♡. An immediate raise to three of a minor is forcing and shows extra strength. After the overcall, however, it is important to get the 3◊ bid in now. Passing would be all right if West also passes, for North will take some action and now South can bid 3◊. Unfortunately, there is the danger that West will raise to 3♠, and if this gets passed around to South (or even if North doubles) South won't know what to do. Life is much easier if South can bid 3◊ (non-forcing) on this hand. If South has a forcing diamond raise, he can cue-bid 3♠. Note that this bid would not have been available without the overcall.

Both vul., South holds: ♠10, ♡KQ954, ◊AQJ96, ♣85

NORTH	EAST	SOUTH	WEST
—	—	1 ♡	Pass
1 NT	2 ♠	?	

South must bid 3◊. If South passes North will almost certainly sell to 2♠, and this figures to be a bad result. Without the overcall the 3◊ bid would have been a game-forcing jump shift, but the overcall makes it strictly competitive and North shouldn't move on without an exceptional hand.

121

N-S vul., South holds: ♠5, ♡J4, ◇AQJ4, ♣KQ10942

NORTH	EAST	SOUTH	WEST
—	—	1 ♣	Pass
1 ♡	2 ♠	?	

South must risk a 3♣ bid. There is too great a danger that North will sell to 2♠ with a flat seven or eight count. Obviously South doesn't have the values for a 3♣ rebid over 1♡, but after the 2♠ bid South must stretch a bit on hands such as this. South could still have a stronger hand, of course, but North should take the conservative view if he has a close decision as to whether or not to bid a game. As in most competitive decisions, this conservatism by the partner of the free-bidder has an extra way to win—it might be the opponents' hand for 3♠ making or down one. Consequently bidding 3NT and going down when 3♣ was making may be a more costly error than normal. There could be a full matchpoint cost against tables where other N-S pairs sold to a spade partial and collected a small plus score on defense.

It is important not to overdo it with this kind of free bid if the bid takes you to a higher level. For example:

None vul., South holds: ♠A5, ♡984, ◇AQ10754, ♣J2

NORTH	EAST	SOUTH	WEST
—	—	1 ◇	Pass
1 ♠	2 ♣	?	

South might as well bid 2◇, since this is what he would have normally bid had East passed. The bid shows nothing more than a sixth diamond. However, after:

NORTH	EAST	SOUTH	WEST
—	—	1 ◇	Pass
1 ♠	2 ♡	?	

South should pass. This hand just doesn't have the playing strength to make it worth going to the three-level. If North takes another call South can bid his diamonds later, while if North sells to 2 ♡ or if West bids 3 ♡ and North passes the hand probably belongs to E-W and selling will be all right.

It must be noted that certain flat minimum hands do not need to be bid in competition, even though they would have been bid without the interference. For example:

Both vul., South holds: ♠ Q974, ♡ Q82, ◊ 96, ♣ Q974

NORTH	EAST	SOUTH	WEST
1 ◊	1 ♡	?	

A 1 ♠ response (or a negative double) isn't exactly a mistake, but pass is probably best. This hand is so square that if North can't find another bid then N-S probably don't have any reason to continue contesting the auction. Of course if East had passed, a 1 ♠ response would be mandatory. On this hand, however, action by South over the overcall is likely to induce North to compete to too high a level.

Contrast with the following hand on the same auction:

Both vul., South holds: ♠ K962, ♡ 42, ◊ J1096, ♣ 532

South should certainly either bid 1 ♠ or make a negative double, depending on his methods, after East overcalls his partner's 1 ◊ opening with 1 ♡. It is important for South to get into the auction because of the good diamond fit. Had East passed, South would probably get best results by passing. A bid might get the partnership too high.

PENALTY DOUBLES

Any time the opponents enter your constructive auction, you have the option of doubling them. Obviously you must expect them to be going down when you double, but this may not be sufficient. If all you can make is a part-score, then down one vulnerable or down two non-vulnerable is quite sufficient. If your side can make a game, however, then your vulnerability is also a factor. In order to beat your game score, you need only a two trick set at favorable vulnerability, a three trick set at equal vulnerability, and a four trick set at unfavorable vulnerability. If the decision is close, you should go for the penalty if you are quite sure of beating their contract for at least +200. This way you have several ways to win. The penalty may be large enough to compensate for your potential game, the game might not make, or even if game does make it may not be bid at other tables. It only costs one-half matchpoint to other tables if you double and are wrong (provided you collect at least +200), but if you bid a marginal game and go down when you could have collected more than the value of a part-score on defense you lose a full matchpoint against other tables playing a part-score with your cards.

The key factor in close decisions is your side's overall high card strength. With marginal game values you should double, with minimal but sufficient game values you should tend to bid the game, and with excess values for game you should usually double and go for the big set. For example:

N-S vul., South holds: ♠52, ♡KJ62, ◇A762, ♣542

NORTH	EAST	SOUTH	WEST
1 NT	2 ♡	?	

South should double. The values for game are marginal, and there certainly is a likely +300 available. Strengthen South's hand a bit to ♠52, ♡KJ62, ◇A762, ♣Q42. Now South should bid 3NT. This contract figures to be secure, but collecting +700 is a bit optimistic. Here, South has minimum but sufficient game values. Improve South's hand a bit more to ♠52, ♡KJ62, ◇A762, ♣A42. Now South should go back on the doubling trail. Game is certain, of course, but the excess strength and the heart stack figure to be enough to set East four tricks for +700 and a top. This is a gamble, of course, but it seems worthwhile. A look at the full hand illustrates the correctness of this strategy:

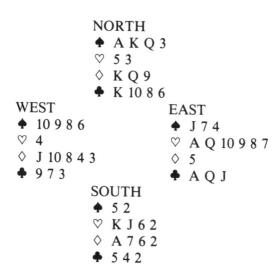

NORTH
♠ A K Q 3
♡ 5 3
◇ K Q 9
♣ K 10 8 6

WEST
♠ 10 9 8 6
♡ 4
◇ J 10 8 4 3
♣ 9 7 3

EAST
♠ J 7 4
♡ A Q 10 9 8 7
◇ 5
♣ A Q J

SOUTH
♠ 5 2
♡ K J 6 2
◇ A 7 6 2
♣ 5 4 2

2♡ doubled is down two, +300, and N-S have no game. Give South East's queen of clubs and 3NT is on, but 2♡ doubled only nets +500. But give South East's ace of clubs and now careful defense collects +700 against 2♡ doubled, beating the 3NT game.

When the opponents choose the wrong time to enter the auction, it is important to double them and collect a number. This is usually difficult to do at the one-level, but penalty doubles at the two-level can be very profitable when your side holds the balance of strength. The most important factor is your holding in the enemy trump suit. A good general guideline is to go for a penalty if your side has six trumps, but to simply bid to your normal contract if your side has only five trumps. When the trumps are stacked behind the overcaller, it is easy. For example:

NORTH
♠ 9 8
♡ 5 2
◇ A J 6 3
♣ A J 8 7 5

SOUTH
♠ A Q J 6 4
♡ K J 8 7
◇ 10 2
♣ K 2

None vulnerable.

NORTH	EAST	SOUTH	WEST
—	—	1 ♠	Pass
2 ♣	2 ♡	Double	Pass
Pass	Pass		

This should produce a comfortable penalty, and N-S probably don't have a game. If the cards do lie favorably enough for N-S to make a game, they may score +500 against 2♡ doubled.

The last hand was easy, and most pairs would properly collect the penalty. Let's shift the hands slightly:

NORTH
♠ 9 8
♡ J 5 2
◇ A J 3
♣ A J 8 7 5

SOUTH
♠ A Q J 6 4
♡ K 8 7
◇ 10 6 2
♣ K 2

N-S have the same cards, and once again it is right to defend. But how do they know? Clearly South can't double, for North would sit with a weaker heart holding as in the first example and be wrong. The answer is that North must do the doubling. The bidding should go:

NORTH	EAST	SOUTH	WEST
—	—	1 ♠	Pass
2 ♣	2 ♡	Pass	Pass
Double	Pass	Pass	Pass

The double in front of the overcaller does not show a trump stack, as does the double behind the overcaller. North's double in this sequence simply shows a fair balanced hand, no fit for partner, and three trumps. Most players looking at the North hand would not consider a double, yet it is clearly the winning action provided South understands that it does not show a trump stack, and so he won't sit without a reasonable trump holding.

Lastly, suppose the player in front of the overcaller holds the long trumps:

NORTH
♠ 9 8
♡ K J 5 2
◊ J 3
♣ A Q 8 7 5

SOUTH
♠ A Q J 6 4
♡ 8 7
◊ A 10 6
♣ K 6 2

You can't get them all the time. With these combined hands and the same auction the opponents will escape unscathed, for South should not sit for the double with two small hearts. Note that this may not be so bad for N-S. With the heart honors lying well for E-W the penalty may not be so secure, and the club fit gives 3NT a good chance to make. Since South holds club support, he shouldn't even pass the 2 ♡ bid around to North. A normal auction might be:

NORTH	EAST	SOUTH	WEST
—	—	1 ♠	Pass
2 ♣	2 ♡	3 ♣	Pass
3 NT	Pass	Pass	Pass

Without the overcall South would rebid 2 ♠, but once the opponents are in the auction it is more important to show the club fit immediately in case the enemy competes to a higher level. The 3NT contract has no guarantees, but it is certainly reasonable and better than defending 2 ♡ doubled.

The second major consideration is support for partner's suit. If you are short in partner's suit you should be quick to defend, but if you have support it is usually correct to show it first.

None vul., South holds: ♠K84, ♡84, ♢J52, ♣AQ963

NORTH	EAST	SOUTH	WEST
1 ♠	Pass	2 ♣	2 ♡
Double	Pass	?	

South should bid 2 ♠, just as he was planning to do before the overcall complicated the issue. It is true that an occasional number may be missed if North has a large heart stack, but there is a great danger that the opponents have a double fit (hearts and diamonds) and the penalty against 2 ♡ may not be sufficient to compensate for a potential part-score or game in spades for N-S. An additional argument for the 2 ♠ bid is that even if North has a good double of 2 ♡, the spade fit may be enough to allow 4 ♠ to make, which may score more than the penalty. Consequently the 2 ♠ bid (as opposed to the pass) has an extra way to win—there may be a spade game. If South's third spade were a small diamond or club, passing the double would be the indicated action.

The importance of a fit in partner's suit when deciding whether or not to defend is so great that it is necessary to strain to raise partner in any competitive auction in order to avoid later problems.

NORTH
- ♠ 8 7
- ♡ J 10 5
- ◇ K J 5 2
- ♣ A Q 4 3

SOUTH
- ♠ K Q J 5 2
- ♡ 7 4
- ◇ A 4
- ♣ K 8 6 2

N-S vulnerable.

NORTH	EAST	SOUTH	WEST
—	—	1 ♠	Pass
2 ♣	2 ♡	3 ♣	3 ♡
Double	Pass	Pass	Pass

If East hadn't overcalled South would have rebid 2 ♠, planning on continuing with 3 ♣ if North rebid 2NT. Once East bids, however, it is essential for South to show his support now. If South had bid 2 ♠ he would be very uncomfortable passing the double of 3 ♡, for North would also double with something like: ♠87, ♡J105, ◇K2, ♣AQJ543. If North holds this hand, both 3 ♡ and 4 ♣ are likely makes. Once South has shown his club support, however, he can confidently pass the double for he knows that North won't be doubling with a long club suit.

If the enemy interference is in the form of an artificial call such as a takeout double, Michaels cue bid, or Unusual Notrump, the next hand to bid has available a double of the artificial bid or redouble of the takeout double to show strength and suggest willingness to defend. This should be used on hands which have all the opponents' suits but one (or better, all the opponents suits) under control. The partner of the doubler or redoubler should double himself if the opponents land in his second suit; otherwise, he should pass it around to his partner unless he has a singleton in the enemy suit. If he has a singleton a low-level double will probably not be profitable, since the opponents are likely to have at least eight trumps, so he should bid out his shape.

Most pairs can handle the following type of hand correctly:

NORTH
♠ 5 4
♡ A Q 10 8 6
◇ 8 2
♣ K J 8 5

SOUTH
♠ A K 9 7 3
♡ 4 3
◇ Q 10 5 3
♣ A 4

Both vulnerable.

NORTH	EAST	SOUTH	WEST
—	—	1 ♠	Double
Redouble	Pass	Pass	2 ◇
Pass	Pass	Double	Pass
Pass	Pass		

North has shown his strength and willingness to defend by the redouble, so he can pass it around to South. South has four trumps so he must double despite his minimum opening bid, and the penalty is likely to be worthwhile. If East had tried 2♣, South would pass it around and North would double.

Problems arise on more balanced hands. For example:

Both vul., South holds: ♠A6, ♡9852, ◇A873, ♣Q32

NORTH	EAST	SOUTH	WEST
1 ♠	Double	Redouble	2 ♣
Pass	Pass	?	

Should South double? Most players would, but if North has only two clubs he will pass the double and it could easily backfire. A better approach is for South to pass first, then double. This should show a fair balanced hand, but no great stack in the probable enemy suits. So after the auction:

NORTH	EAST	SOUTH	WEST
1 ♠	Double	Pass	2 ♣
Pass	Pass	Double	

North will pass with ♠KQ852, ♡AJ4, ◇Q4, ♣J74 but will pull to 2♡ with ♠KQJ82, ♡AJ104, ◇Q4, ♣74 and he will probably be right both times. On the first hand 2♣ should go down, but on the second hand it could well make and N-S have a comfortable heart part-score.

Let's see how this might work against the Unusual Notrump. None vul., the bidding has gone:

NORTH	EAST	SOUTH	WEST
1 ♠	2 NT	?	

a. ♠63, ♡Q10854, ◇A6, ♣KJ42. South should double. He plans to double 3♣, and hopes his partner can double 3◇. If the opponents have a safe landing spot in 3◇, N-S must bid on and hope to find a decent contract.

b. ♠63, ♡Q54, ◇A1086, ♣KJ42. South should double 2NT, planning to double either 3♣ or 3◇. Unless North is very short in the minors, the penalty should be lucrative.

c. ♠643, ♡AJ54, ◇J86, ♣A42. South should pass first, planning to double either 3♣ or 3◇. This sequence shows a hand like this—a balanced fairly strong hand but no stack in either minor. North will know to sit for the double with ♠AQJxx, ♡Kx, ◇Qxx, ♣Jxx but to pull with ♠AQJxx, ♡KQxx, ◇xx, ♣Jx.

131

HIGH-LEVEL INTERFERENCE

SACRIFICES

You have bid to a game that you felt you could make. The opponents now proceed to take what is clearly a sacrifice. What should you do? Should you double them and take the penalty, or should you bid on in the hope of making a higher score on offense. This is a common problem at matchpoints. Analysis of the potential matchpoint costs of the various auctions will help put the problem in the proper perspective.

When your opponents take a sacrifice, they are betting on a parlay. First, your game must make, and second the save must not go for too much. Actually there is a third part to the parlay—the field must bid the game. This third part is not a problem for the game bidders. If they have bid a marginal game that may not be bid at other tables, they won't have much trouble doubling. So for the rest of this discussion we will assume that the rest of the field will surely bid the game, even though it may not necessarily be a make. If the sacrifice is wrong on any part of its parlay, it will be a very bad board for the savers provided that their opponents don't take the push and bid one more.

If your opponents take a 5 ◇ save over your 4 ♠ bid and you choose to push on to 5 ♠, now you are the one who is betting on a parlay. You are betting that 5 ♠ will make, and also that the 5 ◇ sacrifice will not go for more than the value of the game. If you are wrong on either count, you should have doubled rather than taken the push.

It might seem right to bid on if you think that you are a favorite to make your contract and if you believe, but are not sure, that the opponents have taken a good save. This is not necessarily correct. The problem is that the two are often closely inter-related. The finesse that allows you to make your contract when it works may be the same finesse which beats the save more than the value of the game, for it will lose for the opponents. The following example illustrates this point:

NORTH
- ♠ K 10 6 4
- ♡ Q 10 2
- ◊ 9 5
- ♣ A J 3 2

SOUTH
- ♠ A 7 5 3 2
- ♡ A J 8 5
- ◊ 2
- ♣ K Q 8

None vulnerable.

NORTH	EAST	SOUTH	WEST
—	—	1 ♠	2 ◊
3 ♠	5 ◊	?	

Let's suppose that South could see North's hand. What should he do? A superficial analysis would be: If the spades split two-two or if the heart king is onside, then 5♠ will make. This makes 5♠ a favorite, so it is the right bid since I'm not sure whether or not we can beat 5◊ enough. The full hand:

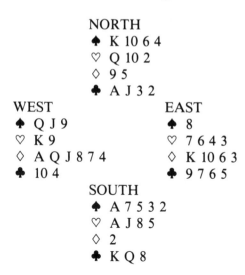

NORTH
- ♠ K 10 6 4
- ♡ Q 10 2
- ◊ 9 5
- ♣ A J 3 2

WEST
- ♠ Q J 9
- ♡ K 9
- ◊ A Q J 8 7 4
- ♣ 10 4

EAST
- ♠ 8
- ♡ 7 6 4 3
- ◊ K 10 6 3
- ♣ 9 7 6 5

SOUTH
- ♠ A 7 5 3 2
- ♡ A J 8 5
- ◊ 2
- ♣ K Q 8

Unlucky! Both suits fail to behave, and 5 ♠ goes down. Furthermore E-W have taken a good save; they only have four losers for − 300. But it isn't only bad luck. Suppose that either hearts or spades behave for N-S. In that case, E-W would have one more loser in the suit that behaves, and would be set 500 in 5 ◊, more than the value of a game. On this hand if E-W do not have a singleton in hearts or clubs, it is never right to bid on. Either 5 ♠ will go down or 5 ◊ will be set at least 500, depending on the lie of the major suits. The fate of both 5 ◊ and 5 ♠ depend on the same things—the E-W distribution and the location of the heart king. Even if N-S were vul. vs. not it would be very questionable to bid on. Twenty-five percent of the time 5 ♠ will go down, and some of the time it makes the same friendly lie of the cards will set the opponents 700.

Now, let's look at the matchpoint costs. Suppose we choose to double 5 ◊ instead of bidding 5 ♠ and are wrong—5 ♠ makes and 5 ◊ goes down less than the value of the game. In this case we get + 300 instead of + 450, so we lose one-half matchpoint to every other table since these are the only possible scores. It might be noted that we lose nothing to any table which somehow fails to bid the game.

Suppose we bid 5 ♠ and are wrong. There are several ways to be wrong. If 5 ♠ is down one but 5 ◊ is a good save we go from + 300 to − 50. This costs one-half matchpoint to other tables at which the decision was at the five-level, but does not cost anything against tables where the save was not taken, since we had no chance against them. Suppose 5 ♠ makes, but 5 ◊ would have gone for 500. Then we go from + 500 to + 450, losing one-half matchpoint to every other table since these are the only two possible results. This indicates that we should be more inclined to take the push when the question is whether or not 5 ♠ will make, rather than whether we can get them enough. This is quite logical. In the first case the assumption is that the opponents have taken a good save which means that if we double them we may get a poor score even if we are right, while in the second case it is not clear whether or not their save is a good one.

There are, unfortunately, more serious errors to be considered. Suppose both that 5 ◊ was going for too much and 5 ♠ doesn't make. Now the decision to bid 5 ♠ swings our score from +500 to −50, costing a full matchpoint to those in 4♠ making, which figures to be a popular result. Suppose that the sacrifice is a phantom—4♠ was, in fact, going down. Now our 5♠ call turns our +300 into −100, which loses a full matchpoint to the common result of 4♠ down one for −50.

What does all this tell us? If you are sure that your game was making, and sure that either you can make at the five-level or that the opponents' save will not go for more than the value of the game then it may well be right to bid on, with more of a tendency to bid on when you know the opponents have taken a good save. However, if it is possible that 4♠ wasn't making or possible that five is going down and they will go for too much in their save, you should definitely double. Bidding on may cost a full matchpoint to most tables if wrong, while doubling can cost at most one-half matchpoint to any other table. Only judgment and experience can really answer the question on any given hand, but it is better to know what we are risking by various actions.

N-S vul., South holds: ♠AJ96, ♡96, ◇A98, ♣KJ52

NORTH	EAST	SOUTH	WEST
—	—	1 ♣	Pass
1 ♠	2 ♡	2 ♠	3 ♡
4 ♠	5 ♡	?	

South should double. He has a minimum opening bid with no great distribution. There is no reason to expect 5♠ or even 4♠ to make, and no reason to be sure the opponents won't go for 700. Admittedly E-W have probably taken a good save, but South's proper course of action is to suggest defending. With a singleton heart South should pass the decision to his partner.

N-S vul., South holds: ♠Q1042, ♡94, ◇86, ♣KQ742

NORTH	EAST	SOUTH	WEST
1 ♠	2 ◇	2 ♠	3 ◇
4 ♠	5 ◇	?	

South should pass. He has an offensively oriented hand with a fourth trump and good club suit, so he should not suggest defending. On the other hand he can't bid 5 ♠ himself, since for all he knows North was stretching for the 4 ♠ bid. As a general rule, a limited hand should never bid on over a sacrifice in the direct seat, unless his partner has previously made a bid which suggested such an action on a suitable hand. South can only pass or double, and North should be well-placed to make the final decision.

N-S vul., South holds: ♠AQJ762, ♡KQ53, ◇5, ♣K2

NORTH	EAST	SOUTH	WEST
—	—	1 ♠	3 ◇
3 ♠	5 ◇	?	

South should bid 5 ♠. There are no guarantees, but it seems certain that E-W will not go down 700 in 5 ◇, and equally certain that 4 ♠ would have made. Consequently, doubling 5 ◇ will probably lead to a poor score even if it is right, since the save may not be taken at all the other tables. Note that South cannot pass. This is not a forcing situation, because N-S have not voluntarily bid game. South must decide one way or the other, and the percentage bid seems to be 5 ♠.

There is one type of situation where it is correct to push on in a close decision. Occasionally it may sound like the opponents are sacrificing. In fact they may think so themselves, but their save just might make. In this case bidding on now has an extra way to win—maybe it is a good sacrifice!

None vul., South holds: ♠7, ♡AQJ632, ◇KJ107, ♣A9

NORTH	EAST	SOUTH	WEST
—	—	1 ♡	1 ♠
2 ♡	4 ♠	?	

South was planning to bid a game in hearts, expecting to be a favorite. 5 ♡ will probably not make unless partner has the right hand, so it seems as if South should double 4 ♠. However, there is a reasonable possibility that 4 ♠ will make. I would bid 5 ♡ as a two-way shot—maybe it will make, or maybe it will be a good save. The full hand:

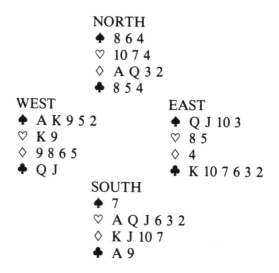

NORTH
♠ 8 6 4
♡ 10 7 4
♦ A Q 3 2
♣ 8 5 4

WEST
♠ A K 9 5 2
♡ K 9
♦ 9 8 6 5
♣ Q J

EAST
♠ Q J 10 3
♡ 8 5
♦ 4
♣ K 10 7 6 3 2

SOUTH
♠ 7
♡ A Q J 6 3 2
♦ K J 10 7
♣ A 9

East meant his bid as preemptive, and West's hand is nothing to get excited about. The hands fit well, however, and the offside king of hearts which defeats your 5 ♡ contract is the onside king of hearts which allows 4 ♠ to make. Once again the bid which has more than one way to win comes through with a surprising victory.

ENEMY PREEMPTS

High level preempts by the opponents early in the auction can make life very difficult. Not only do you not have enough room to find your proper suit or level, but it might not even be your hand. There is no absolute way to guarantee being right all the time, but there are guidelines which will increase your chances of landing on your feet. Remember that other pairs holding your cards are likely to face the same problem.

The most important thing to realize is that extreme accuracy is not nearly as important against preempts as it is in totally constructive auctions. If you have the auction to yourself, it is crucial to get to the very best spot most of the time. Second best will not score well. In a jammed auction, however, second best will often score quite nicely. This is because other pairs will do worse and land in third, fourth, or fifth best contracts. Consequently, the cost of being wrong by finding the second best as opposed to the best contract may not be great, for you will still beat many pairs who land in yet worse contracts. For example:

```
                ♠ Q 5 4 3
                ♡ A J 9 6 2
                ◇ 6 5
                ♣ 8 3


                SOUTH
                ♠ A K 7 6
                ♡ 7 3
                ◇ K 2
                ♣ K Q J 10 5
```

N-S vulnerable.

NORTH	EAST	SOUTH	WEST
—	3 ◇	4 ♣	Pass
Pass	Pass		

I'm not endorsing the N-S auction; in fact, I have no idea what is best. In an uncontested auction it would be a close decision between 3 ♠ and 4 ♠, and any pair who arrived at a contract other than a part-score or game in spades could expect a very poor matchpoint score. After the preempt, however, I would expect the 4 ♣ contract to score pretty well even though it isn't optimal. Look at some of the bad things other N-S pairs might do:

They might speculate 3NT with the South hand and play it there.

They might start with a takeout double and have North drive to 4 ♡, which is certainly not a favorite.

They might go conservative and defend 3 ◊, doubled or un-doubled.

They might find their spade fit via a cue bid by North in response to a takeout double, but overestimate their combined strength and push past 4 ♠ looking for slam.

In addition to all this, if spades split badly, as they are more likely than normal to do after the preempt, then 4 ♠ will not make and the club part-score looks better still. The principle is to settle for any decent landing spot after a preempt rather than look for perfection. Often this means simply bidding a long strong suit instead of exploring other avenues.

Another important principle is to be willing to defend if the decision is close. The preemptor doesn't like this. Put yourself in his shoes. Let's say that RHO opens 1 ♣ and you shoot out 3 ♡ on a marginal hand. If the opponents continue bidding you are always happy. Maybe they will stumble into the right contract, but you know that your preempt has done its dirty work of hampering their constructive auction and that you have escaped unscathed. On the other hand, suppose you are dropped in 3 ♡, doubled or undoubled. Now you are not so happy. You may be a winner, but if partner puts down the wrong dummy you won't like it. You no longer have the feeling that you definitely have the best of it.

If the preemptor isn't happy being dropped there, it follows that it is often right to defend when an opponent preempts. Ob-viously I am not advocating always defending; quite often it is your hand and you simply have to try to get to the best contract. What I am saying is that it is often right to sell when facing a close decision. For example:

Both vul., South holds: ♠K932, ♡J4, ◇AJ, ♣KJ643

NORTH	EAST	SOUTH	WEST
—	—	1 ♣	3 ♡
Pass	Pass	?	

Sure, N-S might have a part-score available in spades, clubs, or diamonds, or there might be a large penalty available if North has a penalty pass of a takeout double (assuming N-S are playing negative doubles). The problem is that South has no real reason to believe that there is a playable contract above 3 ♡, or that North will find the right bid even if there is one. The one piece of information that South has is that North was unable to act over 3 ♡, so it is unlikely that N-S are missing a game. It is a close decision, but I would pass it out at 3 ♡. This can't be too far wrong, while a takeout double or a 3 ♠ bid could be very wrong if North has the wrong hand, and even if he has the right hand he may not find the winning response, whatever it is.

None vul., South holds: ♠AJ6, ♡QJ9, ◇74, ♣AQ1082

NORTH	EAST	SOUTH	WEST
—	—	1 ♣	3 ♡
Double*	Pass	?	

*negative double

South should pass. This should be at worst a reasonable result, and could easily be the best spot available for N-S. Any of the other possible actions (3 ♠, 3NT, or 4 ♣) could work out better, but they could all be calamities. Even if it is right to bid, can South be so sure of finding the right bid?

When making a choice of games decision against an enemy preempt, strain to play notrump if it is at all reasonable. There are two reasons for this. First of all, the bad splits which are suggested by the preempt may doom an otherwise sound suit contract by unlucky ruffs or terrible trump divisions. Secondly, notrump will often put the preemptor's hand out of commission if you can hold up on his suit until his partner is out. The preemptor often does not have any side entries, so the usual timing advantages of a suit contract are no longer needed. A simple holdup play can suffice to stop the run of the enemy suit. For example:

None vul., South holds: ♠A3, ♡KJ84, ♢KQ2, ♣KQ107

NORTH	EAST	SOUTH	WEST
—	3 ♠	?	

South certainly must act, and a takeout double seems automatic. But is it? Somebody has to bid notrump if it is right, and North is unlikely to be able to do so. Even if N-S have a heart fit, the hand could well belong in notrump. I recommend a 3NT overcall with the South hand. It could really backfire if West has three spades or East has a side entry, but the odds favor success. The full hand:

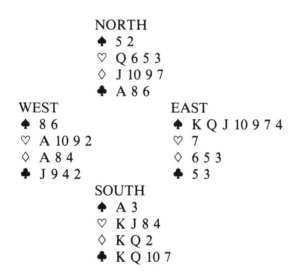

```
                    NORTH
                    ♠ 5 2
                    ♡ Q 6 5 3
                    ♢ J 10 9 7
                    ♣ A 8 6
       WEST                         EAST
       ♠ 8 6                        ♠ K Q J 10 9 7 4
       ♡ A 10 9 2                   ♡ 7
       ♢ A 8 4                      ♢ 6 5 3
       ♣ J 9 4 2                    ♣ 5 3
                    SOUTH
                    ♠ A 3
                    ♡ K J 8 4
                    ♢ K Q 2
                    ♣ K Q 10 7
```

Looking at just the N-S hands without any opposing bidding, 3NT would be a terrible contract compared to 4♡. The 3♠ opening bid changes matters entirely. Note that 4♡ may go down if East has a singleton in hearts, diamonds, or clubs. At 3NT, however, declarer calmly ducks one round of spades and then goes about knocking out West's aces as East sits helplessly

141

by, unable to contribute to the defense. To add insult to injury West eventually gets squeezed in clubs and hearts when declarer cashes dummy's fourth diamond, and notrump makes ten tricks while 4 ♡ goes down. This sort of result is quite common when there is an enemy preempt, so it is wise to get to notrump if at all possible. Make very aggressive notrump overcalls against preempts, particularly if you hold the guarded ace of the preemptor's suit. You can anticipate holding up until the partner of the preemptor is out, and then going about your business setting up tricks with one opponent completely out of the hand.

Another important point when dealing with preempts is for the strong hand to be optimistic about game chances. If the decision is close, it is usually right to overbid to get to game. For example:

N-S vul., South holds: ♠AJ64, ♡8, ◊KQ42, ♣A642

NORTH	EAST	SOUTH	WEST
—	3 ♡	Double	Pass
3 ♠	Pass	?	

If South had doubled an opening 1 ♡ bid on this hand and heard his partner respond 1 ♠, he would barely be worth a raise to 2 ♠. North could have a yarborough, and any higher contract could be overboard. Against the 3 ♡ opening bid, however, it is correct to drive the hand to game! South simply must assume that North has a fair hand, and South cannot expect North to jump to game on some scattered collection such as ♠Q10xxx, ♡xxx, ◊Jxx, ♣Kx. As a corollary, the partner of the strong hand should discount his first six or seven points when choosing his response, because his partner will be playing him for them. On balance, this approach will work well. The preemptor is assumed to have a weak hand, so there are plenty of points to go around and the partner of the strong hand will usually have at least a few of them. This approach will permit fairly light action against preempts without fear that partner will hang you when he has what you were hoping for when you overcalled or doubled. For example:

N-S vul., South holds: ♠A87, ♡AQJ1072, ◊6, ♣AQ9

NORTH	EAST	SOUTH	WEST
—	3 ◊	?	

South should bid 4♡. He hopes that his partner "has his bids" (i.e. holds a few high cards even though he hasn't actually bid anything). If North has a yarborough—unlucky! Against an opening one bid South could start slowly with a 1♡ overcall, knowing that if North does nothing there is probably no game, but against the preempt South must gamble. It should be noted that at other tables E-W may be taking sacrifices (phantom or not) at 5◊, so it is all the more important to shoot out a game.

Both vul., South holds: ♠K63, ♡J53, ◊1075, ♣K952

NORTH	EAST	SOUTH	WEST
—	—	—	3 ◊
3 ♡	Pass	?	

South should pass. He "has his bid"—just what North is playing him for. North may have risked an overcall on as little as ♠Axx, ♡KQ109xx, ◊xx, ♣Qx. This is dangerous, but defending 3◊ when both 3◊ and 3♡ are cold won't be worth many matchpoints, and South certainly wouldn't have balanced. If South raises to 4♡, however, all the good work of the 3♡ overcall is undone. By bidding 4♡ on this hand South is in effect giving his partner a choice of defending 3◊ or playing 4♡. This is inconsistent, since 3♡ could easily be the winning contract, as it is here.

REVIEW PROBLEMS

1. Both vul., South holds: ♠KQ8, ♡QJ63, ◇KQ76, ♣53

NORTH	EAST	SOUTH	WEST
—	—	1 ◇	Pass
1 ♡	Pass	2 ♡	Pass
3 NT	Pass	?	

2. E-W vul., South holds: ♠A9543, ♡K6, ◇105, ♣KQ106

NORTH	EAST	SOUTH	WEST
1 ◇	Pass	1 ♠	Pass
2 ♠	Pass	3 ♣	Pass
3 ♠	Pass	?	

3. Both vul., South holds: ♠Q8742, ♡72, ◇96, ♣AQJ5

NORTH	EAST	SOUTH	WEST
1 ♡	Pass	1 ♠	Pass
2 ♣	Pass	?	

4. None vul., South holds: ♠943, ♡QJ87, ◇76, ♣A654

NORTH	EAST	SOUTH	WEST
1 NT	Pass	2 ♣	Pass
2 ♡	Pass	?	

5. None vul., South holds: ♠62, ♡Q85, ◇K87, ♣AQ974

NORTH	EAST	SOUTH	WEST
1 ♠	Pass	2 ♣	2 ♡
Pass	Pass	?	

6. E-W vul., South holds: ♠A32, ♡J2, ◇AQ2, ♣AQ984

NORTH	EAST	SOUTH	WEST
—	—	1 ♣	Pass
2 ♣*	Pass	2 ◇	Pass
3 ♡**	Pass	3 ♠	Pass
4 ♣	Pass	4 ◇	Pass
4 ♠	Pass	?	

*10+ points
**singleton heart

7. N-S vul., South holds: ♠Q1086, ♡K10832, ◇984, ♣K

NORTH	EAST	SOUTH	WEST
1 ♣	3 ◇	?*	

*you are playing negative doubles

8. Both vul., South holds: ♠J4, ♡J74, ◇KJ3, ♣AQ1092

NORTH	EAST	SOUTH	WEST
1 ♠	Pass	2 ♣	Pass
2 ♠	Pass	?	

9. Both vul., South holds: ♠KQJ5, ♡10762, ◇A2, ♣A104

NORTH	EAST	SOUTH	WEST
1 ◇	Pass	?	

10. N-S vul., South holds: ♠98, ♡AK1062, ◇A6, ♣KQ93

NORTH	EAST	SOUTH	WEST
—	—	1 ♡	Pass
2 ♡	2 ♠	4 ♡	4 ♠
Pass	Pass	?	

145

SOLUTIONS

1. 4♡. South should go for the four-four heart fit. His intermediates in hearts are strong, and his worthless doubleton in clubs also points to the suit contract. Lack of aces does not necessarily mean that the hand is notrump oriented, for N-S may need time to knock out those missing aces, and only a trump suit can provide that time.

2. 3NT. South is certainly strong enough to drive to game, and notrump is still a possibility. Nothing can yet be concluded from North's 3♠ bid except that he has a minimum, for at that point South's 3♣ bid was just a game try. Now when South bids 3NT he clarifies his intentions to North—choice of games with club concentration, and North can make the final decision.

3. Pass. There is a chance that a marginal game will be missed, but a 3♣ bid is more likely to push the partnership overboard. North would certainly bid 3NT with something like ♠x, ♡AK10xx, ◇KQx, ♣Kxxx and it won't have much play. A heart preference could work if North has strong hearts, but South has no way of knowing. The general principle of taking the sure plus score on a part-score hand prevails here.

4. Pass. South should be happy where he is. His Stayman bid was certainly questionable, but it seems to have worked well. Many players will pass 1NT and probably take less tricks than N-S will take in hearts, so South should not jeopardize his already favorable position by pushing to a close game. Even if 4♡ makes, +170 will beat those playing 1NT.

5. Double. In front of the bidder this does not show a trump stack, but a fair balanced hand with some defense. If North has three hearts defending 2♡ doubled will probably be lucrative, and North should usually pull the double with a doubleton heart.

146

6. 5♣. It looks like South must have at least a reasonable play for slam, for the worst North could have is something like ♠KJx, ♡x, ◊Kxxx, ♣Kxxxx, and any improvement makes slam laydown. However, South should settle for 5♣. He made a fortunate decision not to open 1NT; this will certainly be the popular choice at most tables. The likely result at other tables is 3NT down one or two on a heart lead, for North probably has a normal 3NT response despite his singleton heart. 5♣ making five or six should be worth plenty of matchpoints if 3NT goes down at other tables, so South should not jeopardize his favorable position by bidding the slam.

7. Pass. Either 3♡ or a negative double could work well, but there just may not be a safe landing spot. If North also sells out it might be the best action available to N-S, and if North reopens South can reconsider depending on North's choice of actions.

8. 3◊. South is not quite worth a force to game, and his possible value bids are 2NT or 3♣. Unfortunately, neither of these bids will tell North to bid 4♠ with ♠KQ109x, ♡10x, ◊AQx, ♣Kxx but to bid 3NT with ♠KQ109x, ♡AQx, ◊10x, ♣Kxx. South should make the slight overbid of 3◊, driving the hand to a possibly thin game but increasing the chances of arriving in the the best game.

9. 1♠. A four-three spade fit looks good here, while a four-four heart fit might not be missed too much. For example, suppose North holds ♠Axx, ♡Axxx, ◊KQxx, ♣xx. 3NT will probably only make nine tricks, 4♡ will make ten tricks unless the hearts split four-one, but 4♠ will always make ten tricks unless there are very bad splits, and possibly eleven tricks if a heart-diamond squeeze materializes. There are other hands North might hold, of course, but the 1♠ response just has to be the percentage action.

10. Double. South has committed himself to this action. If he had wanted to probe intelligently he should have bid 3♣ rather than 4♡, to get some help from his partner. Instead South

blasted to 4 ♡, which certainly isn't necessarily cold, in order to make the opponents guess what to do. They made their guess, and now South must assume that they have guessed wrong and double. A 5 ♡ bid would be very costly if it turned out that 4 ♠ were a phantom.

COMPETITIVE BIDDING

COMPETITIVE
BIDDING

THE FIGHTING GROUND

Most matchpoint enthusiasts will agree that more match-points are swung by competitive part-score decisions than any other phase of bidding. There is a logical reason for this. Most bidding decisions such as which game to bid, whether or not to bid a game, whether to take a sacrifice, etc., involve only two or three possible contracts at other tables. Consequently, a losing auction is unlikely to cost more than one-half matchpoint against another table. In a part-score competitive auction, however, there are many different possible contracts and results. It is not unusual to see the scores on such a board look as follows:

$$+470$$
$$+200$$
$$+140$$
$$+120$$
$$+110$$
$$+100$$
$$+90$$
$$-50$$
$$-90$$
$$-100$$
$$-110$$
$$-300$$
$$-670$$

With such a variety of results at other tables, any action is likely to swing several matchpoints. Thus, accurate competitive part-score bidding has high priority for a winning matchpoint player.

Where does the battle take place? If you stop at a cozy 2♣ or 2♦ contract, competent opponents simply won't let you play it there if they have their share of the high-card strength and any kind of fit at all. The opponent in the balancing seat will usually find some excuse to get into the auction. Conversely, suppose you bid up to 4♣ or 4♦ in a part-score battle. You may get doubled, but it is unlikely that the opponents will compete higher unless the hand is very distributional. It is at the three-level where the critical part-score decisions are made. The decision to compete to the three-level over the opponents' two or three-level contract is one of the most important decisions in matchpoints, and one that recurs frequently. The three-level is the battleground where part-score fights are won and lost, and your bidding should be geared towards making the right decision when this battleground is reached.

The most important principle is: In a competitive auction (or one that is likely to become competitive), if you know that you will want to compete to the three-level and if it is probable that the opponents will make you go there, then it is best to do it immediately rather than wait for the enemy to describe their hands to each other. This often occurs when you have a good trump fit, the enemy has a fit or a potential fit in a higher ranking suit than yours, and the high-card strength seems to be evenly divided. Vulnerability may be a factor, but it is usually correct to get to the three-level yourself on all vulnerabilities in this type of situation. That quick bid to the three-level prevents your left-hand opponent from bidding his suit or raising his partner at a comfortable level. When the opponents hold the higher ranking suit, they will have to make the critical decision of whether or not to compete to the three-level over your three-level contract. Your quick action at the three-level often prevents the opponents from exchanging the information necessary to make an intelligent decision.

None vul., South holds: ♠108, ♡KJ102, ◇K653, ♣J97

NORTH	EAST	SOUTH	WEST
1 ♡	Double	?	

South should bid 3 ♡. Call it preemptive, call it jamming, call it anything you want, but it is the correct bid. We all know that if South bids 2 ♡ E-W will find their way to 2 ♠, either by a direct 2 ♠ bid by West or a reopening double by East. After this happens, South will undoubtedly want to compete to 3 ♡ anyway, so he should do so now. Imagine poor West holding ♠KQxx, ♡xx, ◇Q10xx, ♣xxx. Over a 2 ♡ call he has an easy 2 ♠ bid, but over a 3 ♡ call he is not so happy. 3 ♠ could easily overshoot the mark, and even if 3 ♠ is right his partner may carry on to 4 ♠ going down; East can't be sure just how competitive the 3 ♠ call is. On the other hand, if West passes his partner may have a moderate distributional hand such as ♠AJxx, ♡x, ◇AJxx, ♣K10xx. Should he reopen over 3 ♡? It could be catastrophic if his partner doesn't have a fit, but selling out could be equally disastrous. Let's look at the entire hand:

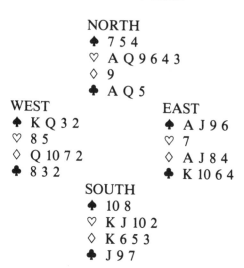

NORTH
♠ 7 5 4
♡ A Q 9 6 4 3
◇ 9
♣ A Q 5

WEST
♠ K Q 3 2
♡ 8 5
◇ Q 10 7 2
♣ 8 3 2

EAST
♠ A J 9 6
♡ 7
◇ A J 8 4
♣ K 10 6 4

SOUTH
♠ 10 8
♡ K J 10 2
◇ K 6 5 3
♣ J 9 7

It is clear that E-W belong in 3 ♠. If South bids only 2 ♡, they will have no problem. West will bid 2 ♠, and East will compete to 3 ♠ over North's 3 ♡ call. If South bids 3 ♡, however, E-W could easily either sell out or overbid to 4♠ without either one of them making a particularly bad bid. Notice that it is correct for either East or West to compete over 3♡ on this hand, but if the opposite hand weren't quite so suitable competition by East or West could be disastrous. The vulnerability was set at none vul., but the 3♡ call would be equally correct and effective at any vulnerability.

E-W vul., South holds: ♠1063, ♡A8, ♢K32, ♣KQ1075

NORTH	EAST	SOUTH	WEST
—	—	1♣	Pass
2♣	Pass	?	

What a nice cozy contract. Do you really think that South will be permitted to buy it there? If West has played enough match-points to know that defending 2♣ contracts is not the road to winning pair games, he will be in there. South will definitely want to compete to 3♣ over whatever E-W get to on the two-level, so he should bid it now. South doesn't know if E-W should be competing over 3♣ or not, and he doesn't care what they do. The important point is that an immediate 3♣ bid makes it more difficult for E-W to determine their best action, whatever it might be.

Both vul., South holds: ♠Q4, ♡876, ♢108, ♣KJ8765

NORTH	EAST	SOUTH	WEST
—	—	—	1♡
Double	Redouble	?	

Without the redouble, South should bid 2♣. 3♣ would be an invitational bid, and South's hand simply isn't worth it. The redouble changes matters. Now, South should immediately bid as high as he is willing to compete, which is the 3♣ level. Let the opponents start exchanging information from here, and they are more likely to do the wrong thing. The strength for this kind of bid can vary from almost completely preemptive to nearly invitational. It doesn't really matter. All that is important is that South is willing to compete to the three-level. Of course if he tries the bid on something like ♠xx, ♡QJ10x, ◇xx, ♣AQxxx (I think he should), he will then double the opponents if they bid 3♡, so the jump to the three-level can also be used as a trap. Only the bidder knows; the opponents must guess.

None vul., South holds: ♠102, ♡Q1065, ◇973, ♣A985

NORTH	EAST	SOUTH	WEST
—	—	—	1 ♣
1 ♡	Double*	?	

*negative double

South should go right to 3♡. It is virtually inconceivable that the opponents will sell to 2♡, and South will compete to 3♡ anyway, so he should put the pressure on before they can determine whether or not they have a fit. Again, the strength of this bid can vary from very preemptive to nearly game invitational. Don't worry about occasionally missing a game. As we have seen this is not so important in competitive auctions, and the matchpoints gained when the opponents misjudge the situation because they have to start guessing at the three-level will more than compensate for any bidding inaccuracy on your part.

Sometimes it is not necessary to go directly to the three-level, even though you are willing to compete there if necessary. This usually occurs when your side holds the higher ranking suit and there is some chance that you may buy the contract at the two-level. It is then not so important to shut the opponents out of their fit, for they will have to go to the four-level to buy the contract, and if your assessment of the hand as a part-score battle is correct this will suit you fine. Careful attention to the tempo of the bidding and awareness of opponents' problems will help you determine whether or not the immediate three-level bid is necessary. Some examples:

E-W vul., South holds: ♠Q87, ♡A876, ♢K9, ♣K632

NORTH	EAST	SOUTH	WEST
2 ♠*	Pass	?	

*weak 2-bid

3 ♠ would not be a bad bid, but I think it is better to pass. There is a reasonably good chance that you will buy the hand for 2 ♠, and this might be all you can make. It is silly to push voluntarily to 3 ♠ down one when the opponents were about to sell to 2 ♠. The only argument for bidding 3 ♠ immediately is to trap them into trying something at the four-level, which you will be willing to test out with a double, but this is not too likely to happen. Of course if E-W find their way to 3 ♢ you will be forced to compete to 3 ♠, but it is not at all inconsistent to pass now, planning on bidding 3 ♠ over 3 ♢. If East makes a takeout double, however, you should definitely bid 3 ♠. Now E-W have committed themselves to acting at the three-level. Since you have no intention of defending at this level, it is better to bid 3 ♠ and make them guess before they have any more chance to exchange information. Of course, you might also make the bid on a very weak hand, but one that did not have enough offensive potential to justify an advance sacrifice of 4 ♠. Since you could have anything, the 3 ♠ bid may goad them into stretching to compete at the four-level, and on this hand you will welcome that.

Both vul., South holds: ♠AQ10953, ♡K95, ♢K85, ♣9

NORTH	EAST	SOUTH	WEST
—	—	1 ♠	Pass
2 ♠	Pass	?	

There is no reason to bid at this point. While you have every intention of competing to 3 ♠ if the opponents get in the auction, you may have already frozen them out. West, who was not strong enough to take initial action, will think twice before stepping in at the three-level after you and your partner have exchanged information and E-W may not have a decent place to play the hand. Many pairs use a 3 ♠ bid by South as preemptive here, but I think it should be an old-fashioned game try for the simple reason that it is usually wrong to make the preemptive reraise with no competition even if you are dealt the perfect hand for it. Of course had West doubled or overcalled, it would be another story. There would be a greater likelihood of his having something else to say, so the 3 ♠ bid should be played as preemptive and made on this hand to stop him from conveniently describing his hand to his partner. Once again, enemy action drastically changes the meaning of certain bids, making them potentially weaker in competitive auctions than they would be in totally constructive auctions.

The type of action which must be avoided when you have the lower ranking suit is to fail to go directly to the three-level when you have the chance, allow the opponents to exchange information, and them compete to the three-level. For example:

Both vul., South holds: ♠54, ♡K62, ◊KJ97, ♣9653

NORTH	EAST	SOUTH	WEST
1 ◊	Double	?	

Are you willing to compete to the three-level over the likely enemy two of a major contract without any encouragement from partner? This is a close decision which is up to you (personally, I would), but the important point is that you must make that decision now with a 2 ◊ or 3 ◊ bid and then stick with your decision. The auction to be avoided is:

NORTH	EAST	SOUTH	WEST
1 ◊	Double	2 ◊	2 ♠
Pass	Pass	3 ◊	

This is a losing sequence, yet many players fall into this trap. South could hardly have been caught by surprise by the 2 ♠ bid, for it is unlikely that E-W with fair high card strength and a likely major suit fit will sell to 2 ◊. So, if South thought the hand was worth competing to 3 ◊ on his own he should have done so immediately and put maximum pressure on the opponents; if not, South should pass 2 ♠ and respect his partner's decision not to compete. Remember that North has heard South's 2 ◇ bid and is quite capable of bidding 3 ◇ himself if he thinks it is the right action. North could well hold something like ♠KQ10x, ♡Q10x, ◇Axxx, ♣Qx. If this is North's hand E-W have misjudged by bidding 2♠, but only if South keeps quiet. If South bids 2 ◇ and then 3 ◇ he is giving E-W a chance to escape if their initial 2♠ bid was wrong, and making it easier for them to find the correct action over 3 ◇ than if South had bid it immediately. So either way, bidding 2 ◇ and then 3 ◇ must be wrong.

It is often necessary to raise partner or get your own suit into the auction when competition starts on hands which normally wouldn't call for these actions. If the opponents are in the auction, you can assume it will be a fight to the three-level. In order to be prepared to win this fight, it is important to lay the foundations early. Some examples:

E-W vul., South holds: ♠AJ, ♡J73, ◇AQJ42, ♣872

NORTH	EAST	SOUTH	WEST
—	—	1 ◇	Pass
1 ♡	1 ♠	?	

If East had passed, many players would prefer a 1NT or 2 ◇ rebid on South's cards to a 2♡ raise. This is largely a matter of partnership style, depending on such things as how likely North is to have a weak four-card heart suit, whether or not the raise promises or implies four trumps, whether North is likely to check back for three-card support after a 1NT rebid, etc. After the 1♠ overcall, however, a 2♡ bid by South is correct regardless of partnership style. If South does anything else (pass, 1NT, or 2 ◇), he is all too likely to hear a 2♠ bid on his left. If this gets passed around to him he will have no idea what to do now that the three-level is approaching. 3♡ will probably be right if North has a five-card suit and a fair hand, but it could be disastrous if North has only four hearts. If South bids 2♡ immediately he can confidently sell to 2♠, knowing that if North wasn't willing to bid 3♡ then N-S don't belong there.

Both vul., South holds: ♠ J8, ♡ 94, ♢ QJ10653, ♣ K96

NORTH	EAST	SOUTH	WEST
1 ♠	Double	?	

If East had passed, South would bid 1NT. The hand isn't strong enough for a 2 ♢ response. After the double, South must bid 2 ♢. The bid no longer shows the same strength that it would if East had passed. Now if West bids the expected 2 ♡ and this is passed around to South, he will not feel compelled to bid on since he has already told his partner about his diamond suit. If South passes over the double and West bids 2 ♡, South won't have any idea what to do in the balancing seat. His failure to prepare earlier puts him at a guess now that the critical three-level decision is at hand.

None vul., South holds: ♠ KJ9862, ♡ 73, ♢ Q73, ♣ 92

NORTH	EAST	SOUTH	WEST
—	—	—	1 ♣
1 ♡	2 ♣	?	

South must bid 2 ♠. No matter that this is an overbid; the suit must be bid now. If South passes West may very well bid 3 ♣ (particularly if he has read this book!), and South will have egg on his face when it then goes pass, pass, to him.

E-W vul., South holds: ♠ 632, ♡ 75, ♢ Q3, ♣ AQ10875

NORTH	EAST	SOUTH	WEST
—	—	—	1 ♡
1 ♠	2 ♡	?	

If East had passed, South might have tried 2 ♣, planning on following with 2 ♠ if somebody took another bid, as somebody usually will. This way, South gets his lead-director in and paints an accurate picture of his hand so North will be well-placed to make the final decision should E-W compete to three of a red suit. East's 2 ♡ bid changes the picture considerably. No longer can South afford the luxury of a club bid. In the first place the auction might die at 3 ♣, which would be bad if N-S belong in spades as they probably do. Secondly, if E-W compete to 3 ♡ South is not strong enough to contest to 3 ♠ on his own, and North cannot help since he doesn't know that South has spade support when South bids 3 ♣. South must content himself with a 2 ♠ bid, and hope that his partner will find the winning auction if the opponents bid to the three-level as they are likely to do. It is true that North won't be able to evaluate his club holding accurately, but at least he will have a fair idea of South's strength and spade support. You just can't have everything, particularly when the opponents make bids which gobble up your bidding room. You simply have to do the best you can with what you have left.

So far we have examined hands on which it is clear to drive to the three-level or describe your hand to partner so he can make the final decision. What if it is not so clear, and it is your decision to make. The next chapter examines an extremely important concept which is the main basis for making that decision.

THE LAW OF TOTAL TRICKS

The problem of which side can make how many tricks with what trump suit is the riddle that both pairs attempt to solve during the auction. Unfortunately, the most accurate bidding system in the world will not always lead to the right conclusion. Even if you could see partner's hand you would not always find the winning contract. Although you could always get to the percentage contract, the location of a couple of key enemy cards or the splits in important suits will in the end determine how many tricks you take.

In competitive bidding, the lie of the cards works both ways. What is good for you is often bad for the opponents, and vice versa. For example, suppose your trump suit is:

North: AQ10x
South: J98x

If the king is onside you will lose no tricks in the suit, while if it is offside you will lose one trick. However, the location of the king will also make a difference to the opponents if they declare in some other suit. Assuming that the suit splits three-two, if the finesse is on for you then it is off for the opponents and they will lose two tricks in the suit, while if it is off for you then it is on for them and they have only one loser in the suit. Note that there is a total of two tricks to be lost in the suit. Either they have two losers and you have none or each side has one. The location of the king determines which side loses how many tricks, but the total number of losers between N-S and E-W remains constant.

Another example:

North: AKxx
South: Qxxx

If this is your trump suit you will have no trump losers if the suit splits three-two, one loser if it splits four-one, and two losers if it splits five-zero. Conversely, if this is a side suit for the opponents in some other trump contract then they will have two, one or no losers depending on how this suit is divided in their hands. Once again, the total number of losers in the suit between both pairs is constant, although the distribution of these losers depends on how the suit is divided.

These examples seem to indicate that for an entire hand the total number of losers for N-S and E-W may be a constant figure, even though the distribution of these losers is unclear. If this is the case, then the number of tricks available to N-S in their best trump suit plus the number of tricks available to E-W in their best trump suit may be constant. Let's look at a full hand and see if this may be the case:

NORTH
♠ K 6
♡ K 6 5 3
◇ A Q 5 3
♣ J 10 9

SOUTH
♠ 8 5 4
♡ A 9 8 7 4
◇ 8 4
♣ A 8 2

How will N-S fare in a heart contract? It depends a lot on the lie of the opposing cards. Let's suppose that everything works. Then N-S have one spade loser and one club loser, for eleven tricks. If this is the case, how will E-W do in spades? They will lose one spade, two hearts, two diamonds (I'm forgetting about the ruff), and two clubs, so they will take only six tricks.

Conversely, suppose hearts are three-one and all finesses lose for N-S. Then N-S lose two spades, one heart, one diamond, and two clubs, so they take seven tricks. E-W on the other hand lose only one heart, one diamond, and one club for ten tricks.

In both cases, the total number of tricks available to the two pairs was seventeen. In the first case it was eleven plus six, in the second case seven plus ten. Try arranging the E-W cards in various ways so that some finesses win for N-S and some for E-W. Provided that E-W don't have unusual distribution such as a five-two club fit, the total number of tricks available to the two pairs will remain at seventeen regardless of how you distribute the E-W cards.

Now we notice something very interesting. N-S have nine hearts between them, and E-W have eight spades. So the total number of trumps held by the two pairs in their respective trump suits is also seventeen, the same as the total number of tricks. Is this just a coincidence? It turns out that this is a quite common occurrence. Examination of a large number of hands has shown that the total number of tricks available to both pairs (i.e. the tricks N-S can take if they declare in their best trump suit plus the tricks E-W can take if they declare in their best trump suit) averages out to be the total number of trumps held by the two pairs in their respective trump suits. It quite often comes out exactly right, and is seldom off by more than one trick. This remarkable fact is called the law of total tricks. It tends to break down at the four and five levels or when one or both pairs have wild two-suit fits or a lot of distribution. For the run-of-the-mill part-score hand, however, the law of total tricks is surprisingly accurate, and can be used very effectively to judge what to do at the three-level.

Let's see how we can use the law of total tricks to aid us in competitive part-score decisions. First of all, look at what our goals should be. Suppose the opponents are in 2♠, and we are considering whether or not to compete to 3♡. If both contracts make, it is correct to compete. If neither contract makes, it is correct to defend. What if only one of the contracts will make and the other is down one? This is not so clear, but the scoring at matchpoints is such that it is usually right to compete under these circumstances. The reason, of course, is that a part-score scores more than +100 at contracts higher than two of a minor. Consequently it is better to make a part-score than to defeat the opponents one trick, and it is better to be set one trick than to allow the opponents to make a part-score. The exception is when one or both sides are vulnerable. If the opponents are vulnerable and you can ascertain that they will be the ones who go down, then doubling them and collecting +200 will be more profitable than making your part-score. Conversely, if you are vulnerable and you believe that your contract will be down one and the opponents will be sharp enough to double, then it will be better to sell out. In practice this kind of pinpoint determination is impossible, particularly about the doubles, so on balance it will pay to bid on rather than sell if you think that one but not both contracts will make. An added bonus is that the opponents may bid still one more, and if your initial judgment was correct this will definitely be favorable for your side.

How can we incorporate the law of total tricks into the decision-making process? First of all, what about the opponents' trump length? On balance, you may assume that they have an eight-card fit. Occasionally they may have a seven-card fit, but this is difficult to determine. Often they will have a nine-card fit, and sometimes this can be diagnosed from the bidding. Usually your side will also have an eight or nine card fit. We can already see why it is almost always wrong to sell to a two-level contract when you can bid a higher ranking two-level contract. Even if both sides only have eight-card fits the total number of trumps is sixteen, so the trick total figures to be sixteen also. Consequently it is likely that at least one if not both sides can make their contract, so it is right to compete.

It is at the three-level where the decisions get close. There are four different possibilities, and we will examine them separately.

Case 1: You have an eight-card trump fit and the opponents have the higher ranking suit. For the sake of simplicity, let's suppose for the rest of this discussion that the suits are hearts and spades. This means that the opponents have stopped in 2 ♠. You are considering whether or not to compete to 3 ♡, and there are sixteen combined trumps. Therefore the opponents have done the right thing, since the trick total expectancy is also sixteen. Bidding 3 ♡ would be a one trick "overbid" by trick-total analysis, and as we have seen it is usually correct to make this overbid because one of the contracts figures to make. Once again, vulnerability may be a deterrent factor, even if a double is unlikely. For example, suppose both sides are vulnerable. There is the possibility that the cards lie very favorably for either you or your opponents, which means that somebody may go for 200 even if they aren't doubled. If this is the case, it is better to sell out regardless of which pair is unlucky. This doesn't mean that selling out will necessarily work; it simply means that with both sides vulnerable there is an extra way to win by defending that wouldn't exist if one or both pairs weren't vulnerable. Consequently, if the decision is really close it is worth keeping an eye on the vulnerability. On the other hand, it is possible that the opponents have a nine-card fit. In this case, trick-total indicates that it is definitely correct to go to the three-level over their two-level contract, for both contracts might make. Furthermore even if bidding on is wrong you have another way to win—the opponents may misjudge and bid one more. So all other things being equal, it will usually pay off to bid on in this situation.

Case 2: You have a nine-card heart fit, and the opponents are in 2♠. Now the trick total is presumed to be seventeen, so it is clear to compete to 3♡; there is a good chance that both contracts will make. Furthermore, you now give the enemy a difficult decision as to whether or not to bid on to 3♠. As we saw in several examples from the previous chapter, hands that fall into this category should usually be bid to the three-level immediately, to make the decision tougher for the opponents.

Case 3: You have an eight-card spade fit, and the opponents are in 3♡. The presumed trick total is sixteen, and the enemy has already "overbid" the trick total by one. Hence it is almost always incorrect to compete to 3♠, because it would be a two-trick overbid by trick-total standards. There is a good chance that both contracts will go down one or that one of the contracts will be defeated two tricks; in either case, bidding on is wrong. You should bid on only if you have a two-suit fit, unexpected distribution, or reason to think that the opponents have a nine-card fit, which would make your 3♠ call only a one-trick overbid.

Case 4: You have a nine-card spade fit, and the opponents are in 3♡. Once again, the decision is close, since bidding on would be only a one-trick overbid if the opponents have eight trumps. There is now a better chance that they have nine trumps since they were willing to compete to the three-level. If so, bidding on will probably be right, for then the trick total is eighteen, which means that both contracts might well make. On the downside, you don't have the extra chance that you may push them one level higher, since they are unlikely to compete to the four-level without substantial distribution.

All this can be summarized by a good rule of thumb: In a competitive part-score auction, be willing to contract for the same number of tricks as your side has trumps. In other words, you should generally compete to the three-level with a nine-card fit, but with an eight-card fit it is often correct not to compete to the three-level. This is just a general guideline and there are plenty of exceptions, but it is surprising how often following this rule leads to the correct action in a close competitive situation.

I must point out at this juncture that I have been discussing only the decision of whether to bid or defend. There is, of course, a third possibility, and that is to double the opponents. Doubling is really a subset of defending; only you think that they are probably going down or possibly that you will get a terrible result if they make it so you might as well double even though they will make the contract over half the time. This subject will be discussed in a later chapter. The best way to look at a competitive part-score decision is to first determine whether or not it is correct to bid, via the law of total tricks. If you decide that it is right to defend, only then do you consider whether or not to double. The only time the doubling decision should come first is when the double stands out, usually because you have a stack in the enemy trump suit.

Enough of this theory. Let's look at some examples to see how the law of total tricks is applied in actual auctions.

None vul., South holds: ♠ J73, ♡ J7, ◇ Q863, ♣ K973

NORTH	EAST	SOUTH	WEST
1 ♠	2 ♡	2 ♠	3 ♡
Pass	Pass	?	

South should pass. He knows that his side has only eight spades. How does he know this? Because North would have bid 3 ♠

himself on almost any hand with a six-card spade suit, on exactly the same trick-total reasoning. The opponents may or may not have a nine-card fit; that is not clear. If they do then the 3 ♠ bid is only a one trick overbid and may turn out right, but if the opponents have an eight-card fit the 3 ♠ bid is very likely to be a losing action. Even with neither side vul., which is the vulnerability most conducive to aggressive part-score competition, South is advised to pass. This will probably surprise a lot of players who think that a 3 ♠ call is automatic in this situation, but the law of total tricks says otherwise.

E-W vul., South holds: ♠97, ♡KJ43, ◇Q98, ♣AK98

NORTH	EAST	SOUTH	WEST
—	—	1 ♣	1 ♠
Double*	2 ♠	?	

*negative double

South should bid 3 ♡. In the worst case he will be overbidding the trick total by one, when North has four hearts and E-W have only eight spades. As we have seen, this may not be bad. It should be noted that this is not a constructive bid; competition is more important. If South has a game invitational hand in hearts he should just bid the game and let the opponents guess what to do.

Both vul., South holds: ♠Q653, ♡AK62, ◇8, ♣A874

NORTH	EAST	SOUTH	WEST
—	1 ◇	Double	Pass
1 ♠	2 ◇	2 ♠	3 ◇
Pass	Pass	?	

South should try 3 ♠. The bidding indicates that E-W have a nine-card diamond fit, so North should, therefore, have at least a four-card spade suit since he probably has only three diamonds. Thus, South is overbidding the trick total by at most one trick. The singleton diamond and the excellent card placement (queen in the trump suit, aces and kings outside), argue in favor of the 3 ♠ bid. It should be noted that if North had held a five-card spade suit he probably would have bid 3 ♠ himself almost without looking at the rest of his hand, relying on trick total to see him through. Also, South's 2 ♠ bid does not particularly show extra strength, as it would if East had passed. The bid simply shows four-card support, which the takeout double doesn't guarantee. This enables North to make the proper competitive decision at the three-level. If South had, say, ♠ Qxxx, ♡ AQxx, ◇ xx, ♣ KQx he should still bid 2 ♠. The difference is that he could then comfortably pass out 3 ◇, knowing then that a 3 ♠ bid would be too high. If South passes on this hand and West bids 3 ◇ as in the actual auction, South will have a very uncomfortable feeling when it gets passed back to him, for both sides could have nine-card fits. This shows why it is important that raises and free bids not show extra values in competitive auctions.

Both vul., South holds: ♠ K73, ♡ QJ3, ◇ K9842, ♣ 82

NORTH	EAST	SOUTH	WEST
1 ◇	Double	?	

Many players would try a cute 1NT bid on this hand, planning to bid 3 ◇ if E-W compete to two of a major or 3 ♣. This isn't the worst bid in the world, but it just doesn't do the job. Trick total analysis shows that South must compete to 3 ◇ anyway, and it is very unlikely that the opponents will sell out to a lower contract if they have any strength at all, so South should bid 3 ◇ now. If South bids 1NT, West can get his suit in at a safe level, and East can make the final decision at the three-level. Over the 3 ◇ bid, however, E-W don't have that luxury. West is in a bind, and he may sell out when it is his hand or bid at the wrong time and take a minus score. If West does try three of a major, South should bet that West has guessed wrong and double him. This kind of bidding puts a lot of pressure on the opponents, and will induce them to misjudge the auction quite often.

N-S vul., South holds: ♠32, ♡KJ64, ◇82, ♣KQ654

NORTH	EAST	SOUTH	WEST
1 ♠	2 ◇	Double*	Pass
2 ♡	Pass	Pass	3 ◇
Pass	Pass	?	

*negative double

South could speculate a double if he chose, although it would be pretty chancy. A 3 ♡ bid, however, is a definite no-no. With only eight trumps and the opponents already at the three-level, it is generally wrong to bid on. On this auction, South can't even be 100% sure that North has four hearts. Bidding on hands like this is a common error of aggressive matchpoint players. The law of total tricks says not to bid, and it is a good law to obey.

Both vul., South holds: ♠Q53, ♡875, ◇KQ3, ♣AJ52

NORTH	EAST	SOUTH	WEST
2 ♠*	Double	?	

*weak two-bid

Over East's double, South should bid 3 ♠ immediately. He will have to bid it eventually according to the law of total tricks, for West will undoubtedly take the double out to his best suit. By bidding 3 ♠ now, South makes the opponents guess immediately. Also, a delayed 3 ♠ call is more likely to get doubled for the deadly −200, since the opponents will be better able to judge the fit of the hand if they have a chance to bid their suits. South can't be sure that he can make it; in fact, he has no idea whose hand it is. If he just follows the law of total tricks, he is likely to be right regardless of who can make what.

Laws are made to be broken, and the law of total tricks is no exception. There are several factors which should sway the astute bidder to overbid or underbid the total trick count.

1. Distribution. A singleton in the opponents' suit is often sufficient reason to stretch the law a tiny bit. The reason is that they are more likely to have a nine-card fit, so an overbid may

not be that much of a stretch. For example:

None vul., South holds: ♠AQ1096, ♡3, ◇KQ83, ♣Q103

NORTH	EAST	SOUTH	WEST
—	—	1 ♠	2 ♡
2 ♠	3 ♡	?	

Normally South should have a sixth spade for a 3 ♠ call in this sequence, and the bid could easily turn out wrong. However, the singleton heart suggests the overbid of 3 ♠. The opponents may well have a nine-card fit on this auction, and if North is looking at three spades and three hearts he certainly won't bid on, yet competing to 3 ♠ will probably turn out best. If South's small diamond were a small heart, a 3 ♠ call would definitely be wrong.

On the other side of the coin, exceptionally flat distribution often argues for conservatism. For example:

N-S vul., South holds: ♠K985, ♡764, ◇A85, ♣852

NORTH	EAST	SOUTH	WEST
1 ♠	2 ♡	2 ♠	3 ♡
Pass	Pass	?	

South should pass. His fourth trump argues for a 3 ♠ call, but his total lack of distribution says otherwise. He has a good clue that North doesn't have a singleton heart, since North might have bid 3 ♠ himself if he did, and North also should have only five spades for the same reason. If North has tripletons in both minors, prospects in 3 ♠ are rather bleak. If South's minor suit distribution were four-two either way on this hand, the 3 ♠ call would be correct.

2. Two-suit fits. When you have a good fit for partner's second suit, it often pays to be a bit aggressive. The extra fit means that the opponents are likely to have a two-suit fit also, and the second suit is sort of another trump suit, so both you and your opponents may take more tricks than the law of total tricks would predict even on relatively balanced hands.

For example:

E-W vul., South holds: ♠QJ83, ♡98, ◊KJ76, ♣972

NORTH	EAST	SOUTH	WEST
1 ◊	1 ♡	Double*	2 ♡
2 ♠	3 ♡	?	

*negative double

North's 2♠ bid doesn't show any extra strength, of course, merely the possession of four spades. Normally South would pass with an eight-card fit and the opponents at the three-level. However, the fit in diamonds, North's first suit, argues in favor of bidding on. A look at all four hands illustrates the point:

```
                    NORTH
                    ♠ A K 5 4
                    ♡ 5 3 2
                    ◊ A Q 8 2
                    ♣ 10 6
     WEST                          EAST
     ♠ 10 7 6                      ♠ 9 2
     ♡ A 7 4                       ♡ K Q J 10 6
     ◊ 9 4 3                       ◊ 10 5
     ♣ K J 8 4                     ♣ A Q 5 3
                    SOUTH
                    ♠ Q J 8 3
                    ♡ 9 8
                    ◊ K J 7 6
                    ♣ 9 7 2
```

No nine-card fits, no singletons, yet both sides can make nine tricks. What happened to the law of total tricks? The answer is that both sides have a good two-suit fit, so the hands will tend to make more than one would normally expect. To illustrate how important the two-suit fit is, let's try interchanging the minor suit holdings of the South and West hands. N-S still make 3♠ with all the cards onside for them, but these same finesses cause E-W to lose two tricks in each side suit and be down two in 3♡.

This looks more like what the law of total tricks would predict. If the gods had been fairer with the distribution of the honors, then both contracts would be down one. With the new hand (three small diamonds and KJxx of clubs), South knows there is no double fit, so it is clearly correct to pass.

3. Location of intermediates. While aces and kings will score tricks in any contract, queens and jacks are more effective trick takers on offense in long suits than in short suits. This is an important principle of hand evaluation. We all know that ♠Ax, ♡KQJ10x, ◇Axxx, ♣xx is a stronger hand offensively than ♠AJ, ♡K10xxx, ◇Axxx, ♣Qx even though the "point count" is the same for both hands. The reason is that queens and jacks are more likely to score on the third and fourth rounds of suits, and this will only be of help in trump suits or long side suits. If there is no third or fourth round of a suit, the lower honors may not be of much value on offense.

Conversely, queens and jacks in short suits may provide extra tricks on defense which they don't provide on offense. A holding of Qx opposite Jxx will produce at most one possibly useless discard on offense, yet it is worth a full trick on defense if that is the enemy trump suit or a side suit that splits four-four or five-three. Queens and jacks in long suits, however, are not likely to produce tricks on defense, because the late rounds of the suit will be ruffed by declarer. Thus, we say that the first hand in the previous paragraph is offensively oriented, while the second hand with the minor honors in the short suits is defensively oriented.

In competitive part-score bidding, we are concerned with both the offensive and defensive potential of the hand. The law of total tricks gives us a good idea about who can make what, but this can be fine-tuned by examining the location of the minor honors. If they are concentrated in long suits, the trick total is likely to be higher than the law of total tricks suggests. If the queens and jacks are in the enemy suit, however, this is an indication that the trick total may be lower than we expect. For example:

None vul., South holds ♠Q106, ♡A973, ◊AJ76, ♣Q7

NORTH	EAST	SOUTH	WEST
—	—	1 ◊	Pass
1 ♡	1 ♠	2 ♡	2 ♠
Pass	Pass	?	

Presumably both sides have eight-card fits, since North didn't try 3♡. With neither side vulnerable and the opponents at the two-level, it is usually right to bid on, since 3♡ would be a one trick "overbid" by the law of total tricks. The location of South's queens should persuade him to pass. These cards are all in short suits, so they are more likely to score tricks on defense than on offense. Therefore, the trick total count will tend to be on the low side. The full hand:

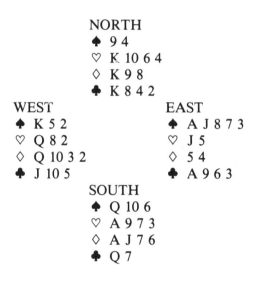

NORTH
♠ 9 4
♡ K 10 6 4
◊ K 9 8
♣ K 8 4 2

WEST
♠ K 5 2
♡ Q 8 2
◊ Q 10 3 2
♣ J 10 5

EAST
♠ A J 8 7 3
♡ J 5
◊ 5 4
♣ A 9 6 3

SOUTH
♠ Q 10 6
♡ A 9 7 3
◊ A J 7 6
♣ Q 7

N-S can make eight tricks in hearts and E-W can make seven tricks in spades, one less than the law of total tricks predicts, so selling out turns out to be correct. The importance of the location of the minor honors can be seen if we simply exchange South's queen of spades for West's queen of hearts, leaving all distributions the same. Now hearts makes nine tricks, while spades makes eight tricks, one more total trick than anticipated.

This should make a difference to South in his choice of actions. With ♠1062, ♡AQ93, ◇AJ76, ♣Q7 the 3♡ call is indicated.

MATCHPOINT DOUBLES

The penalty double in a competitive part-score auction is one of the most important actions for the successful matchpoint competitor. Understanding when to double and when to sell out in a part-score battle will swing many matchpoints for any duplicate player. The utopian goal should be: Double when they are going down, don't double when they are making. This is analogous to the Rabbi's Rule: When the king is singleton, play the ace. It is true, of course, that the prime consideration in doubling the opponents is whether or not you think they can make it. However, often you are not very sure one way or the other. In these situations, it is important to understand the matchpoint odds you are getting on your double. Sometimes the double figures to win far more matchpoints when it is right than it will lose when it is wrong; at other times exactly the opposite is true. You want to double frequently when there is much to gain and little to lose, but to avoid close doubles when there is little to gain and a lot to lose.

First of all, let's see how the matchpoint odds on a tight part-score double differ from the IMP odds. We all know that it is wrong to double the opponents into game at IMPs if it figures to be close. Suppose we are not vulnerable against vulnerable opponents. We have bid to 3 ♡, and they have outbid us to 3 ♠. Let's further suppose that the contract is 3 ♡ at the other table, either making or down one. We are considering whether or not to make a close double of the 3 ♠ contract. Let us further suppose that 3 ♠ is also either making or down one. This last assumption is consistent with our assessment that a double of 3 ♠ would be close.

If we double and are right, we go from + 100 to + 200. If 3 ♡ makes at the other table for + 140, then we win two IMPs instead of losing one IMP for a three IMP gain. At matchpoints, we gain a full matchpoint against the other table. If 3 ♡ is down one for − 50, then the double takes us from plus four IMPs to plus six IMPs for a two IMP gain. At matchpoints, the double makes no difference; we win the board anyway.

If we double and are wrong, we go from − 140 to − 730. If

$3 \heartsuit$ makes, then we turn a seven IMP loss into a thirteen IMP loss for a six IMP cost. At matchpoints the cost is zero; the board was lost once the opponents bid $3 \spadesuit$. If $3 \heartsuit$ goes down, then we lose twelve IMPs for doubling instead of three IMPs for passing for a nine IMP loss. Once again, the double costs nothing at matchpoints.

Putting all this together, we see that on the average we are risking about three times as many IMPs by doubling as we stand to gain if we are right. Consequently, we should be pretty sure about the double. At matchpoints, however, the double gains a full matchpoint if it is right against $3 \heartsuit$ making at another table, and never costs if it is wrong against other $3 \heartsuit$ contracts. Therefore, if we judge that most of the field will buy the hand our way for $3 \heartsuit$, which may make, then the double is virtually a no lose proposition which may gain a lot if it is right, so we should double on almost any excuse. Another way of looking at it is that we are headed for a very bad score if $3 \spadesuit$ makes whether we double or not if the field buys the contract our way for $3 \heartsuit$. Therefore the double will only turn a bad score into a zero if it is wrong, while it will definitely net us a top if it is right.

Does this mean that we can take a pot shot at the opponents every time they outbid us, since we have everything to gain and nothing to lose? Not at all. It is quite possible for the double to cost substantially when it is wrong. The following occurrence in a recent Life Masters Pairs illustrates this: With both sides vulnerable, our opponents had competed to $3 \spadesuit$ over our $3 \heartsuit$ contract in an aggressive competitive sequence. I gave some thought to doubling, but finally decided to sell out. They played it well and made exactly nine tricks, clearly all that were available, so I naturally estimated an average-minus. Imagine my surprise when we got 27½ out of 29 matchpoints on the board! What had happened? One look at the recap sheet told the story. The hearts split badly and so eight tricks was the limit in our heart contract, and nearly everybody in the room was doubled in $3 \heartsuit$ or $4 \heartsuit$, going for -200 or -500. Obviously I had made a good decision not to bid on, but even more important was the decision not to double. If I had doubled we would have been -730, losing to all those -200's and -500's instead of beating them, for virtually a full board swing. This example is extreme, but it shows that indiscriminate doubling in part-score battles can be very costly.

In order to determine the potential gain or loss of a double, we must run it through the matchpoint cost analysis. Let us suppose as before that we are N-S and have bid to 3 ♡, the opponents have competed to 3 ♠, and we are considering doubling. What are some likely results at other tables? One possibility is that they also play 3 ♠, doubled or not. Against these tables the gain and loss is easy to figure—you gain one-half matchpoint if you double and are right, but lose one-half matchpoint if you double and are wrong. Some of the other possibilities are more interesting:

1. E-W buy the hand for 2 ♠. This means that your 3 ♡ bid was somewhat of a push, not taken at other tables, and it was successful in that you pushed the opponents to 3 ♠. In this case the double gains nothing if it is right, for any plus score beats − 110, but the double costs a half matchpoint if it is wrong, since − 140 would have tied the other table.

2. E-W bid up to 4 ♠. If you are considering doubling 3 ♠, then 4 ♠ will surely be doubled. If you are right you gain nothing, for the pairs defending 4 ♠ will collect a larger number. If you are wrong you lose nothing if exactly nine tricks are the limit, since you were dead anyway, but if ten tricks are available the double costs a full matchpoint, for the double will make you − 630 or − 930 depending on vulnerability, worse than − 590 or − 790.

3. N-S buys the hand for 3 ♡. This is likely to be a common result if your decision is really close. Here the gain or loss from the double depends a lot on what happens to 3 ♡. If 3 ♡ makes, then the double has nothing to lose if wrong, and may gain a full matchpoint when it gets you a score greater than + 140. This will happen if you set them exactly one trick vulnerable, or two tricks non-vulnerable. On the other hand, suppose 3 ♡ is going down. Now the double gains nothing when it is right, but may lose a full matchpoint when it is wrong if the penalty you avoided in 3 ♡, doubled or not, is more than the value of the opponents' part-score.

4. N-S bid up to 4 ♡. If this makes, it won't matter whether

or not 3 ♠ is doubled unless the penalty against 3 ♠ is greater than the game your way (which indicates that the double wasn't so close). If 4 ♡ is going down the double of 3 ♠ cannot gain, but it might lose if 4 ♡ is doubled and set more than the value of the opponents' part-score.

So far, all we have seen is that sometimes tight part-score doubles have more to gain than to lose, and sometimes they have more to lose than to gain. The odds on the double are greatly affected by what is happening at other tables. Let's now examine the key factors which determine what is likely to be going on around the room. What we are looking for are factors which may cause the double to gain a full matchpoint against another table if successful, or, conversely, cost a full matchpoint if unsuccessful.

1. Vulnerability. This is very important when considering a close part-score double. We have already seen that the primary gain for a successful double comes when the increased penalty is greater than the part-score you could have made, while the undoubled penalty would be less. If our 3 ♡ contract is making at other tables and we double our opponents in 3 ♠, we only need to set them one trick if they are vulnerable to outscore the 3 ♡ contracts, while a two trick set is necessary if they are not vulnerable. Consequently, the double is more likely to gain when it is right if the opponents are vulnerable. This type of successful double is called "protecting your score". You must double to protect the +140 that you could have scored. Of course the opponents can also see the vulnerability, so the downside of doubling vulnerable opponents is that they are less likely to be out on a limb than if they were not vulnerable, so they are more likely to make the contract.

Not too many players realize that your own vulnerability is also of prime importance when considering making a tight double. It won't matter if the double is successful, but what if it fails? The instinctive reaction is "If the double fails I get a zero, so what difference does it make." As we have seen, it can make quite a difference. We are not so concerned with the matchpoint score we get, but how many matchpoints our action will cost if it is wrong. The greatest cost of doubling and being wrong comes when pairs holding your cards go for numbers which are greater than the part-score available to the opponents. Consequently, there is potentially a much greater cost of doubling and being wrong when you are vulnerable, for others may go −200 on your cards which your −140 would have beaten. If you are non-vulnerable it is likely that −140 would be almost tied for bottom anyway, so the double won't cost as much if they make.

To summarize: Your most profitable part-score doubles occur at favorable vulnerability, your least profitable at unfavorable vulnerability, with equal vulnerability in between.

2. Balance of power. When your side holds more than half the high card strength, it is much safer to make a tight part-score double. This is not only because high cards generate tricks, but also because results at other tables will tend to favor the double. Looking back to our 3 ♠ vs. 3 ♡ example, if your side holds the balance of power there figure to be a lot of pairs buying the hand for 3 ♡, and they probably won't get doubled. As we have seen, this is the situation where the double gains the most if right and loses the least if wrong. In other words, it may be "your hand", and you must double the opponents once they have outbid you.

Conversely, suppose the opponents hold the balance of power. Now, many pairs your way may sell out to 2 ♠, and if they bid 3 ♡ they may well get doubled because of the outstanding high-card strength. If either of these results occurs at another table, the double will not gain anything against that table if it is right, but may cost a full matchpoint if it is wrong. To look at it another way, you have pushed the opponents one trick higher and escaped unscathed while doing so. It is likely to be their hand, so any plus score should be good, and doubling risks turning a fair result into a bottom if wrong. This is somewhat analogous to taking a sacrifice against a game and pushing the opponents to the five-level. You would never double in this situation without having a sure set, because just beating them will be a very good board. In a part-score battle it is never clear who is pushing whom, but if the opponents hold the majority of the high card points it is likely that you are pushing them. Consequently, a double tends less to be the indicated action.

3. The success of your contract. Suppose at another table,

your side buys the hand for 3 ♡. If 3 ♡ makes, then your double of 3 ♠ may gain if it is right, but it will not cost anything to that table even if it is wrong. Conversely, suppose 3 ♡ is going down. Then the double has nothing to gain if right, but everything to lose if wrong. Consequently, you should be more inclined to double 3 ♠ if you liked your chances in 3 ♡, but less inclined to double if the 3 ♡ contract seemed doubtful.

These factors are not necessarily independent. For example, the more high card strength you hold, the more likely you are to make your contract. Never forget that the most important criterion of all for a double is: Are they going down? If it is quite likely that they are, go ahead and double regardless of potential gain and loss. You never know what crazy things may be happening at other tables, so you might as well collect as big a number as you can. Conversely, if it seems unlikely that you will set them, then it is silly to double even if you anticipate a bad board if they make. There is no reason to turn an average-minus into a zero. Occasionally the field will surprise you, and your bad board for −140 becomes a good board in the most unexpected ways. These factors should be taken into consideration only if it seems close as to whether or not the opponents' contract will make.

There are two more points to consider. First of all, you should tend to avoid doubling them if your double may tell them how to play the hand. There is no more costly bid than a double which tells declarer how to make a contract he would have otherwise gone down in. This is more likely to happen at the game or slam level. Declarer can't put too much faith in the meaning of a tight part-score double, since you might simply be doubling because you have been outbid and you think it is your hand. If the opponents have the preponderance of the high card strength, however, then declarer may deduce that your double is based on a bad trump split and play the hand accordingly.

The other important point about doubling is that your own contract comes first. If you believe that you can outbid your opponents and make your contract or if the law of total tricks suggests further competition, then it is much better to bid on than to try a speculative double. The only exception occurs when you are quite sure you can defeat the opposing contract. In this case, if your score may be larger than what you could get by bidding on you can forget the law of total tricks—just double and collect your number.

In the following examples, there is a good bit of judgment involved as to how likely various contracts are to make. If your assessment of the situation differs substantially from mine, you may come up with a different conclusion. Nevertheless, these examples will demonstrate how to weigh the important factors to put the odds in our favor in doubling situations.

E-W vul., South holds: ♠A53, ♡J64, ◇J9742, ♣K3

NORTH	EAST	SOUTH	WEST
1 ♠	2 ♡	2 ♠	3 ♡
Pass	Pass	?	

This is a model matchpoint double. Trick total argues against bidding 3 ♠. N-S figure to hold only eight spades since North failed to bid 3 ♠, and E-W are likely to hold only eight hearts because North might have pushed to 3 ♠ with a singleton heart. It appears close whether or not 3 ♡ will make. As for the other factors:

1. Vulnerability is perfect for the double. If you are right and set them one trick you collect +200 for a top when +100 would probably have been a bad score, while if you are wrong, doubling (as opposed to passing) does not figure to cost too much since N-S are not likely to go for more than 100 in a spade partscore.

2. N-S have the balance of strength since South has nine high-card points and North has opened the bidding. This argues in favor of the double.

3. The 2 ♠ contract figured to make. This makes the double more likely to gain when it is right and less likely to cost when it is wrong.

The full hand illustrates the correctness of the double:

```
                    NORTH
                    ♠ K Q J 10 2
                    ♡ 7 5
                    ◇ A 6 5
                    ♣ Q 10 4
        WEST                    EAST
        ♠ 8 7 4                 ♠ 9 6
        ♡ 8 3 2                 ♡ A K Q 10 9
        ◇ Q 8                   ◇ K 10 3
        ♣ A J 8 7 2             ♣ 9 6 5
                    SOUTH
                    ♠ A 5 3
                    ♡ J 6 4
                    ◇ J 9 7 4 2
                    ♣ K 3
```

Everybody's actions are reasonable, yet both 3 ♡ and 3 ♠ go
down one, as the law of total suggests. You may claim that this
is an unfair example, because so much depends on those minor
suit tens which can't really be considered in the bidding. If E-W
had the ten of clubs they would make 3 ♡, while if N-S owned
the ten of diamonds then 3 ♠ would also make. However, this is
compensated for by the internal solidity of the trump suits. For
example, suppose North held the queen of hearts instead of the
queen of spades, with the distribution around the table otherwise the same. Now E-W must lose an additional trick at hearts,
and N-S may have an additional loser at spades. As a percentage
action the double stands out, but the bid would not occur to
many players who would think their choice was between pass
and 3 ♠. On this hand the double will produce a top, pass would
be well below average since not all E-W pairs will compete to
3 ♡, and bidding 3 ♠ would be worst of all.

Both vul., South holds: ♠K84, ♡J76, ◇K7, ♣97652

NORTH	EAST	SOUTH	WEST
1 ♡	1 ♠	2 ♡	2 ♠
3 ♡	Pass	Pass	3 ♠
Pass	Pass	?	

South should pass. Obviously a 4♡ bid is out of the question; North would have bid game himself if it were close. Should South double? It appears to be pretty much of a toss-up whether or not 3♠ will make. What about the other critical factors?

1. Vulnerability. So-so. The opponents are vulnerable, which means that the double is more likely to gain when it is right, but N-S are also vulnerable, which means that other N-S pairs may be −200 in 3♡, doubled or not, so the double may cost substantially if it is wrong.

2. Balance of power. Not clear, but South has no particular reason to think that his side has more than half the high card strength. North's 3♡ bid doesn't show extra strength—all it shows is a sixth heart.

3. Success of 3♡. Again, not clear. It might make, but South has no particular reason to think that it will.

All things considered, South is wisest to pass. It may be that E-W are the ones who took the questionable push, and any plus score is likely to be good. A typical hand for North is: ♠xx, ♡AQxxxx, ◇xx, ♣AQx. Who can make what will depend completely on how the E-W cards are divided. N-S could make anything from ten tricks on a good day to six tricks on a bad day, while E-W might make from eleven tricks to seven tricks depending on the location of the key cards. On balance, doubling will cost more when it is wrong than it will gain when it is right. Note how the law of total tricks comes up with seventeen tricks, a very good estimate of the combined trick total for N-S and E-W.

None vul., South holds: ♠QJ943, ♡K1096, ◇Q4, ♣84

NORTH	EAST	SOUTH	WEST
—	—	—	1 ♡
Double	2 ♡	2 ♠	3 ♡
Pass	Pass	?	

Although the double might be tempting, South should prefer 3 ♠. The first priority is to bid your own contract, unless you are pretty sure you can set the opponents more than the value of a part-score. South cannot at all expect a two-trick set of 3 ♡; in fact, he might not beat it. The law of total tricks says to bid on, since N-S presumably have nine spades between them. Admittedly North doesn't absolutely guarantee four spades with his takeout double, but he will have them far more often than not. This makes a likely trick total of seventeen, so with neither side vulnerable bidding 3 ♠ is the indicated action. It would not be correct for North to compete to 3 ♠ simply because he has four spades and a singleton heart. South would certainly bid 2 ♠ with a four-card spade suit and four hearts, so from North's point of view the trick total might easily be only sixteen. Therefore, it is South's decision to make, and the fifth spade points to the 3 ♠ bid. A typical North hand might be: ♠K10xx, ♡x, ◇AKxx, ♣Qxxx. Opposite this hand the fate of 3 ♡ is not clear—down one is the probable result. 3 ♠ is very likely to make, so it is better than defending 3 ♡ doubled.

A small change in the hand or the conditions would make the double a better choice. For example, make one of South's small spades a diamond, giving him ♠QJ93, ♡K1096, ◇Q43, ♣84. Now the double stands out. The trick total is lower, and the hand certainly meets the most important criterion for a double—South expects 3 ♡ to go down! Note that taking away one of South's spades both improves the defensive potential against 3 ♡, because the opponents are less likely to hold a singleton spade, and decreases the offensive potential in 3 ♠, for that ninth trump is a very valuable asset in the play. This is exactly what the law of total tricks anticipates.

Another change would be to make E-W vulnerable. Now the arguments for the double are very strong in spite of the five-card spade suit. The double is simply a bet that they will not make it. If they go down N-S get a top, while if they make E-W get a top. In this particular situation N-S vulnerability does not matter, because South's choices are doubling and bidding 3 ♠ rather than doubling or passing. The 3 ♠ bid is likely to be an average result, while double is top or bottom. If South thinks that 3 ♡ will go down more often than not, then he should double. It's as simple as that.

N-S vul., South holds: ♠86, ♡Q10853, ◇K72, ♣J32

NORTH	EAST	SOUTH	WEST
1 NT	2 ◇*	2 ♡	2 ♠
Pass	Pass	?	

*spades and a minor

This is a frustrating hand. It seems as though South should take some action holding six high card points opposite a strong notrump. Unfortunately, no action makes much sense. North doesn't have four hearts or he would have bid 3 ♡ on a trick-total basis, and if he had three hearts and two spades he might have tried 3 ♡ anyway. Consequently, trick total argues against bidding on. What about doubling? The problem with that is that South isn't particularly optimistic about defeating 2 ♠; maybe even money at best. The vulnerability argues against doubling, since you would need a two-trick set to compensate for a heart partial, and that doesn't seem very likely. The double can lose heavily at this vulnerability if it is wrong, for other pairs holding the N-S cards may go for −200 or more due to bad splits. The wisest course of action is to pass and hope for some protection at other tables. You may be headed for a below average board, but that is still better than a bottom. The full hand:

```
                    NORTH
                    ♠ Q 9 5
                    ♡ A 6
                    ◊ A J 8 3
                    ♣ K Q 7 4
      WEST                      EAST
      ♠ 7 4 3 2                 ♠ A K J 10
      ♡ K J 9 7                 ♡ 4 2
      ◊ 5                       ◊ Q 10 9 6 4
      ♣ A 10 9 5                ♣ 8 6
                    SOUTH
                    ♠ 8 6
                    ♡ Q 10 8 5 3
                    ◊ K 7 2
                    ♣ J 3 2
```

Partner has full values, but you can't do much damage to 2♠.
2♡, on the other hand, will go down two if the defense is
careful. Quietly selling out to 2♠ will not lead to a bad score at
all, but if South takes any further action the only question is
what number will he go for, −470 or −500. This type of result
is not at all uncommon when the opponents have a fit and
distribution, while your side has no great fit. Holding the majority of the high cards doesn't guarantee that it is your hand.

Both vul., South holds: ♠K72, ♡KJ104, ◊94, ♣Q652

NORTH	EAST	SOUTH	WEST
1 ♠	2 ♡	?	

This time the law of total tricks can be ignored. South simply expects to beat 2♡, and that's all that matters. Even if N-S hold
eight spades and E-W hold eight hearts, defending 2♡ doubled
figures to be the winning action. South should make a penalty
double (or pass, hoping for a reopening double if playing
negative doubles). +200 beats any spade part-score, and South
figures to get at least that against 2♡ doubled. If North holds a
good enough hand to make a spade game, then N-S could easily
score +800 on defense. It is true that South would expect to

make 2 ♠, but this is the one situation where you don't bid for your contract first; namely when you see a profitable set.

NUISANCE BIDS

The concept of a nuisance bid can best be understood by seeing the effect it has on your own bidding. First, let's look at:

None vul., South holds: ♠K32, ♡A9653, ◇842, ♣AQ

NORTH	EAST	SOUTH	WEST
—	—	1 ♡	Pass
2 ♣	Pass	?	

This is not a particularly comfortable rebid. 2 ♡ on this weak suit is not satisfactory, 2NT with an unbid suit completely unstopped is also an unhappy choice, and anything else such as a 2 ◇ rebid is likely to lead to trouble later in the auction. Now, suppose East overcalls 2 ◇ instead of passing. Suddenly, South's problems are solved. He has a very easy and accurate call available—a pass! This conveys the message that South has nothing more to say, which is certainly true. In addition, South will be happy to pass if North doubles. The interference was not a nuisance at all; in fact, it made South's bidding much easier.

Contrast with the following situation:

None vul., South holds: ♠94, ♡AQ973, ◇8, ♣KQJ32

NORTH	EAST	SOUTH	WEST
—	——	1 ♡	Pass
1 ♠	Pass	?	

Obviously South has no rebid problems at all. He has a very happy 2 ♣ rebid which goes a long way towards describing his hand perfectly. Now let's try it with East overcalling 2 ◇. Suddenly, South is not so happy. This little overcall does a lot of damage. South simply isn't strong enough for a 3 ♣ bid, but if he passes or bids 2 ♡ the club suit is likely to be lost forever, particularly if West now raises to 3 ◇.

It is interesting that in the first case the 2 ◇ overcall solved South's problems, while in the second case it created problems where there were none. This is what I call a nuisance bid. To some extent it has the same effect as a preempt, although it is not a jump. A nuisance bid is simply a bid that takes away from an opponent a bid he would like to be able to make, such as the 2 ♣ rebid on the previous hand.

Nuisance bids come in different shapes and sizes. The most common form is a bid which blocks an opponent from bidding a suit naturally that he would like to bid at a convenient level, but there are several other possibilities, some of which can be quite subtle. Robbing an opponent of a jump raise (so that his raise may be competitive rather than constructive), interfering with an artificial sequence and causing confusion, or even stealing a cue bid from an opponent are a few of the possibilities.

A player may make a bid in a competitive auction which appears to serve no purpose. His side can't buy the hand, there is no lead-directional value to the bid, and a sacrifice is out of the question. All the bid seems to do is give the opposition a fielder's choice. They can double and collect a number if it is right, or they can ignore the bid and go after their own contract. Such a meaningless bid can still be correct if it serves to hamper the opponents' constructive auction in any way. The wise player listens to the auction, anticipates the problems his left-hand opponent is likely to face, and determines whether such a bid will help or hinder the enemy. Also, if a player has a close choice of whether or not to enter the auction or of which bid to make, he will do better to choose the bid which will make life more difficult for the opponents by stealing their bidding room.

N-S vul., South holds: ♠K9, ♡K84, ♢95, ♣KJ9754

NORTH	EAST	SOUTH	WEST
Pass	1 ♢	?	

I don't need to tell you the risks involved in a 2 ♣ overcall. At this vulnerability it could be a disaster, even undoubled, and partner's pass indicates that the hand probably belongs to the opponents. Also there is the danger that partner may play the overcaller for a better hand and make a losing competitive decision later in the auction. Despite these risks, I believe that 2 ♣ is the winning action because it gobbles up so much bidding space. It is true that most opponents have the negative double available to help find four-four major suit fits after interference, but there may still be plenty of problems. Picture poor West holding something like: ♠xxx, ♡QJ9xx, ◊Qxx, ♣Ax. If South doesn't overcall, West has an easy 1♡ response and probably few rebid problems later. What does he do over a 2♣ overcall? A 2♡ bid risks getting the partnership overboard, particularly if East has a minimum opening bid without heart support. West could try a negative double, but we all know that East will bid spades (partners always do in this situation), and then what? 2◊ is all right on value, but it probably loses any heart fit forever. West could pass and hope to recover later, but this involves some unpleasant possibilities such as 2♣ getting passed out when E-W have a part-score or a 3♣ raise passed around to West who now must make a guess at the three-level with nothing to go on. Personally I would bid 2♡ on the West hand since I believe it is best to be aggressive early in competitive auctions, but I'm not particularly happy with the bid. Anybody who says they are comfortable with their choice in this situation is probably a liar. There is no doubt that this simple overcall can cause plenty of problems for the opponents, enough to justify the risk.

It is important to see that as the space consumed by the overcall decreases the nuisance value of the bid goes down, making it less attractive. If the opening bid had been 1♡ only the spade suit would be shut out by the 2♣ overcall, and even this might not be a serious problem since many pairs play Flannery, so responder could assume that his partner didn't have four spades. Consequently, the risks of the overcall probably aren't compensated for by the nuisance value. If the opening bid had been 1♠ the overcall wouldn't shut out anything except a 1NT response, which responder might be just as happy not making, so there is no nuisance value at all and the 2♣ bid is clearly wrong. In fact, the 2♣ bid may actually ease responder's problems, for it gives him a negative double to play with which was otherwise unavailable. For example, suppose responder had ♠xxx, ♡AQxx, ◊KJxx, ♣xx. Without the overcall responder must either bid 2♣, a slight underbid which also loses a poten-

190

tial four-four heart fit if opener can't move on, or bid 2 ◊ (or 1NT forcing if available), both of which will certainly get the partnership to at least the three-level. After the overcall he can make a negative double, convert 2 ◊ to 2 ♠, and he will have described his hand and permitted a stop at the two-level.

Another consideration: Suppose West were a passed hand. Now the 2 ♣ overcall over 1 ◊ loses much of its nuisance value. The reason is that West's biggest problem hand, the ten-pointer with a five-card major, is no longer a great problem. West simply bids two of the major, and the danger of getting too high is no longer present since West has already limited his hand by his initial pass, so the bid is now non-forcing. Once again, the loss of nuisance value now makes the already marginal overcall no longer the percentage action.

The general priniciple illustrated in the preceding paragraph is that the more the oppponents know about each other's hands, the less valuable a nuisance bid becomes. For example:

None vul., South holds: ♠ KJ972, ♡ A9, ◊ 107, ♣ 10975

NORTH	EAST	SOUTH	WEST
—	1 NT	?	

After a normal notrump opening bid, a 2 ♣ overcall would be very questionable. West knows approximately what his partner has, and is therefore reasonably well-placed to find a decent contract even after the nuisance bid, so the opponents don't figure to be too badly hampered. In addition, West is in excellent position to double and collect a number if South has picked the wrong time to try this bid. Most experienced partnerships have conventional understandings such as Lebensohl which will help them cope with the 2 ♣ overcall if it gets in their way (the bid would be more effective against a pair which does not have these understandings). However, suppose the 1NT opening bid were a "dynamic notrump" (part of the Romex system) showing a very strong unbalanced hand. Now the 2 ♣ overcall will have much more effect as a nuisance bid, since East hasn't defined his shape yet. In addition to causing problems for the opponents the bid will be hard to double, since the opponents haven't found out much about the hand. Along the same lines, risky overcalls can be made freely over strong artificial club openings since the shape of the hand is not defined, but these same overcalls may be too dangerous over a standard 1 ♣ opening. Conversely, more daring overcalls may be made against a standard one of a major opening than against a Precision one of a major, since the latter is very well-defined so the nuisance value of the overcall is considerably less.

Both vul., South holds: ♠8, ♡982, ◇J1095, ♣KQJ65

NORTH	EAST	SOUTH	WEST
Pass	Pass	Pass	1 ◇
1 ♡	Double*	?	

*negative double

There is a lot to be said for a 2♣ bid by South. The lead-directional value is obvious, and it is impossible to be dropped there since the opponents have presumably located a four-four spade fit. There can be little doubt that West's next bid will be 2♠ (or 3♠ or 4♠ if his hand is stronger), so 2♡ by South has no more nuisance value than 2♣. Since N-S have no intention of sticking their vulnerable necks on the chopping block at the three-level and since E-W will certainly compete to at least 2♠, there is no real reason to raise hearts.

However, suppose on the same auction South holds: ♠J1095, ♡982, ◇8, ♣KQJ65. Now a 2♡ bid is better. The point is that with South holding a singleton diamond it is quite likely that West has a long diamond suit which he will rebid in response to the negative double. If South bids 2♣ West will rebid 2◇ with a minimum opening, 3◇ with extras, and will have completed a good description of his hand. Suppose instead that South makes the nuisance bid of 2♡. Things are not so easy for West any more. What should he do with, say, ♠Kxx, ♡xx, ◇AQ109xx, ♣Ax. If he passes the diamond suit may get lost, particularly if North re-raises to 3♡, but if he bids 3◇ his partner may play him for a stronger hand and get overboard. If 3◇ seems right,

then what should West rebid with a stronger hand such as
♠AQx, ♡xx, ◇AQJ10xx, ♣Ax. 3 ◇ still seems right, but if he
bids 3 ◇ on both of these hands East may have to guess whether
to play his partner for the stronger hand or the weaker one.

N-S vul., South holds: ♠3, ♡K653, ◇KQJ3, ♣Q843

NORTH	EAST	SOUTH	WEST
—	—	1 ◇	Pass
2 ◇	Double	?	

Offhand, it seems silly for South to bid 3 ◇. The opponents
hold the balance of strength and presumably at least nine
spades, since North failed to respond 1 ♠, so they can compete
to 3 ♠ and might well have a game. Why should South risk
– 200 if E-W decide unexpectedly to double, when there doesn't
seem to be anything to gain? However, close examination shows
that there is a hidden gain to the 3 ◇ bid. E-W are close to a
spade game, and must judge whether or not to bid it. Even
though South has no idea if this game will make, he wants to
make it as hard as possible for his opponents to assess their
values. If South passes, West can bid 2 ♠ on a moderate hand
such as ♠QJxxx, ♡QJx, ◇xx, ♣xxx but jump to 3 ♠ on a
somewhat stronger hand like ♠QJxxx, ♡QJx, ◇xx, ♣Axx,
and East is likely to judge correctly. If South bids 3 ◇ it is
another story. West will be nervous about passing on the first
hand, for with the five-card spade suit it is probably correct to
compete to 3 ♠ and he does not know if his partner has enough
strength or distribution to reopen. If he does bid 3 ♠ on this
hand his partner may play him for the stronger hand with the
extra ace, on which a 3 ♠ bid is also reasonable, and bid a game
that doesn't make. The 3 ◇ call has the nuisance value of deny-
ing West the option of voluntarily jumping to 3 ♠. Consequently his 3 ♠ bid may be either competitive or constructive, and it is
very difficult for East to make a borderline decision about
whether or not to bid a game. If South passes West has a wider
choice of actions available, so East is more likely to go right
since West's hand will be more closely defined.

None vul., South holds: ♠32, ♡1074, ◊A1096, ♣QJ42

NORTH	EAST	SOUTH	WEST
3 ♡	3 ♠	?	

What earthly good could a 4♡ call do? E-W have already found their spade fit and can certainly make game, which a 4♡ bid won't stop them from bidding. It is possible that E-W can make eleven or twelve tricks in spades, depending on whether or not North has the ace of hearts and how the E-W minor suit cards are distributed. South has no interest in sacrificing against an E-W game or slam with neither vulnerable; in fact, 4♡ might go down too much if South bids it and E-W stop off to double. In spite of all this, South should still bid 4♡. The reason is that it robs West of a 4♡ cue bid. To illustrate this, let's look at a couple of possible West hands and see what his problems might be. First, suppose West holds: ♠Kxxx, ♡xx, ◊QJx, ♣Kxxx. West will bid 4♠ whether or not South bids 4♡. No guarantees, but it should at least have a play. Now, let's add an ace to West's hand, making it: ♠Kxxx, ♡xx, ◊QJx, ♣AKxx. With this hand West has good reason to think of slam if his partner has a strong overcall. Unfortunately if East has a minimal overcall such as ♠AQJ10xx, ♡xx, ◊Ax, ♣Q10x even 5♠ might be in jeopardy. What West would like to do is to suggest a spade slam without going above the 4♠ safety level. If South passes West can bid 4♡, a cue bid which carries exactly the desired message. However, if South bids 4♡ West can no longer make this cue bid. Consequently West is faced with the choice of conservatively bidding 4♠ and possibly missing a slam, or making a slam move above the game level and possibly getting to 5♠ down one. It is not a happy choice, particularly since the 3♠ overcall has a rather wide range. The 4♡ bid by South has the nuisance value of taking away West's slam try below the game level.

Both vul., South holds: ♠3, ♡KJ10652, ◊AJ106, ♣106

NORTH	EAST	SOUTH	WEST
—	—	—	1 ♠
Pass	2 ♣	?	

South's hand is below par for a vulnerable 2 ♡ overcall against a two over one response, and certainly risks going for a number in the face of a misfit. In addition, it is unlikely that N-S will be able to buy the contract. Does the 2 ♡ overcall create enough of a nuisance to make it worthwhile? A little thought will show that the 2 ♡ bid probably has no nuisance value at all; in fact, it is likely to help the opponents. South has a singleton spade, so West may very well have a six-card suit. If South passes and West bids 2 ♠ East cannot be sure if this shows a six-bagger, for West had to do something and 2 ♠ may have been his only convenient rebid even if on a five-card suit. However if South overcalls, West doesn't have to do anything. He can pass on a nondescript hand, so his 2 ♠ rebid now definitely shows a six-card suit. Consequently, the 2 ♡ overcall is likely to help E-W rather than hinder them. But change South's hand to ♠ AJ106, ♡ KJ10652, ◊ 3, ♣ 106 and it is a different picture. Now West is likely to have an easy 2 ◊ rebid, and the 2 ♡ overcall will shut that out. In addition, if North has some heart support a 3 ♡ raise will probably be much more damaging than if South had a singleton spade, for now E-W no longer have the higher-ranking suit and may be faced with a very difficult decision.

It may seem like a little thing that the 2 ♡ overcall in the previous example is more effective when South has spades than when he has diamonds, but these little things make the difference between winners and losers over the course of a session. Anybody can make an obvious overcall or avoid a ridiculous one. The player who consistently puts the odds in his favor on the close decisions will in the long run have an edge on his opponents. In this situation the 2 ♡ overcall becomes a better percentage action when it is more likely to damage the opponents through its nuisance value, and this factor is sufficient to swing the marginal overcall from a losing percentage action to a winning one.

BALANCING

Balancing decisions present a unique problem in competitive bidding. A player in the passout seat has the option of passing and ending the auction right away, for better or worse. Since his partner has done nothing but pass he knows less about the hand than in a normal competitive part-score decision, so the total trick count is often a guess.

The decision of whether or not to balance is extremely critical, and can swing many matchpoints. What to balance with can also be important, but the big decision is usually whether or not to bid at all. Paradoxically the conservative decision is usually to balance, while the aggressive decision is to pass and end the auction. If you balance and are wrong you will have several ways to recover. The opponents may fail to collect a number that they have coming to them, they may be pushed one level higher when they should have defended, or they may fail to find a superior contract which became available when you entered the auction. However, if you pass and are wrong it is all over—there is no second way to win. Consequently, most close decisions in the balancing seat should be resolved in favor of bidding.

There are four major types of balancing decisions, each of which has its own characteristics. These are against an opening one of a suit bid, against a preempt, after you have opened and an opponent has overcalled, and after the opponents have found a low-level contract. We shall examine each one separately.

AFTER AN OPENING BID

The law of total tricks tells us that it can virtually never be correct to allow the opponents to buy the hand at the one-level if they are in a reasonable contract. Even if neither side can muster up an eight-card fit, which is quite rare, the trick total will still be fourteen, so it is a losing action to sell out. When you pass out an opening one bid, you are betting that the opponents have made a mistake. It is unlikely that this mistake is missing a game, for if they have a game usually either the opening bidder would have opened 2♣ or 2NT, or his partner would have found a response. The more common mistake is that they have landed in the wrong part-score, and if you bid you give them a chance to recover. This is not so uncommon. How often have you opened 1♣ on something like ♠AQxx, ♡KJx, ◇Axx, ♣KQx, heard it go pass-pass, and prayed that RHO would do something. Or haven't you held a hand like: ♠—, ♡J10xxxx, ◇Jxxxx, ♣xx and passed partner's opening 1♣ bid in the hope that LHO would reopen so you could get to a better contract. The trick is to determine when the opponents have landed in the wrong suit. There are three important factors to consider.

First of all, consider your overall strength. If your hand is strong enough that there is a reasonable chance that your side holds the balance of power then it is usually wrong to sell out unless you expect to slaughter the opponents' contract. Since there are many twelve or thirteen point hands on which your partner would not have acted, you should usually bid with nine or ten points unless your distribution indicates that your partner can't have a good hand.

A second important consideration is length in the enemy trump suit. If you have four or more trumps, you know that either partner is short in trumps or the opponents are in a terrible contract. If partner is short in trumps he would have found an overcall or takeout double with a reasonably good hand, so you can safely assume that either he doesn't have a good hand or that the opponents are in a bad contract. Therefore, you may pass moderate strength hands. Conversely if you have two or fewer trumps partner may well have the balanced thirteen or fourteen count on which he couldn't find a convenient call because of his length in the enemy suit. In this case, you should strain to reopen on almost any hand unless you are extremely weak.

A third consideration is shortness in an unbid major suit. If you have a doubleton or especially a singleton, this is an indication to drop the opponents in one of a minor if you have a close balancing decision rather than stir up the animals. Who has the missing major? If it is partner, his failure to overcall tells you that he does not have a good hand, so the opponents clearly have the balance of power and may well have a better contract. If partner does not have the missing major the enemy does, so why give them a chance to improve their contract.

These factors are not independent. What it boils down to is the longer you are in trumps and the shorter in unbid majors the more you need in high cards to balance, while the shorter you are in trumps and the longer in unbid majors the less you need in high cards and the more you should strain to balance.

A few examples:

None vul., South holds: ♠93, ♡KJ43, ◇Q1062, ♣K42

NORTH	EAST	SOUTH	WEST
—	—	—	1 ◇
Pass	Pass	?	

Drop this one. You have only nine HCP and the other factors (long diamonds and short spades) argue for a pass.

N-S vul., South holds: ♠KQ93, ♡105, ◇A963, ♣1087

NORTH	EAST	SOUTH	WEST
—	—	—	1 ♣
Pass	Pass	?	

It could be right to pass, but the strong spade suit argues for a 1 ♠ balance. If South's spades and hearts were reversed a pass would be more reasonable, because now the opponents might hold the ranking major. Personally I would still balance, because I hate to stake the entire board on this decision when I have so little information.

Both vul., South holds: ♠Q64, ♡K64, ◇AJ43, ♣J86

NORTH	EAST	SOUTH	WEST
—	—	—	1 ♠
Pass	Pass	?	

Bid 1NT. Who knows? When in doubt, bid rather than pass in a one-level balancing situation.

E-W vul., South holds: ♠53, ♡A94, ◇AJ8, ♣KQ1082

NORTH	EAST	SOUTH	WEST
—	—	—	1 ♣
Pass	Pass	?	

This is the type of hand on which to gamble a pass, in spite of the excess strength. You have two ways to win, since the opponents are almost certainly in the wrong suit. If it is not your hand you are quite happy to sell out here rather than let the opponents improve their contract. Even if it is your hand you may collect +200 against 1♣ and still not have a game. The pass could easily backfire, but it is a good gamble. If the clubs were shorter or if E-W were not vulnerable then the second way to win by defeating 1♣ by more than the value of your part-score would be less likely, so I would prefer a 1NT reopening.

Once you have decided to balance, your action should be as natural as possible depending on your distribution. If you have a decent suit bid it, if you have support for the other suits make a takeout double, and if you have a balanced hand bid 1NT. Bidding your shape is far more important than bidding your strength, since it is probably a part-score hand and it is more important to concentrate on playing in the right denomination than in getting to game. Don't worry if your hand isn't perfect for the action. You may occasionally have to double with less than ideal pattern, balance in a four-card suit, or bid notrump without a stopper in the enemy suit, but this is all part of the game. The reason is that it is necessary to balance with hands on which you would never consider taking direct action. Therefore, the requirements for a balancing call cannot be as narrow as those for the same call in direct position. There can never be much precision after a balancing action due to the extremely wide range of hands on which you must balance, so accept this fact, make your most descriptive bid, and things will usually work out reasonably well.

There is one special problem involved in balancing that doesn't occur in normal auctions. If you hold: ♠KQ94, ♡—, ◇A8543, ♣K984, and RHO opens 1♡ you will, of course, make a takeout double. You won't like it if partner leaves it in, but this is such an infrequent occurrence that it is not worth distorting your bidding to guard against it. However, if you reopen with a double on this hand after 1♡-P-P, there is a significant chance that partner has a heart stack behind the opening bidder and will pass the double. Usually this won't work out well unless you have at least one heart to push through declarer. Consequently, it is best not to double in the balancing seat on this type of hand. A balancing cue bid should be used to show a void in the opponents' suit and a hand on which you can't stand to have a double left in. Occasionally you may miss a number, but you will come out ahead more often than not by avoiding a double with a void in the balancing seat.

AFTER A PREEMPT

While the same factors (strength, trump length, and shortness in a higher ranking suit) are still the critical factors when considering whether or not to balance against a preempt, it is far more often correct to sell out. There are two reasons for this. First of all, the law of total tricks isn't necessarily hanging over your head the way it is at the one-level. If it goes 1♡-P-P to you, total tricks almost demands a bid on any excuse. However if it goes 3♡-P-P to you, it may well be that the opponents have already bid to or overbid the total trick count, and any further action by you would overshoot it still more. Secondly, the partner of the preemptor knows exactly where he stands, and if you guess wrong by bidding he will be sure to apply the ax. This is not true at the one-level; there you are likely to escape unscathed even when you could be going for a number.

On the other side of the coin, there is an argument for bidding over a preempt which doesn't exist at the one-level. If you drop the opponents in one of a suit they may simply be playing in the wrong trump suit. The preempting side usually belongs in the preemptors suit (although perhaps not at the level of the preempt), so you have little fear of pushing the opponents to a better contract by balancing. Consequently, you should compete over a preempt if you feel you have a bigger plus score coming to you than you would get on defense against the preempt undoubled.

N-S vul., South holds: ♠Q10932, ♡104, ◇A82, ♣KJ3

NORTH	EAST	SOUTH	WEST
—	—	—	3 ♡
Pass	Pass	?	

A 3♠ bid could work out, but the odds are against it. South doesn't know much about the hand, but he can conclude that North probably doesn't have a good hand and four spades, since North failed to act over 3♡. Consequently either N-S are outgunned or don't have enough spades to make 3♠ a winning

201

action, so passing seems indicated. The problem with bidding is that if it is wrong there is no recovery possible. Passing can work out very well if West has picked a misfit on which to preempt (note this is exactly the situation in which 3♠ will be worst, potentially a top to bottom swing), and the pass can still get a reasonable score if 3♡ is simply the normal level to which the hand should be competed. If the opening bid had been 1♡ a reopening would be mandatory, and after a weak 2♡ bid 2♠ is probably correct. This is much closer, but the law of total tricks indicates that reopening will be right more often than not.

N-S vul., South holds: ♠104, ♡KJ9, ◇AJ98, ♣AQJ4

NORTH	EAST	SOUTH	WEST
—	—	—	3 ◇
Pass	Pass	?	

Passing could be right, of course, but South's hand is just too strong to risk selling out and the penalty against 3 ◇ undoubled might not even compensate for a part-score, Personally, I would bid 3NT and hope for the best. Even though this could go for a telephone number if East has a good hand, I consider it a more conservative bid than the pass. Despite my strong diamond holding I can't count on the opponents being in the wrong suit after the preempt as I might at the one-level, so I must bid for the plus score to which I think I am entitled.

One more important point about balancing against a preempt is that you should use the takeout double freely, even if somewhat off-shape. The reason is that it is often right to defend when the opponents preempt, and doubling leaves this option open while overcalling does not. For example:

None vul., South holds: ♠AK105, ♡95, ◇93, ♣KQ1032

NORTH	EAST	SOUTH	WEST
—	—	—	3 ♡
Pass	Pass	?	

If the opening bid had been 1 ♡, double would be a bad call.

Partner is likely to bid 2 ◊, and now what? It would be nice if partner were planning to pass the double, but that just isn't likely to happen. Either 1 ♠ or 2 ♣, depending on your mood and preference, is better than doubling. After the 3 ♡ opening, however, double is the best bid assuming you choose to balance. Partner may well leave it in, which would probably be very good, or he could bid a black suit or 3NT. If he goes all the way to 4 ◊ he probably has a long suit, so things might turn out all right anyway. There is no guarantee with any action, but double is recommended because it is the most flexible bid and keeps all options open, including defending.

AFTER AN ENEMY OVERCALL

Suppose the bidding has gone:

NORTH	EAST	SOUTH	WEST
—	—	1 ♡	2 ♣
Pass	Pass	?	

This time we do know something about North's hand, based on what he didn't do. He certainly doesn't have heart support unless he has a very weak hand, or else he would have raised hearts to the appropriate level. Also he doesn't have the strength and/or suit for a new suit bid, and he doesn't have an appropriate hand for a negative double. (I am assuming negative doubles are in use, since most pairs play them. If you don't play negative doubles, some of these arguments may have to be modified a bit.) He could have a hand with which he wants to penalize the opponents, or he might have some nondescript garbage which wasn't suitable for any bid.

This time, the most important criterion is the number of cards held in the overcaller's suit. With two or fewer cards it is almost always right to reopen. There is a good chance that partner is planning a penalty pass, and even if he isn't, total trick analysis will show that some kind of competition is probably better than selling out. Extra high card strength isn't important. Even if you have a minimum, partner is bound to have some cards or else the opponents probably would have bid more. Furthermore, if you get in trouble it will be difficult for them to double you because they don't really have a very good idea of their combined assets.

If you have three or more cards in the overcaller's suit, you should give serious thought to passing. A takeout double almost can't be right since there must be some suit for which you don't have support. If you don't have the strength for a notrump reopening or an easy rebid of your first suit or another suit, then passing is probably correct. Even if partner has planned a penalty pass it would probably turn out all right, for with your side having so many trumps the opponents undoubtedly have a better contract, so the undoubled undertricks should amount to a good score. If partner isn't able to raise, make a negative double, or bid a suit of his own he either is very weak or has at least three cards in the opponent's suit, in which case total tricks suggests defending.

Both vul., South holds: ♠103, ♡A10852, ◊KJ6, ♣A62

NORTH	EAST	SOUTH	WEST
—	—	1 ♡	1 ♠
Pass	Pass	?	

South should reopen with a double despite his minimum point count. It is true that the hand probably belongs to E-W, but South just won't get rich if he sells to 1 ♠ with spade shortness. N-S probably have a playable fit somewhere, and South must make some effort to get a plus score either by buying the contract or pushing E-W up higher.

Both vul., South holds: ♠KJ975, ♡75, ◊A92, ♣AK6

NORTH	EAST	SOUTH	WEST
—	—	1 ♠	2 ◊
Pass	Pass	?	

South should sell out in spite of his extra strength. He just doesn't have any place to go. A takeout double with a doubleton heart doesn't make any sense. North is unlikely to have adequate spade support since he didn't raise, and North's silence suggests that there is no future in the hand. It would not be surprising if neither side had an eight-card fit, in which case selling out is indicated by the law of total tricks even at this low level.

The choice of reopening action should not be influenced much by the possibility of partner's having a penalty pass. It is necessary to be able to handle a bid in your shortest suit if you reopen with a double. If a penalty is missed that is just too bad, but it is more important to get to the right contract. For example:

E-W vul., South holds: ♠AQJ863, ♡76, ◊A85, ♣K8

NORTH	EAST	SOUTH	WEST
—	—	1 ♠	2 ♡
Pass	Pass	?	

South should bid 2 ♠ even if playing negative doubles. His partner might have been planning to sit for 2 ♡ doubled, but if so N-S should still get to a reasonable contract. The danger in doubling is that North will bid three of a minor when the best contract is quite likely to be 2 ♠.

If the opponents' overcall is a preemptive jump, pretty much the same criterion for reopening applies. The only difference is that with a doubleton in the enemy suit and a minimum opening bid you might tend to sell out. The reason is that the opponents may have already bid to or surpassed the trick total, and any action by your side could well be overboard. Also, the partner of the preemptor may have a strong hand and be in position to punish you if you step out of line. For example:

N-S vul., South holds: ♠K63, ♡AJ954, ◊84, ♣AJ9

NORTH	EAST	SOUTH	WEST
—	—	1 ♡	3 ◊
Pass	Pass	?	

If West had overcalled 2 ◊ South would have a routine reopening double, but after the 3 ◊ overcall it is probably right to pass. North will strain to raise to 3 ♡ on any decent hand with heart support, and N-S certainly don't have a game or North would have found some bid. Therefore it is best to assume that the pushing to the three-level has already been done, so there is no reason to compete further.

THE OPPONENTS HAVE ARRIVED

This is the most difficult balancing decision of all. The opponents have bid to a low-level contract, accurately describing their hands to each other, while you and your partner have remained silent. Now it is two passes to you, and you must decide whether or not to balance. It is the most dangerous type of balance, for both opponents know something about their partner's hand and they will be quick to double you if you are wrong. Nevertheless, this type of balance is often necessary to get matchpoints on a board.

The following is a classic example of such a balance:

None vul., South holds: ♠Q1052, ♡54, ◊AJ95, ♣Q63

NORTH	EAST	SOUTH	WEST
—	1 ♡	Pass	2 ♡
Pass	Pass	?	

South should reopen with a double. He didn't have the strength to double the opening bid, although his shape is right. Now that the opponents have subsided in 2♡, he must get in the auction and the double is the best descriptive bid. Note that South is in some sense trusting his opponents to make his bid correct. Since East made no move toward game E-W should have at most 23 or 24 high card points, which means that North figures to have at least eight or nine, probably more. Also E-W probably have at least eight hearts between them, which increases the likelihood of N-S having an eight-card fit and making it correct to bid by total trick analysis. Of course the reopening could backfire, particularly if E-W have only a seven-card fit, but on balance it will pay off.

The main indicators for this type of balance are that the opponents have found a fit, which suggests that your side also has a fit, and they have stopped at the two-level where you may be able to outbid them or push them one level higher. Vulnerability is a far more important consideration here than in other balancing situations. The opponents know where they are, so they will be able to double you if you step the least bit out of line. Consequently you must be very cautious when you are vulnerable, for down one doubled will be −200 and a bottom. If you are not vulnerable a close balance is more attractive, for you still have an extra way to win—down one when their contract is making.

E-W vul., South holds: ♠K985, ♡A9, ◇1043, ♣Q542

NORTH	EAST	SOUTH	WEST
—	—	—	1 ◇
Pass	1 ♡	Pass	2 ◇
Pass	Pass	?	

A reopening double could work out, but passing will be right more often than not. The opponents do not necessarily have a fit, which means that N-S might not have one either. A particular concern is South's doubleton heart. If the opponents don't have an eight-card heart fit, as suggested by their choosing diamonds rather than hearts, then North is marked with at least four hearts. Consequently North can't have both four spades and a reasonable hand, or he would have made an initial takeout double, so the odds swing against balancing. If West had raised to 2♡, the balancing double would be much more attractive.

Both vul., South holds: ♠109, ♡93, ◇KJ52, ♣KQ1085

NORTH	EAST	SOUTH	WEST
—	1 ♠	Pass	2 ♠
Pass	Pass	?	

Should South back into the auction with the Unusual Notrump? It could be right, but the vulnerability argues for selling out. If 3♣ or 3◇ is going down it is quite likely to be doubled, and a one-trick set is −200 for a bottom. If South were not vulnerable then 2NT would be the percentage bid, for three of a minor down one could still be a good result, giving South a second way to win. If the opponents were bidding hearts and one of South's suits were spades the balance would again be more attractive, since it might only be necessary to contract for eight tricks. As it is, the odds seem to be slightly against balancing, so the pass is recommended.

THE LAST GUESS

It is apparent that if you can put your opponents in a position where they must guess what to do, then you have a good chance of getting a favorable result for they may guess wrong. Conversely, if you are the one who has to make the guess, then your prospects on the board are not too good. It follows that it is to your advantage to maneuver competitive auctions so it is the opponents and not your side who have to make that last guess.

Let's look at a couple of similar examples which illustrate this point:

N-S vul., South holds: ♠AKJ986, ♡A8, ◊76, ♣KJ4

NORTH	EAST	SOUTH	WEST
—	—	1 ♠	2 ◊
2 ♠	3 ◊	4 ♠	?

West is thinking about taking a 5 ◊ save. How do you feel sitting South? Pretty good! You know exactly what to do if West bids 5 ◊. It certainly isn't right to bid 5 ♠; in fact, the 4 ♠ call was somewhat of a stretch. You have put the opponents in the position of having to make the last guess on the hand; namely, whether or not to sacrifice. You don't particularly care which way they go since you have no idea whether or not 4 ♠ will make, but you know that if they guess wrong you are headed for a very good board. The key is that if they bid 5 ◊ you don't have any guess—it is quite clear to double. Consequently, E-W have to make the last guess on this hand.

Contrast with the following hand:

N-S vul., South holds: ♠AQJ1072, ♡AQ2, ◊3, ♣Q72

NORTH	EAST	SOUTH	WEST
—	—	1 ♠	Pass
3 ♠*	4 ◊	4 ♠	5 ◊
Pass	Pass	?	

*Limit raise

E-W certainly seem to have taken a good sacrifice. 4♠ figures to be cold, and it is extremely unlikely that 5♢ can be set more than three tricks. The question is, should South bid 5♠? If he does, E-W will have no problem passing. They won't consider taking a 6♢ sacrifice, for fear that either it will go for too much or that N-S can't make 5♠. E-W will be happy to have pushed N-S to the five-level. Consequently, South must make the last guess on this hand, and it is a difficult one. If South guesses wrong he will wind up with a very poor result, while a right guess will probably only be a normal result. South might have alleviated his problem by bidding 4♡ rather than 4♠ to give his partner the picture, but there would still be a problem. South is not in a comfortable position. He must make the last guess on the hand, and he must guess right to avoid a bad score. East probably has no idea what South's right action is and doesn't really care what South does. He is just hoping that South guesses wrong.

Your goal in a competitive auction should be to maneuver the bidding so that the opponents have to make that last guess. Naturally this will not always be possible, particularly if the opponents are trying to do the same thing. You know that you have achieved this goal when you have bid the limit to which your side will compete, and you don't know what the right action for the opponents is. Since you have bid the limit of the hand you do not have a guess if they bid on, except perhaps whether or not to double. If it is clear to you either that the opponents should defend or that they should bid on it will usually be clear to them also, so they won't really have a guess, but if you don't know what their correct action is the chances are that they have a really close decision and may well guess wrong.

Both vul., South holds: ♠93, ♡AK10762, ♢Q103, ♣A7

NORTH	EAST	SOUTH	WEST
—	—	1 ♡	1 ♠
2 ♡	Pass	?	

South could conceivably pass, bid 3♡, or bid 4♡. If he passes there is no question in his mind that it is correct for E-W to compete. If he bids 4♡ E-W will certainly do well to defend, probably doubled. However, if South bids 3♡, he doesn't really have any idea what the correct E-W action is. In addition, South has no intention of bidding higher. Consequently, the 3♡ bid gives E-W the last guess, and the guess won't be easy. It is not surprising that this is consistent with total trick analysis.

E-W vul., South holds: ♠7, ♡Q105, ◇AJ92, ♣Q10976

NORTH	EAST	SOUTH	WEST
3 ♡	3 ♠	?	

If South bids 4♡, he knows that it must be right for E-W to bid 4♠; this contract figures to make. If South bids 6♡ he can be pretty sure that E-W should double; South has enough defense so that 6♠ will probably go down. However, if South bids 5♡, he has no idea what the correct E-W action is. 5♠ might make or it might not, and South really doesn't care. He has taken a good advance sacrifice at the highest level his side will reach, and now E-W have to make the last guess.

N-S vul., South holds: ♠AQJ965, ♡2, ◇A4, ♣AQ83

NORTH	EAST	SOUTH	WEST
—	—	1 ♠	3 ♡
4 ♠	5 ♡	?	

There doesn't figure to be a grand slam, for North would have bid 4♡ rather than 4♠ if he had the necessary cards to make a grand. A small slam, on the other hand, could be cold, reasonable, or hopeless depending on what North has, and there is no way to find out. If South meekly bids 5♠ this will undoubtedly end the auction, and South will have made the last guess. If N-S have a small slam, E-W must have a good save. Therefore, South should bid 6♠. Now the last guess is thrust back on E-W. They must guess whether or not South can make his slam. South doesn't know what action he is rooting for, but the problem is back in the opponents' court where it belongs.

E-W vul., South holds: ♠Q83, ♡1094, ◇A5, ♣KJ873

NORTH	EAST	SOUTH	WEST
—	—	—	1 ◇
2 ♠*	Double**	?	

 *preemptive
 **negative double

South cannot tell if E-W have a game. This will depend some-what on whether or not E-W have a four-four heart fit, how the spades split, and the lie of the club suit. A 4♠ call by South simply doesn't give the opponents any problem. They will just double for lack of anything else to do as they can't very well be going to the five-level with South holding this many high cards, and they will probably be right. A pass by South won't give E-W a problem either. It is extremely unlikely that West will pass the negative double, so he will just bid his hand. A 3♠ call, however, is just right. South does not plan to compete to 4♠, so he has no further problems. He does not know what the best ac-tion for the opponents is, so E-W must now make the last guess.

This last hand presents an interesting paradox. Suppose South bids 3♠ as recommended, and West does, in fact, bid 4♡. Should South save? We have already determined that the answer is no. If South does take the sacrifice, he will be thrust-ing the last guess back upon himself. However, if 4♡ makes then 4♠ would certainly be a good save, as it can hardly be go-ing down four tricks. So if South is not going to save, he is bet-ting that the opponents have done the wrong thing, and 4♡ won't make. Well, if South thinks 4♡ is going down, then is there any reason that South shouldn't back up his judgment with a double? The answer in this case, which will surprise a lot of players, is no, there is no reason, and South's correct action is to double 4♡! This seems strange. South wasn't exactly bid-ding 3♠ to make, although on a good day it might, and the hand certainly seems to belong to E-W on high cards. Yet, it is recommended that South double 4♡.

Let's look at the matchpoint cost analysis. If South doubles 4♡ and is wrong he only costs one-half matchpoint to other tables which are in 4♡, doubled or not, and costs nothing to any other result since 4♠ clearly can't go for 700. In other words, there is no possible score between −620 and −790. Conversely, if 4♡ is going down, then South gains one-half matchpoint from other tables in 4♡ by doubling. So far, this isn't quite enough justification for the double. South might think that 4♡ is slightly more likely to make than not and still not save for fear that not enough tables will bid 4♡ to make the sacrifice pay off even if it is right. There is, however, a third possibility. The hand just might belong to N-S for a spade partial. If this is the case, the double can gain a full matchpoint if it is right against other pairs who buy the hand for 3♠, making. The full hand illustrates how this might be:

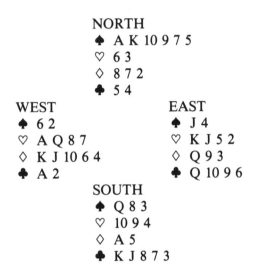

NORTH
♠ A K 10 9 7 5
♡ 6 3
◇ 8 7 2
♣ 5 4

WEST
♠ 6 2
♡ A Q 8 7
◇ K J 10 6 4
♣ A 2

EAST
♠ J 4
♡ K J 5 2
◇ Q 9 3
♣ Q 10 9 6

SOUTH
♠ Q 8 3
♡ 10 9 4
◇ A 5
♣ K J 8 7 3

Everybody's actions are quite reasonable. West was pushing slightly for his 4♡ call; had South passed he probably would have bid only 3♡. It is not a bad bid, however, and it may give N-S the last guess as to whether or not to save. North has a good hand for South, and with a winning club guess 3♠ is a make while 4♡ is clearly down one, so there is likely to be a big swing on doubling 4♡.

Does this mean that every time we give the opponents the last guess and they bid on we should double them? No, that would be ridiculous. For example, on the earlier hand on which we took the premature 5♡ save we would not double if E-W bid

5 ♠, even if we felt that we had a good save available in 6 ♡ and we did not think that 5 ♠ was a favorite to make, for there would be no reason to double. If 5 ♠ were going down we would get a good board anyway, because not everybody will push the opponents to the five-level, while if 5 ♠ were making the double would needlessly cost one-half matchpoint against other tables who bought the hand for a spade contract at the four or five level. This type of double should only be made when the opponents have outbid us by bidding a game, and there is some chance that our contract would have made. On the hand where the opponents bid 4 ♡ over 3 ♠, had they bid 4 ♢ instead a double would not be recommended. There are several possible scores between −130 and −710, so the double could cost a lot if wrong. Over the 4 ♡ bid, however, the double may gain a lot if right and lose little if wrong once we decide not to sacrifice.

The general idea in these "who knows who can make what" auctions is to bid the limit of your hand quickly to make the opponents guess, and if they outbid you make them pay for guessing wrong if you might have made what you bid. This is particularly true when your last bid is one under an enemy game contract, and they then bid the game. In this type of situation a preemptor who has been raised is allowed to violate his usual oath of silence and join in with a double or a bid if his hand is exceptionally offensively or defensively oriented for his preempt. A bid which is one level under the opponents' potential game is called a "one-under" bid, and allows these unusual competitive actions. For example, on the previous hand North might well have doubled 4 ♡ himself after South bid 3 ♠ if the partnership style is extremely light weak jump overcalls at favorable vulnerability, for he has extra defense with his ace-king of spades.

Another example:

E-W vul., South holds: ♠4, ♡AQJ10763, ♢A4, ♣K84

NORTH	EAST	SOUTH	WEST
Pass	Pass	4 ♡	4 ♠
Pass	Pass	?	

215

South's 4 ♡ bid is not a classic preempt, but it is a reasonable tactic opposite a passed hand and certainly makes E-W guess. Once West guesses to bid 4 ♠, however, South must assume that West has guessed wrong and double him. There is too great a danger that 4 ♡ will make even though South couldn't know if it would when he bid it, and 4 ♠ must be doubled to guard against this possibility. Note that North couldn't double on a scattered nine-count, for South might have a normal 4 ♡ opening bid for all North knows. Sometimes the 4 ♠ contract will make, but South can't just sit there and pass, nor does he have any reason to believe that 4 ♠ will make and take a 5 ♡ save. If you are going to adopt tactics such as opening 4 ♡ in third seat on this type of hand (winning tactics, in my opinion), then you must be prepared to assume that the opponents have guessed wrong if they bid and double them. The general principle is: Make them guess, and then make them pay!

It is not always necessary to bid immediately to the highest level you are willing to reach. Sometimes you may be able to buy the contract one level lower, even though you will go higher if necessary. Keep in mind that this approach gives the opponents a chance to exchange information which may help them when they have to make the final guess. Also, make sure that you have already decided it is correct to compete further if you take the slow approach. If you are not sure, it is best to make your decision now one way or the other and then stick with it; otherwise, you will be the one who is making the last guess.

E-W vul., South holds: ♠KQ10632, ♡84, ◇AJ7, ♣K7

NORTH	EAST	SOUTH	WEST
—	—	1 ♠	2 ♡
2 ♠	Pass	?	

A 3 ♠ call by South certainly couldn't be criticized, and if E-W go to the three-level South will certainly compete to 3 ♠ since he has six spades. However, a good case can be made for passing. South knows that it is correct for West to bid on, but West may not know that. There is a reasonable chance that West will be afraid to compete to the three-level vulnerable, and N-S will then buy the hand for 2♠. In my opinion, this possibility out-weighs the danger of allowing E-W to exchange further information.

E-W vul., South holds: ♠A765, ♡86, ◇753, ♣Q654

NORTH	EAST	SOUTH	WEST
3 ♠	Double	?	

E-W probably have a slam somewhere, and South is fully prepared to take a save against it. But there is no rush in taking that save, for the slam hasn't been bid yet. A simple 4♠ bid by South may be sufficient to deprive E-W of the bidding room they need to assess their combined values, and they may make the mistake of doubling 4♠ or of stopping at the five-level. If E-W bid their slam, South will, of course, take the save. This is not inconsistent bidding, for South has already made up his mind as to what he will do. Consequently South will not be making the last guess if E-W bid a slam, for South already knows what his right action is. The only danger in this approach is that E-W may exchange enough information to bid a grand, but this is unlikely and the possible gain from bidding only 4♠ is well worth the risk.

Suppose, on the same auction, South had held: ♠K976, ♡9, ◇A9874, ♣864. Now it is not at all clear whether or not E-W have a slam, for N-S might have two aces or North may have a diamond ruff coming. South will certainly want to take a 5♠ save over 5♡, which E-W will undoubtedly bid if South bids only 4♠. Consequently, South should leap to 5♠ immediately and let E-W guess whether or not they have a slam. Obviously if E-W then bid the slam South should not save; he must assume that his opponents have guessed wrong rather than risking making the wrong last guess himself.

None vul., South holds: ♠Q963, ♡32, ◇A75, ♣QJ63

NORTH	EAST	SOUTH	WEST
2 ♠*	3 ♡	?	

*Weak 2-bid

This is not the sort of hand with which to fool around. If South bids 3 ♠ the opponents almost certainly will bid 4 ♡, right or wrong. South simply must decide right now whether 4 ♠ will be a good save against 4 ♡. If he thinks so he should bid it now to make West guess if he has a possible 5 ♡ call, while if South doesn't think 4 ♠ will be a good save (either because 4 ♡ might go down or because 4 ♠ will go for too much) he should merely bid 3 ♠ and then bow out of the auction. Both actions are reasonable. The one thing South must not do is bid 3 ♠ (or pass) now and then take a 4 ♠ sacrifice when E-W bid 4 ♡. This allows E-W to exchange maximum information and puts the last guess back on South. Since South isn't sure what the right guess is over 4 ♡, he should make his decision early in the auction and stick with it. In this way, he has put the last guess back in the hands of the opponents, where it belongs. The time to wait and see if the opponents get to their best contract before saving is when there is a good chance that they won't. On this hand there is little practical chance that the opponents will fail to bid 4 ♡, so South should make an immediate decision and act on it.

HIGH-LEVEL DECISIONS

Both partnerships have good distributional fits, and the bidding soon soars up to the four or five level where either or both pairs might or might not be able to make their bids. At some point, you have to make the crucial decision—to double, pass, or bid on. Many matchpoints can ride on this decision. While there is no substitute for good judgment, it is possible to load the dice so that you gain the most when your decision is right and lose the least when it is wrong.

Suppose your side has a spade fit, the opponents have a diamond fit, and they have competed to 5 ◇ over your 4 ♠ bid. Unless one side is taking a sacrifice which is down more than the value of game, it is clearly correct to bid 5 ♠ if either 5 ◇ or 5 ♠ makes, but to double if neither does. At IMPs or rubber bridge the odds always favor bidding on if the decision is close. If you bid when both contracts are down one you go from + 100 to − 100 (assuming neither vulnerable and that the final contract will be doubled), for a five IMP loss. If you double when they make and you are down one you get − 550 instead of − 100, costing ten IMPs, and if it is your contract which is making you get + 100 instead of + 650 for an eleven IMP swing. If both contracts happen to make, the swing may get as high as fourteen or fifteen IMPs. Consequently the IMP odds always favor bidding on if it is close, simply because you lose more by defending and being wrong than by bidding and being wrong.

At matchpoints, the amount by which you are wrong is not significant. Being − 100 instead of + 100 can be just as costly as being − 550 instead of + 100. The object is simply to be right as often as possible. Unfortunately total trick analysis, so accurate at lower levels, tends to be of little use at the four-level or higher. Long trump holdings matter, of course, but factors such as distribution and two-suit fits come into play much more at the higher levels than in part-score competition.

If the decision is really close and you really have no idea who can make what, it is usually better to bid on. By buying the contract you give yourself two ways to win—either you might make or they might make. If you defend, you are right only when both contracts are going down. Bidding on actually has a third way to win. Even if both contracts are going down, there is the possibility that the opponents will misjudge the situation and bid still more. For example:

North deals
Both vul.

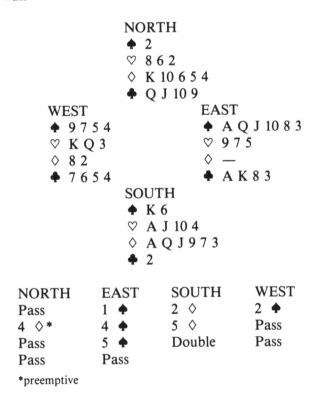

NORTH
♠ 2
♡ 8 6 2
◊ K 10 6 5 4
♣ Q J 10 9

WEST
♠ 9 7 5 4
♡ K Q 3
◊ 8 2
♣ 7 6 5 4

EAST
♠ A Q J 10 8 3
♡ 9 7 5
◊ —
♣ A K 8 3

SOUTH
♠ K 6
♡ A J 10 4
◊ A Q J 9 7 3
♣ 2

NORTH	EAST	SOUTH	WEST
Pass	1 ♠	2 ◊	2 ♠
4 ◊ *	4 ♠	5 ◊	Pass
Pass	5 ♠	Double	Pass
Pass	Pass		

*preemptive

This is a typical sequence on a distributional fitting hand. When East bids 4♠ South doesn't know if 4♠ will make, and he also doesn't know if 5◊ will make. His 5◊ bid is a good two-way shot. It might either make, or be a good save. On the actual hand both 4♠ and 5◊ happen to go down one trick, largely due to the lack of fit in the heart and club suits, which can't be diagnosed during the bidding. However, the auction isn't over yet. West has nothing more to say, and when it gets passed back around to East he is in the same position that South was in when he bid 5 ◇. From East's point of view 5 ♠ could well make, or 5 ◇ might be making, in which case 5 ♠ will certainly be a good save. His 5 ♠ call turns out very badly, but it is not a terrible bid and certainly could have worked. Finally, South knows what to do. He can't be 100% sure of beating 5 ♠, but it is still correct to double since 5 ♠ figures to go down and 5 ◇ might make. The interesting point about the hand is that South was "wrong" in bidding 5 ◇, since both 4 ♠ and 5 ◇ are down one, yet the bid worked out beautifully because the opponents made the mistake of bidding one more. This is another example of giving the opponents the last guess. East guessed, and he guessed wrong.

One can't always buy the contract. The bidding has to stop someplace. The point is that in a high-level competitive bidding decision, if either the contract the opponents have just bid or the one you are thinking about bidding might make it is usually correct to bid on, for you give yourself several ways to win. Once it is clear that you can't make your contract if you bid further, it is time to defend. On the previous hand South thought he might make 5 ◇ on a good day, but 6 ◇ is certainly out of the question. Consequently the 5 ◇ bid is correct, but bidding 6 ◇, while it could be right if E-W can make 5 ♠, is not a wise action. It is seldom right in a who knows who can make what auction to deliberately settle for a minus score. East's 5 ♠ bid is justifiable only on the grounds that it might make; if it could have no play it would probably be better to defend. Once you have taken what is definitely a sacrifice, you have committed yourself to the last guess.

If you choose to defend in a high-level competitive auction, it is always correct to double rather than sell out undoubled if your previous bid had been for a make rather than a save. For example, at neither vulnerable you bid 4 ♡ with the hope of making, and the opponents now bid 4 ♠. A double, if wrong, as opposed to a pass, will only cost one-half matchpoint against other tables in 4 ♠, since there is no possible score between −420 and −590 (presumably if you bid 4 ♡ to make then others holding your cards will not be going for −500 even at the five-level). However, the double gains one-half matchpoint against these same tables if it is right. Since you have chosen to defend you must believe that 4♠ is more likely to go down than not, for if you thought 4♠ was a favorite to make you would have bid 5♡ as a save with the outside possibility of making. Consequently, the odds favor the double. In addition, there is the possibility that 4♠ was bid as a sacrifice against your 4♡ game. If this is the case not doubling would be very costly, particularly if the sacrifice happens to go down more than the value of your game. Allowing the opponents to get away with an undoubled save is very expensive at matchpoints. This is a situation where the double stands to gain more when it is right than it will lose when it is wrong, and you must believe it is a favorite to be right or you would bid on. Therefore, doubling becomes very attractive.

None vul., South holds: ♠2, ♡KQJ954, ◇A105, ♣AQ9

NORTH	EAST	SOUTH	WEST
—	—	1 ♡	1 ♠
2 ♡	2 ♠	4 ♡	4 ♠
Pass	Pass	?	

What should South do? When he bid 4♡ it was with every intention of making it, although there were no guarantees. Bidding 5♡ in the hope of making would be much too optimistic. Partner would need a perfect hand and it would still probably be on a finesse. What about the opposing 4♠ contract? If South feels 4♠ will make he should bid 5♡ as a save, but I don't think this is a good bid. There is no particular reason to expect 4♠ to make, although it certainly might. If South bids 5♡ he commits himself to a minus score when it might have been the opponents who were saving, so there is no reason to take this action. However, South must not pass simply because he doesn't know who can make what. It is essential to double! Since South is betting that E-W can't make 4♠ he might as well up the stakes, since there is no likely score between −420 and −590. For all South knows, it is E-W who are saving.

The previous hand is a "double or save" situation. N-S can

certainly make at least nine tricks in hearts, so South knows he has a good save if E-W can make 4♠. Therefore, pass cannot be the best action. If the opponents are making it is right to save, while if they are going down it is right to double. You must do one or the other, particularly if it is at all possible that you could have made your bid and it is the opponents who are saving.

The exception to the double or save principle occurs when you have already taken a sacrifice and the opponents have bid on. You may be sure that a further sacrifice is still safe, but choose to defend undoubled. The reason is that the further sacrifice might not gain much when it is right, because some pairs may buy the hand your way at a lower level. This situation can only occur at favorable vulnerability when a three-trick set is a good save. At any other vulnerability either the further sacrifice will be too expensive or you were only going down one, and so had some chance of making your bid. If the further sacrifice is too expensive it is no longer a double or save situation, while if you might have made your bid you must double as we have seen.

E-W vul., South holds: ♠7, ♡A865, ◇A652, ♣QJ86

NORTH	EAST	SOUTH	WEST
—	—	—	1 ♠
3 ◇*	4 ♠	5 ◇	5 ♠
Pass	Pass	?	

*preemptive

When South bid 5 ◇ it was fully intended as a sacrifice—even the best hand North can have for a weak jump overcall at favorable vulnerability won't produce eleven tricks. 6 ◇ figures to be a good save, for N-S can certainly take nine or ten tricks. What about 5 ♠? This is not so clear. If South feels that 5 ♠ is more likely to go down than to make he might as well double, since it is not likely that other N-S pairs will fail to find the save at the 5 ◇ level. Suppose South feels that 5 ♠ is 60% to make. Does this mean that he should take the 6 ◇ sacrifice? Not necessarily. It would be the correct action if all other E-W pairs pushed to 5 ♠, but this will not happen. Suppose at other tables half the

E-W pairs double 5 ♦, and the other half bid 5 ♠. If South takes the save he gains one-half matchpoint only from those tables in 5 ♠ even if he is right, since the board has been lost to those who bought it for 5 ♦. On a twelve top he will gain three matchpoints, getting six instead of three. If he takes the save and is wrong he loses one-half matchpoint to other tables in 5 ♠, and a full matchpoint to those who bought it for 5 ♦ doubled. This action will cost nine matchpoints, for he will get a zero instead of nine on a twelve top. Consequently he is giving three to one matchpoint odds by saving, which is too much to give if 5 ♠ is 60% to make. It is also incorrect to double, for the gain or loss in doubling is a half matchpoint to other tables in 5 ♠, so if 5 ♠ is a favorite to make double is also a losing action. Consequently, it is correct to pass even though pass cannot be the "perfect" bid. Either doubling or saving is the winning action, but passing is the percentage bid and will give South the highest matchpoint expectation if this assessment of the hand is correct. This is the exception to the double or save principle.

THE FORCING PASS

The concept of a forcing pass is confusing to many players. A forcing pass is just a call showing no preference for defending but insufficient values to bid on unilaterally in a high level competitive auction where the logic of the situation demands that the partnership either bid one more or double. The most common case is when the opponents have taken a sacrifice, but forcing passes can also crop up in the "who knows who can make what" type of auctions or even in double or save positions. The important condition is that it cannot be correct for the partnership to sell out without doubling. The forcing pass throws the decision to the passer's partner, and his decision should be final. If he doubles, the initial passer must pass. If he were planning to bid on, he should have done so immediately, thereby telling his partner that he has extra offensive values in case the key decision must be made at the next higher level.

When is a pass forcing? A lot of players have trouble deciding this, and any good partnership should work out precise agreements as to which passes are forcing and which are not. It is most embarrassing and quite costly to sell out undoubled when one partner thought he was making a forcing pass and showing extra values while his partner did not think the pass was forcing. A good general rule is that passes are forcing when the partnership has found a fit and has shown at least game-invitational values. This does not necessarily mean that the hand belongs to the partnership. It is not uncommon to see a forcing pass lead to a good sacrifice in the "who knows who can make what" type of auction, even though the player taking the sacrifice and his partner might not have thought it was a sacrifice at the time.

A forcing pass invites partner to bid on, so it must show a hand with offensive orientation. Usually this will mean shortness in the enemy trump suit if it is possible that the passer is short. If the passer has already indicated a balanced hand, then his pass shows nothing wasted in the enemy trump suit and invites partner to bid on if he has the singleton. This is not mandatory, of course, With extra strength it might be right to make a forcing pass with a doubleton in trumps, while with a minimum hand it could be correct to double with a singleton simply because you judge that you can't make anything higher but still think you can beat the opponents' contract. In general, however, length in the opponents' trump suit should be the key to the decision.

Consider the following common type of auction with none vul.:

NORTH	EAST	SOUTH	WEST
—	—	1 ♡	1 ♠
3 ♡*	4 ♠	?	

*limit raise

By our definition if South passes it is forcing, since the partnership has a fit and game invitational values. It might be N-S who are saving if they bid 5 ♡, but it cannot be correct to sell out undoubled. We can assume that North doesn't have a singleton spade since he didn't bid 4 ♡, make a splinter bid, make a fit-showing jump, or do any of the other things he might have done with a singleton, depending on partnership agreements.

   a. ♠97, ♡AQJ53, ◇KQ3, ♣973. South must double. There is no guarantee that 4 ♠ will go down, but South would rather defend 4 ♠ than play 5 ♡ opposite a normal limit raise. A pass would invite North to bid on with no wasted spade cards, which South doesn't want North to do.

   b. ♠2, ♡AQ9764, ◇Q74, ♣A87. This is a classic forcing pass. If North has nothing wasted in spades it will probably be correct to go on to 5 ♡. For example, if North holds ♠xxx, ♡KJxx, ◇Kx, ♣QJ10x then 5 ♡ depends on the club finesse. However, if the club finesse is off for N-S it will be on for E-W, so 4 ♠ will probably make. Either way, it would be right to bid 5 ♡, which might be a make and might be a good save. If North instead holds: ♠Kxx, ♡KJxx, ◇xx, ♣QJ10x, he will double 4 ♠. This is certainly the right action on the combined hands, since 5 ♡ has no play and 4 ♠ will probably go down.

226

c. ♠2, ♡AKQ832, ◇AJ8, ♣K65. South should simply bid 5♡, since this is what he thinks he can make. He will probably lose a spade trick and one minor suit trick opposite a normal limit raise such as ♠Qx, ♡Jxxx, ◇KQxx, ♣Qxx. There is no reason to pass the decision to North since South knows where he wants to play the hand, and the penalty against 4♠ is not likely to be sufficient.

d. ♠85, ♡AQJ943, ◇A5, ♣AQ7. This is one hand on which South should make a forcing pass despite his doubleton spade. If North has no wasted spade cards he probably has enough strength in the other suits to cover all of South's losers, so all N-S will lose will be two spade tricks. However, if North has some spade strength it is probably right to defend. Either South will have an extra loser, or the penalty against 4♠ just might be 500 if North produces a trump trick.

e. ♠2, ♡KQJ10742, ◇65, ♣KQ6. This hand is an exceptional case. Despite the fact that North has shown game-invitational values, South can be pretty sure that the hand belongs to E-W and that he should bid 5♡ as a sacrifice. In order to distinguish this from a strong hand, South must pass first and then pull North's double. This type of sequence which should normally be avoided shows a very offensively oriented hand with little defense, and alerts partner not to be too fast to double if the opponents bid one more.

f. ♠—, ♡AQJ643, ◇AQJ32, ♣93. South certainly will not defend 4♠, but he is worried about what to do over 5♠. His best bid is 5◇. This is not meant as a slam try as it would be in an uncontested auction, although slam isn't completely out of the question. The bid simply shows a strong offensively oriented hand with values in hearts and diamonds. Now if E-W compete to 5♠, North will be well-placed to make the final decision. If South had a real slam try he would just go ahead and bid the slam, letting E-W guess whether or not to sacrifice.

Let's look at the view from the other side of the table.

None vul., South holds: ♠863, ♡QJ82, ◊K6, ♣A643

NORTH	EAST	SOUTH	WEST
1 ♡	1 ♠	3 ♡*	3 ♠
4 ♡	4 ♠	?	

South should make a forcing pass. This basically denies any wastage in spades. South's hand is limited and he has implied a balanced hand, so that's all the pass shows. It is up to the partner of the limited hand to make the final decision here. If South instead held ♠Q83, ♡J862, ◊K6, ♣A643 he should double 4♠. North can still do what he wants, of course, but South must show his spade wastage. There is no hand on which South can bid 5♡, because he doesn't know whether or not his partner was stretching for the 4♡ call. If North wanted South to make the final decision, he should have bid something other than 4♡. For example, none vul.

NORTH	EAST	SOUTH	WEST
1 ♡	1 ♠	3 ♡*	3 ♠
4 ◊	4 ♠	?	

*limit raise

4◊ is not a slam try, as it would be in an uncontested auction. North is simply showing his values, preparing for a 4♠ bid by the opponents.

a. ♠Q74, ♡J1087, ◊A3, ♣KJ97. South should double. He has most of his points in the black suits opposite North's presumed shortness, which makes his hand defensively oriented.

b. ♠764, ♡QJ87, ◊A3 ♣K1097. South should pass. This is a forcing pass. South is not sure what to do. His king of clubs argues for defending, but the rest of his hand is offensively oriented. It will be best if North makes the final decision.

c. ♠764, ♡KJ87, ◊AQ3, ♣1097. South should bid 5♡. This is it—the big double fit. If North has interest in competing

228

to the five-level, as indicated by his 4 ◊ call, then South has the perfect hand for him so he should go straight to 5 ♡. If North knew that he did not want to go to the five-level opposite any limt raise he would have bid 4 ♡ rather than 4 ◊ , and now South could only pass or double.

REVIEW PROBLEMS

1. None vul., South holds: ♠105, ♡AQ98, ◇1064, ♣AQJ3

NORTH	EAST	SOUTH	WEST
—	—	1 ♣	Pass
1 ♡	2 ♠	?	

2. Both vul., South holds: ♠AQ10974, ♡985, ◇95, ♣43

NORTH	EAST	SOUTH	WEST
—	—	—	1 ◇
1 ♡	2 ◇	?	

3. Both vul., South holds: ♠K9832, ♡53, ◇K94, ♣K94

NORTH	EAST	SOUTH	WEST
1 ♣	1 ◇	1 ♠	2 ◇
2 ♠	3 ◇	?	

4. N-S vul., South holds: ♠A85, ♡Q762, ◇Q84, ♣J83

NORTH	EAST	SOUTH	WEST
1 ♡	1 ♠	2 ♡	2 ♠
3 ♡	3 ♠	?	

5. None vul., South holds: ♠Q108654, ♡106, ◇AJ3, ♣A10

NORTH	EAST	SOUTH	WEST
—	—	—	1 NT
Pass	2 ♣	?	

6. Both vul., South holds: ♠84, ♡K642, ◇K754, ♣1062

NORTH	EAST	SOUTH	WEST
—	—	—	1 ♣
1 ♡	Double*	?	

*negative double

7. E-W vul., South holds: ♠653, ♡K876, ◊A3, ♣AQ108

NORTH	EAST	SOUTH	WEST
2 ♡*	2 ♠	4 ♡	4 ♠
Pass	Pass	?	

*weak 2-bid

8. E-W vul., South holds: ♠AQ653, ♡J1076, ◊72, ♣107

NORTH	EAST	SOUTH	WEST
—	—	—	1 ♡
Double	Redouble	?	

9. Both vul., South holds: ♠KQ93, ♡92, ◊76532, ♣A8

NORTH	EAST	SOUTH	WEST
—	—	—	1 ◊
Pass	1 ♡	Pass	2 ♡
Pass	Pass	?	

10. N-S vul., South holds: ♠KJ75, ♡AJ10, ◊9642, ♣K7

NORTH	EAST	SOUTH	WEST
—	1 ♣	Double	1 ♡
2 ◊	2 ♡	?	

231

SOLUTIONS

1. 3♡. It is imperative for South to show his heart support, even if it involves a slight overbid. N-S have at least eight hearts, maybe nine, and E-W probably have at least eight spades, so the law of total tricks argues for bidding. North should give South some leeway in this type of auction. If South were worth a jump to 3♡, he would take the bull by the horns and bid game himself.

2. 2♡. It would be nice to be able to introduce the spade suit, but it simply can't be done conveniently. If South bids 2♠ and the opponents compete to 3◊, South won't know whether or not to bid 3♡ since he won't know how many hearts North has. If South bids 2♡, North can make the proper trick-total evaluation on the heart suit, which is probably the most important basis for the competitive decision.

3. Double. This is a good matchpoint double. South has extra strength, good defense, and vulnerable opponents at the three-level. There is a good chance that North has only three spades, for he is likely to have several hearts since E-W haven't bid hearts. If North has four spades and a singleton diamond he will probably pull the double; otherwise, the double figures to work out well.

4. Pass. North's 3♡ bid is not invitational. It only shows a sixth heart or a singleton, so South should not go to 4♡ without an exceptional hand. Even though N-S may have ten trumps, this is not justification for a ten trick contract, as the law of total tricks tends to break down at higher levels. South should not double, for 3♠ is quite likely to make and a one trick set still won't beat +140. The vulnerability argues for conservatism, so South should sell out and hope that others holding his cards get into worse trouble by acting over 3♠.

5. Pass. This is a marginal overcall at best, as it could well go for a number and South doesn't necessarily want a spade lead.

What about the nuisance value of shutting out the opponents' potential heart fit? A little thought shows that this nuisance value is imaginary. If West has four hearts he can pass and see what East does. When East fails to double 2♠ West can deduce that East has four hearts, else why did he bid Stayman in the first place. Consequently, the 2♠ overcall won't hinder the opponents in their search for a heart fit. If the overcall were directly behind the 1NT opener it would be a different story, for now the enemy has had less opportunity to exchange information.

6. 3♡. South should go right to the three-level without delay. He knows that his side has at least nine hearts and that the opponents probably have eight spades, so there is no reason to hold back. A lesser bid gives E-W too much room to exchange information.

7. Double. A classic double or save hand. N-S certainly have a good save at 5♡ if 4♠ is making. South has no particular reason to think that 4♠ will make, so taking the save is wrong. As long as South is betting that 4♠ is going down he should double, for there is certainly some chance that 4♡ is making. The double has far more to gain when it is right than it has to lose when it is wrong, and South is willing to bet that it is right.

8. 3♠. South can assume a nine-card spade fit, and the opponents certainly won't sell to 2♠ after East's redouble. Consequently, South should bid the limit of his hand immediately. This is likely to produce a bonus if East has a heart fit and tries 4♡, for South can now spring his trap and double. Any lesser bid allows East to describe his hand at the three-level, and gives the opponents a chance to get off the hook.

9. Pass. This is a close decision. The danger in bidding 2♠ is that South has no place to run, and the opponents know enough about the hand to penalize South when he is wrong. North's silence and the vulnerability argue in favor of passing.

10. 3◊. Never mind the minimal values and the strong major suit holdings. South has four diamonds, so he must compete to

the three-level opposite his partner's presumed five-card suit.
This bid does not show any extra values—simply possession of a
fourth diamond.

DEFENSIVE BIDDING

DEFENSIVE BIDDING

ENTERING THE AUCTION

It is very important to get into the auction if at all possible after the opponents have opened the bidding. Players who have stiff requirements for overcalls and takeout doubles are hurting their chances in matchpoint competition. Look at it from the opening bidder's point of view. After you open the bidding, wouldn't you prefer that the opponents stay silent so you and your partner can exchange information as you please? It is much more difficult to arrive at the best contract if the enemy starts throwing bids in your face, gobbling up bidding room and making the exchange of information more difficult. What is bad for the opener's side must be good for the other pair, and vice versa. Consequently, it will generally be better to get into the auction than to pass quietly.

The main ways to get into the auction after a one of a suit opening bid are the simple overcall, the takeout double, and the 1NT overcall. Preempts are also important, and will be discussed in a later chapter.

OVERCALLS

The most important competing bid is the overcall. There are four main reasons one might want to overcall. They are: constructive bidding, lead-direction, space consumption, and sacrificial.

1. For constructive purposes: This is the most common reason, and certainly the most important. The opponents' opening bid does not give them a claim to the contract; it could well belong to you. Consequently, an overcall is often simply an attempt to get to the right contract. For example:

Both vul., South holds: ♠ J8532, ♡ A74, ♢ K72, ♣ AQ

NORTH	EAST	SOUTH	WEST
—	1 ♡	?	

South should overcall 1 ♠ despite the weak suit. If East had passed South certainly would have opened 1 ♠, so why not bid it over the opening bid? It will be noted that this overcall doesn't satisfy any of the other reasons for overcalling, but this doesn't matter. South's hand is strong enough to compete and he holds the master suit, so now is the time to act. Some players feel that they can pass now and balance later if it is correct to do so. This is a losing tactic. In the first place the 1 ♠ overcall is very unlikely to be penalized, while a later balance at a higher level after the opponents have exchanged information is much more dangerous. Secondly, you lose the opportunity of having partner raise spades and taking up enemy bidding room. Thirdly, if you balance later you can't be sure of finding a fit, while if you bid now partner will raise only with appropriate trump support.

This type of overcall should not be overdone. With a weaker hand such as ♠ Jxxxx, ♡ Axx, ♢ Kxx, ♣ Qx South should pass. If North can't get into the auction there probably is no constructive future for the hand. Also, if South holds a hand with a lower ranking suit such as ♠ AQ, ♡ Axx, ♢ Kxx, ♣ Jxxxx a pass is advisable. A 2 ♣ overcall is much more likely to be penalized than a 1 ♠ overcall, and since hearts outranks clubs the chances of winning the part-score battle are small, while with the spade suit there is a good chance of outbidding the opponents. These two factors are sufficient to make the 2♣ overcall unattractive, while the 1♠ overcall on the same type of hand is correct.

2. Space consumption: This concept has already been discussed under nuisance bids. It is a prime consideration when deciding whether or not to make a marginal overcall. For example:

Both vul., South holds: ♠A95, ♡Q9873, ◇92, ♣KJ3

NORTH	EAST	SOUTH	WEST
Pass	1 ◇	?	

A 1♡ overcall would be pointless. The danger isn't so much that it may go for a number, but that partner may later over-compete or make a disastrous heart opening lead. However, change a few suits to:

Both vul., South holds: ♠Q9873, ♡92, ◇KJ3, ♣A95

NORTH	EAST	SOUTH	WEST
Pass	1 ♣	?	

Now, South should overcall 1♠. The disadvantages of the over-call are still the same, but the gain in space consumption outweighs them. It is true that most opponents have things such as negative doubles available to help recover lost heart suits, but their bidding still won't be quite as accurate. This is particularly true if partner can muster up a 2♠ raise. Now the opponents will be floundering at the critical three-level before they have any idea what they have, and they are far more likely to go wrong than if they had been left alone. This overcalling policy reaps hidden matchpoints that super-sound overcalls don't realize. They see the occasional disaster, but they don't under-stand that opponents will bid less accurately when faced with space consuming bids. The "lucky" pair which gets many gifts from their opponents usually has taken actions such as these to make life difficult for the opponents and so deserves the gifts.

3. Lead-direction: The premium on overtricks at matchpoints makes lead-direction overcalls far more important than at IMPs. The overtrick saved by the right lead can be worth several matchpoints. Consequently, it is often worth sticking your neck out to get a lead-director in. For example:

Both vul., South holds: ♠A7, ♡872, ♢KQ10765, ♣75

NORTH	EAST	SOUTH	WEST
—	—	—	1 ♠
Pass	2 ♣	?	

The 2 ♢ overcall has little value other than as a lead-director, and the bid could certainly go for a number. Despite this, I still think the overcall is a winning action. If West becomes declarer, as is likely, a diamond lead is the only lead South's hand can stand, and the occasional catastrophe is more than compensated for by the times the oppponents simply bid to their normal contract and the diamond lead saves a trick. However, with ♠72, ♡A87, ♢KQ10765, ♣75 South should pass. Now South doesn't particularly mind a heart lead; in fact, it might turn out better. If the opponents' black suits are solid and partner has something like KJxx in hearts, it is the heart lead, and not the diamond, that will cut down the overtricks in a spade contract. On the first hand, the diamond lead may be necessary both to set up a diamond trick and avoid blowing a heart trick, so the gain may be substantial. On the hand with the ace of hearts the risk of the overcall is not worthwhile, for it may not gain anything even if it is not penalized.

4. Sacrificial: A fourth reason for overcalling is to set up a possible sacrifice. For example:

E-W vul., South holds: ♠Q106432, ♡9, ◇KJ6, ♣542

NORTH	EAST	SOUTH	WEST
—	—	—	1 ♣
Pass	2 ♡	?	

South should stick his nose in with a 2 ♠ overcall, despite the risks. The opponents have already announced game-going strength, so 2 ♠ would have to go for 700 to be too expensive. This isn't very likely, and even if the penalty is available the opponents may not be in a position to collect it. If North has a spade fit there is a good possibility of a successful 4 ♠ save over 4 ♡ (or even a 6 ♠ save over 6 ♡), so the possible gain justifies the risk. At any other vulnerability the 2 ♠ overcall would be downright reckless. The likelihood of a good save would be greatly diminished, and the danger of going for too much at 2 ♠ and getting caught would increase dramatically.

It should be noted that many overcalls satisfy more than one of these reasons. For example:

E-W vul., South holds: ♠KQ10643, ♡105, ◇K2, ♣A73

NORTH	EAST	SOUTH	WEST
—	1 ♣	1 ♠	

The obvious 1 ♠ overcall might work for any of the four reasons, depending on what happens later in the auction. The important point is that you should have at least one of these reasons for any overcall, otherwise there is no purpose in the bid. For example:

E-W vul., South holds: ♠A75, ♡K8, ◇Q8763, ♣1092

NORTH	EAST	SOUTH	WEST
—	1 ♣	?	

There is no reason to bid 1 ◇ just to hear yourself speak. Admittedly the bid is not likely to come to harm, but it can't gain anything. If partner can't bid on his own the hand belongs to

E-W, no space is consumed, South doesn't particularly want a diamond lead, and South's hand is not oriented toward a sacrifice. Overcalling on hands such as these may cause partner to misjudge a competitive auction later on. However, any change in the hand may make the overcall fit one of the reasons. Make the hand stronger such as: ♠A75, ♡K8, ◇Q8763, ♣A92 and now the overcall is correct for constructive value. Make your suit the higher ranking suit as in: ♠Q8763, ♡K8, ◇A75, ♣1092 and the overcall becomes right for space consuming purposes. Strengthen the suit such as: ♠875, ♡K8, ◇AQ763, ♣1092 and the overcall is worthwhile for lead-directional value. Give South better distribution like: ♠A7, ♡K865, ◇Q87632, ♣9 and now the overcall is reasonable due to the sacrificial possibilities.

The most important thing for the partner of the overcaller to do if he has trump support is to raise immediately to whatever level he thinks best and then stay out of the auction. This is particularly true if the partner of the opening bidder acts. The proper level is usually determined by the law of total tricks. Preemptive jump raises of overcalls are a must for any pair wishing to put maximum pressure on the opponents. A convention such as the Rosenkranz Redouble (redouble of a negative double is automatic with a top honor in the suit) is simply ineffective—it gives the opponents too much room. Only when the partner of the overcaller is strong enough to invite a game should he go slowly and start with a cue bid.

None vul., in each case the auction has gone:

NORTH	EAST	SOUTH	WEST
—	—	—	1 ♣
1 ♠	Double*	?	

*negative double

a. ♠Q53, ♡83, ◇Q10763, ♣652. Bid 2♠. So what if it is under strength. Trick-total says to compete to 2♠, and this bid won't make life any easier for the opponents.

b. ♠Q53, ♡83, ◇K10763, ♣A52. Still just a 2♠ bid. The

242

hand isn't quite strong enough for a cue bid. We may have a tough decision later at the three-level, but that is for later. Now, we let the opponents guess first.

c. ♠Q653, ♡83, ◊Q10763, ♣52. Bid 3♠. A perfect trick total bid. This will make life very difficult for E-W.

d. ♠Q653, ♡A3, ◊K10763, ♣52. Still bid 3♠. Again put the pressure on the opponents, making them guess. This time if they guess to bid at the four-level we will bet that they guessed wrong and double to make them pay.

e. ♠Q653, ♡A3, ◊AJ763, ♣52. This hand should start slowly with a 2♣ cue bid. The hand figures to belong to N-S for at least 3♠, and a game is quite possible, so it is wrong to pre-empt. South wants to discover if North has any extra strength, and he is not too worried about the opponents. If the overcalled suit had been hearts and South had held ♠A3, ♡Q653, ◊AJ763, ♣52 it would not be unreasonable to go right to 4♡ as a two-way shot. It might make, or the opponents might have an accident competing to 4♠ over the 4♡ bid. Since N-S hold the spade suit, this kind of preemption is not necessary.

f. ♠Q6532, ♡3, ◊K10763, ♣52. Simply bid 4♠ and let the opponents guess. It might make, it might be a good save, and E-W might now have an accident by being forced to guess at this high level.

THE TAKEOUT DOUBLE

The idea behind the takeout double is entirely different from the overcall. When you overcall you are suggesting that your suit is likely to be the best trump suit. When you make a takeout double, you are suggesting that partner pick the best trump suit. Since he may pick any of the other three suits, you must be prepared to handle a bid in any of them. This means that you should usually have at least three-card support for each unbid suit in order to make a takeout double. Keep in mind that the opponents are likely to preempt vigorously against a takeout double if they have a fit, since your side still hasn't located a trump suit. Partner will strain to bid his five-card suits at the two or even three-level in competition, particularly a suit which outranks the enemy suit. If you don't have support for any suit he might bid, it could be disastrous.

None vul., South holds: ♠K6, ♡AQ108, ◇1075, ♣KQ62

NORTH	EAST	SOUTH	WEST
—	1 ◇	?	

South must either pass or overcall 1 ♡ if it suits his fancy, but a double is out of the question. North is just too likely to bid spades at any level in competition, and this will probably turn out badly. If the opening bid had been 1♠, however, South would have a fine takeout double. Change South's hand to: ♠KQ62, ♡AQ108, ◇1075, ♣K6 and now the takeout double of a 1 ◇ opening bid becomes a reasonable gamble despite the doubleton club. Partner will not strain as hard to bid a lower ranking suit in a competitive auction, since it means going one level higher, so if he bids clubs over a diamond raise he will certainly have five and maybe six. The double could backfire, but with both majors and opening bid strength it is worth getting into the auction.

The question of whether to double or overcall has always plagued players. Strength is not an important factor in making this decision. As we have seen, in competitive auctions it is more important to find the right trump suit and determine the extent of fit than it is to determine strength. The law of total tricks will see us through the three-level if we can find our best trump suit.

None vul., South holds: ♠J762, ♡AQJ32, ◇8, ♣K85

NORTH	EAST	SOUTH	WEST
—	1 ◇	?	

Despite the strong heart suit and the minimal strength of South's hand, I prefer a takeout double to a 1 ♡ overcall. The hand is quite suitable as a dummy for either spades or clubs, so South should let his partner pick the suit. The fourth spade is the key to this decision. If South overcalls 1 ♡ any four-four spade fit will almost certainly be lost forever, for North will need five spades to voluntarily bid the suit, particularly in competition. Switch the black suits so that South has: ♠K85, ♡AQJ32, ◇8, ♣J762 and now a 1 ♡ overcall is preferable. The main danger in doubling is that North might have four spades and three hearts, and then the partnership will probably wind up in the four-three fit rather than the five-three fit. As a general rule, when the opponents open one of a minor and you have a five-card major it is right to double if you have four cards in the other major but better to overcall with fewer than four.

N-S vul., South holds: ♠KQ4, ♡AQ4, ◇3, ♣AQ6543

NORTH	EAST	SOUTH	WEST
—	1 ◇	?	

A simple 2♣ overcall is best. A double could land N-S in an awkward four-three major suit fit when the hand belongs in clubs. The plan is to overcall first and then reopen with a double if the opponents bid more diamonds. This is much more efficient than doubling first and then bidding clubs. Which auction would you rather have:

a.	NORTH	EAST	SOUTH	WEST
	—	1 ◇	2 ♣	3 ◇
	Pass	Pass	?	

b.	NORTH	EAST	SOUTH	WEST
	—	1 ◇	Double	3 ◇
	Pass	Pass	?	

In the first auction South can comfortably reopen with a double and feel that he has accurately described his hand. All contracts are still open, including defending 3 ◇ doubled. In the second auction, however, South is in a bind. If he doubles again North will bid 3 ♠ on something like ♠ Jxxx, ♡ xx, ◇ Qxx, ♣ Jxxx and the hand will not play very well while 4 ♣ is comfortable. On the other hand, if South bids 4 ♣ he may find his partner with ♠ J10xxx, ♡ xxx, ◇ Qxx, ♣ Jx. Now the hand belongs in spades, but 3 ♠ is probably the limit of the hand. By overcalling first and then doubling South can have his cake and eat it too—he will get to the right contract opposite both of these hands.

There are two types of hands on which it is correct to make a takeout double without support for all unbid suits. One is a hand so strong that you fear you may miss a game even if partner cannot muster up a response to your overcall. For example:

N-S vul., South holds: ♠ AKJ1094, ♡ A8, ◇ K9, ♣ AJ8

NORTH	EAST	SOUTH	WEST
—	1 ◇	?	

South should double. This is just a bit too strong to risk having a 1 ♠ overcall get passed out. South can bid spades over whatever North bids. If the hand were slightly weaker, say no king of diamonds, then a 1 ♠ overcall would be preferable.

The other type of hand is one in which you have two suits and can convert to your longest suit at the same level if partner bids the suit you don't have. For example:

None vul., South holds: ♠A876, ♡3, ◇AQJ865, ♣Q7

NORTH	EAST	SOUTH	WEST
—	1 ♡	?	

A 2 ◇ overcall risks losing a spade fit, while a double risks partner bidding clubs. This is all right on this hand, for you can convert clubs to diamonds at any level he bids, and you will have described a hand like this. This is called equal-level conversion, and is the one sequence where a double followed by a new suit doesn't necessarily show a powerhouse. Note that the order of suits is very important. If you had instead held: ♠A876, ♡3, ◇Q7, ♣AQJ865 you would have to overcall with 2♣ and try to get back to spades later if it is right. You couldn't risk a double, for you would have to bid clubs at the next higher level if partner bid diamonds, and the hand is not nearly strong enough for this action.

THE 1NT OVERCALL

The 1NT overcall covers many hands which don't qualify for an overcall because there is no good suit and aren't suitable for a takeout double because of distribution, yet are strong enough to act. All the 1NT overcall shows is something resembling an opening 1NT bid with a stopper in the enemy suit. Many players choose to pass with these hands. Either they think they are being clever by "trapping", or they are afraid of going for a number in 1NT. I think they are making a big mistake. If you pass on this sort of hand you are going to have to guess what to do later in the auction at a higher level, after the opponents have described their hands to each other. However if you make your 1NT overcall you have told your story. You can then sit back and relax, watching the opponents guess while your partner knows exactly what you have. For example:

Both vul., South holds: ♠K4, ♡A765, ◊K94, ♣AJ73

NORTH	EAST	SOUTH	WEST
—	1 ♡	Pass	1 ♠
Pass	2 ♠	?	

This is the type of bind that players who pass on this hand out of fear or cleverness find themselves getting into. What should South do now? Any action is extremely dangerous, but a pass is equally dangerous for the opponents may have stolen you blind. It is far better to get the 1NT overcall in on the first round of bidding and avoid a guess like this later. True, you would rather have some spot cards in hearts, a little more strength, or a source of tricks, but you aren't always dealt the perfect hand for any bid.

Let's look at a few auction entry decisions:

None vul., South holds: ♠Q73, ♡AQ63, ◊Q109, ♣K86

NORTH	EAST	SOUTH	WEST
—	1 ♣	?	

I recommend a takeout double. The hand is unfortunately too weak for a 1NT overcall, which would otherwise be ideal. If you pass you will just have the same problem at a higher level later in the auction. A 1 ♡ overcall would be favored by many, but it is a losing proposition. First of all, the hand may play well in diamonds or spades if partner owns either of these suits, which is the message conveyed by the double but not the overcall. Secondly, you should avoid overcalling on four-card suits if there is a reasonable alternative. The reason isn't that it is dangerous at the one-level, for you seldom go for a number there. The real danger is that partner will play you for a five-card suit and overbid the trick total if he has support.

None vul., South holds: ♠AQ8, ♡J8763, ◇AJ9, ♣86

NORTH	EAST	SOUTH	WEST
—	1 ♣	?	

In the long run a 1 ♡ overcall will work out best, even on this ragged suit. If partner has heart support it will be as good a trump suit as any, and if not he can bid his own suit if he has anything to say. A takeout double risks landing in the wrong suit, and passing isn't the road to matchpoints.

E-W vul., South holds: ♠A86, ♡A7, ◇KQ1098, ♣Q87

NORTH	EAST	SOUTH	WEST
—	1 ◇	?	

Don't get clever with a trap pass. Get your 1NT overcall in there now. The opponents aren't likely to stay in diamonds, so by passing you give them freedom to find out where they really do belong and at the same time make it harder for partner to enter the auction if he has a long suit.

None vul., South holds: ♠AKJ9, ♡84, ◇A864, ♣1053

NORTH	EAST	SOUTH	WEST
—	1 ◇	?	

This is the perfect hand for the four-card overcall. You want a spade lead, the bid consumes space, and the overcall has constructive value. Also notice that this is exactly the type of hand that may play well in a four-three fit—good trumps and no intermediates in the side suit. In fact, you would probably choose to open the bidding 1 ♠ on this hand as dealer if system permitted, for the same reasons.

None vul., South holds: ♠A865, ♡102, ◇K86, ♣AQ94

NORTH	EAST	SOUTH	WEST
—	1 ◇	?	

Sometimes we just have to pass. This isn't meant as a trap pass. South would like to take action; only nothing is at all suitable. The doubleton heart rules out a takeout double, the spade suit is too weak to overcall on a four-bagger, and the hand is not strong enough for a 1NT overcall. South doesn't like it as he may be faced with a difficult guess next round, but there simply is no good bid available.

OVERCALLING ARTIFICIAL BIDS

When the opponents open with a strong artificial bid such as 2♣ or a Precision 1♣, the gain from getting into the bidding is much greater. Anything which can disrupt the auction will be beneficial since you are taking the opponents out of carefully prepared sequences and forcing them into natural auctions without the benefit of having named their long suit. In addition it is very difficult for them to double you, since they don't know how well their hands fit. Constructive bidding is not too important since it probably isn't your hand, but lead-direction and especially space consumption have a very great value.

None vul., South holds: ♠KQ102, ♡63, ◇1076, ♣J752

NORTH	EAST	SOUTH	WEST
—	1 ♣*	?	

*17+ artificial

A 1♠ overcall is automatic, although it would be quite reckless over a natural club. The bid has both space consumption and lead directional value, and even if partner overbids the trick total the opponents may not know it. Partner should go a little easy on his jump raises, for he knows that you may have a hand like this.

E-W vul., South holds: ♠92, ♡QJ1076, ◇K763, ♣63

NORTH	EAST	SOUTH	WEST
—	1 ♣*	?	

*17+ artificial

I recommend a preemptive jump overcall of 2♡. You are unlikely to get caught even if you are going for your life, and this bid will do far more damage to the enemy than a mere 1♡ overcall.

Both vul., South holds: ♠KJ8, ♡A5, ♦Q9874, ♣A87

NORTH	EAST	SOUTH	WEST
—	1 ♣*	?	

*17+ artificial

Over a natural 1♣ opening South should overcall 1♦ for constructive purposes. Over the strong and artificial bid the 1♦ overcall serves little purpose since it consumes no space. South does not particularly want a diamond lead, and the hand is unlikely to belong to N-S, so South should pass.

PREEMPTS

The preempt is one of the most valuable tools of the winning matchpoint player who realizes the importance of making life difficult for the opponents. Any pair playing in a tournament can get to a reasonable contract most of the time if left on their own. A preempt creates problems for the best of experts. It is quite difficult to arrive confidently at the best contract when you have to start searching at the three-level. Players who say that preempts don't interfere with their bidding accuracy are just kidding themselves.

Suppose you have opened 3 ♡. There are only three auctions that you don't want to hear. They are as follows:

1.	NORTH	EAST	SOUTH	WEST
	—	—	3 ♡	Double
	Pass	Pass	Pass	

This is dangerous, but it might not be too bad. East may have had no satisfactory bid and gambled the pass as the least of evils, so your contract might well make. At least if the hearts are stacked they are in front of you.

2.	NORTH	EAST	SOUTH	WEST
	—	—	3 ♡	Pass
	Pass	Pass		

This is actually worse than the first sequence. It is possible that you have stolen the hand from the opponents, but it is more likely that they didn't bid because they didn't have anything. If this is the case you can only hope that 3 ♡ is your best contract, for if it isn't there is no way to recover. In addition, if the hand is a misfit, as it so often is when a preempt gets dropped, you will probably wind up with the worst of it.

3.	NORTH	EAST	SOUTH	WEST
	—	—	3 ♡	Pass
	Pass	Double	Pass	Pass
	Pass			

This is the really bad one. If the heart stack is behind you, you will go for a number. That is one of the risks you take when you preempt.

Any other auction figures to be favorable for your side. If partner bids something he does so knowing what you have, so whether he is bidding for a make or a sacrifice you are happy. If the opponents go after their own contract you are also pleased. Not only have you taken away their bidding room making it less likely that they will find the right spot, but you have described your hand to your partner so you can relax while he takes the proper action, which might be anything from punishing the opponents for stepping in at the wrong time to taking a sacrifice against a slam.

In order to determine whether or not to preempt on a given hand, we must see if we have a reasonable chance of landing on our feet if one of the auctions we don't want to hear occurs. There are several factors which determine the likely outcome of a preempt, and they must all be taken into account when deciding whether or not to make a marginal preempt.

First of all, let's look at the model preempt: None vul., South deals and holds: ♠3, ♡KQJ10843, ◇96, ♣982. This is the perfect 3♡ opening bid. South has a very good heart suit, no defense at all, and no possibility of playing anywhere else. Even on the auctions South doesn't want to hear, he figures to come out reasonably well.

Naturally you can't wait until you pick up this hand before you preempt. If you do you are not preempting nearly often enough; consequently, not giving your opponents enough problems. However, every preempt should approximate this hand to some extent. We will examine the factors which load the dice for or against a preempt.

1. Internal trump strength. This is probably the most important factor of all. If you are left playing the contract, that

queen, jack, or ten in the trump suit will often mean the different between making and going down; or if you are doubled between going for that extra undertrick that costs more than the opponents' game. QJ109xxx is a much better suit for preemptive purposes than AQ9xxxx. If the suit breaks terribly you could lose three trump tricks with the second trump suit, but there will be only two trump losers with the first suit.

2. Possession of the ace of trumps. Oddly enough, this is a liability rather than an asset for preemptive purposes. The reason is that card is a big factor on defense. If you wind up playing the hand in your preempt, which is the dangerous situation, the success of your preempt will often be determined by how well pairs at other tables holding your opponents' cards will do if they buy the hand. That ace in your suit might mean ace and a ruff at other tables, which is why it is a liability rather than an asset. You would rather have KQ10xxxx than AQ10xxxx when you preempt.

3. High cards outside your suit. These are definite liabilities. Once again, if you wind up playing the hand you want E-W contracts to be making. That side queen-doubleton, of no value to you for offense, just might be the card that sets E-W contracts at other tables.

4. Possible alternative contracts. If you have support for another suit, it is possible that your side belongs in that suit. Obviously it will be very difficult to get there after you preempt, so this side support is a liability. It is very unfortunate when you are dropped in a preempt, even undoubled, and find yourself in the wrong trump suit. Major suit support is the most dangerous of all. A 3 ♦ opening on ♠x, ♡xx, ♦KQ109xx, ♣xxxx with neither vul. is quite reasonable, but with ♠xxxx, ♡xx, ♦KQ109xx, ♣x it is very risky. There is too great a danger that you belong in spades. Obviously the longer your preempt suit is, the more likely it is to be the best trump suit.

There are other important factors which determine the success of a preempt that have nothing to do with the hand. They are:

1. Vulnerability. This is a very important consideration. The big danger with a preempt is that it will be set for more than the value of an opposing game or part-score. At unfavorable vulnerability this is a distinct possibility since if the opponents double they need only a two trick set to beat their game, so you must toe the line very closely. At favorable vulnerability they need a four trick set and may not be able to tell that it is available even if it is, so you can be very frisky with your preempts. You can be looser with your preempts with none vul., than with both vul. It won't matter if the opponents have a game, but if the hand is a part-score hand you are far more likely to be wrong when you are dropped in your preempt with both vul., than with none vul., for you might go down −200 undoubled. Consequently, the preferred order of vulnerability for preempting is:

      a. Not vul. vs. vul.
      b. None vul.
      c. Both vul.
      d. Vul. vs. not vul.

2. Position. This can have quite a bit of influence on the success or failure of a preempt. If you are in first seat nobody knows anything, so it is anyone's guess. Second seat is a different story. If RHO dealt and passed, there is a greater chance that the hand belongs to your side, as your partner and LHO are equally likely to hold the strong hand. Furthermore, the opponents are less likely to have an accident because they have already exchanged some information—RHO doesn't have an opening bid and his partner knows this. Consequently, the gains from the preempt diminish and the losses increase, so you should toe the line pretty carefully. Third seat is entirely different. Now partner is a passed hand, so if you have a preemptive type of hand you don't have to worry about the hand belonging to your side. LHO is marked with the strong hand, so you can be very frisky with your preempts since it is unlikely that you will be dropped. No longer are you concerned if it goes all pass, for that probably means that you have stolen the contract.

3. Exchange of information. The more information the opponents have had a chance to exchange, the less effective your preempts are likely to be. They will be better placed to penalize you if it is right, and more likely to get to the right contract otherwise. This is a big factor when considering whether or not to make a preemptive jump overcall. If RHO opens 1NT the preempt loses much of its power since he has already described his hand pretty accurately, so a jump overcall had better be pretty sound. A preempt is more effective over a one of a minor opening than over a one of a major opening, because the major suit bid is better defined, usually a five-card suit, while the minor suit opening might be anything. Against a strong and artificial 1♣ opening bid it is open season for preemption. The 1♣ bid says nothing at all about distribution, so the preempt is likely to be most effective. In addition there is now a very high probability that the hand belongs to the opponents, so it is unlikely to go all pass and you probably do not have a bad result if it does.

Let's now look at a few examples and decide whether or not the odds favor a preempt. Keep in mind that preemptive styles vary greatly. A player who tends toward sounder preempts may think the odds are against preempting on a given hand, while a player who favors frequent preempts may think the odds are right for the preempt. Nevertheless, any player considering a preempt should run through the important factors, check out the plusses and minuses, and use these to draw his own conclusions.

None vul., South holds: ♠Q83, ♡AJ109765, ◇7, ♣98

NORTH	EAST	SOUTH	WEST
—	Pass	?	

Fair intermediates in hearts, ace of hearts is bad, outside queen is bad, spade holding for potential support is bad, vulnerability is good, second seat is bad. All in all it looks like too many minuses, so South should pass. I consider myself an aggressive preemptor, but this hand just has too much going against it. Remove one of the minus factors (say make South dealer) and it becomes a marginal preempt. Remove a second minus factor, and the preempt is clear-cut.

Both vul., South holds: ♠6, ♡106, ♢6432, ♣AQJ975

NORTH	EAST	SOUTH	WEST
—	—	?	

The only bad features are the vulnerability (which isn't terrible), the ace of clubs, and six-card suit. I consider it correct to open 3♣. In my opinion, there is more to gain than to lose. If that side four-card suit were spades I would definitely pass, and if it were hearts I would consider it a close decision.

E-W vul., South holds: ♠74, ♡KQ1065, ♢K742, ♣105

NORTH	EAST	SOUTH	WEST
Pass	Pass	?	

This hand has just enough going for it to justify a weak 2♡ bid, despite the five-card suit. The position (third seat) and the vulnerability are perfect, and the suit is reasonable for a five-bagger. The bid could turn out badly, but it will gain more often than not.

E-W vul., South holds: ♠A1087652, ♡8, ♢Q4, ♣K75

NORTH	EAST	SOUTH	WEST
—	—	?	

Despite the good position and vulnerability, this hand should be passed. This is the worst type of suit on which to preempt—the ace and no intermediates. In addition, South has way too much stuff outside. This is the kind of hand on which if you open 3♠ and it goes all pass you just know that you are headed for a bad result even before you see the dummy. On a normal preempt you expect to have a chance even when you are dropped there, but not on this hand.

N-S vul., South holds: ♠2, ♡102, ♢KQ109754, ♣987

NORTH	EAST	SOUTH	WEST
—	Pass	?	

Despite the vulnerability and position, I would chance a 3 ◇ opening. The hand is otherwise absolutely perfect for a preempt. It could go for a number, but often the opponents won't be able to catch you even when you are in trouble. If the hand had so much as one flaw, I would refrain from preempting at this vulnerability in second position.

None vul., South holds: ♠7,   ♡10843,   ◇K2,   ♣AQ10965

NORTH	EAST	SOUTH	WEST
Pass	1 ◇	?	

I would try a 3 ♣ bid despite the marginal trump holding and the outside king of diamonds. Partner is a passed hand, so we don't have to worry about messing his bidding up. If we don't get stuck here the 3 ♣ bid will give the opponents plenty of head-aches. Had the opening bid been 1 ♠ the 3 ♣ bid would be less effective, for it would be more likely that the opponents had already found their trump suit.

Assuming you have chosen to preempt on a hand, the next question is: How high do you go? The old rule of one, two, and three (be at most down one at unfavorable vulnerability, two at equal vulnerability, and three at favorable vulnerability) has long been discarded by winning players as too conservative. If you want to make life difficult for the opponents you have to take some chances yourself.

A better philosophy is: Preempt as high as you dare, given the conditions (vulnerability, strength of suit, etc.). Occasionally you will go for a number, but the damage you do to the op-ponents will more than make up for it. An extra level of pre-emption really does make a big difference. Look at it from the other side:

N-S vul., South holds: ♠87,   ♡AQ,   ◇K96,   ♣AQJ1087

NORTH	EAST	SOUTH	WEST
—	2 ♠*	?	

*weak two-bid

No problem at all. South has a clear-cut 3♣ overall, with a reasonable expectation of getting to the right contract. If notrump is right North will probably bid it, and if North has a long heart suit, making that the right denomination, he can introduce it safely. Furthermore, if North doesn't have anything 3♣ is probably where we belong. However, let's try the same hand on a different bidding sequence:

NORTH	EAST	SOUTH	WEST
—	3 ♠	?	

Not so happy now! South is too strong to pass, a 3NT bid without a spade stopper would be a wild gamble, and a takeout double risks a 4♡ response on an inadequate suit. It looks like South is stuck with a 4♣ overcall as the least of evils, but this is no bargain. 3NT is lost forever, 4♣ might be too high, and partner with short clubs and a long heart suit may be afraid to introduce his suit for fear of a misfit. Whatever South does he is quite likely to wind up in the wrong contract, and may land in a ludicrous one. No question about it; the 3♠ opening bid on this hand is far more effective than the 2♠ opening bid. In keeping with Newton's law of gravitation, it is not unreasonable to say that the accuracy of the opponents' bidding varies inversely with the square of the level of the preempt.

There is, of course, a major drawback to preempting too high. As we have seen, the auctions which we tend to like the least when we preempt are those which leave us playing in the preempt, doubled or not. The higher we preempt, the more likely we are to buy the contract. A weak 2♢ opening bid may not damage the opponents too much, but we are unlikely to get dropped there. A 4♣ opening bid, on the other hand, is quite likely to end the auction. Consequently, we better be happy to play it there. It should be noted that the rank of the preemptor's suit is important when considering how high to go. A 3♠ opening bid is a much "higher" preempt than a 3♣ opening bid even though they are on the same level, because the 3♠ opening bid wipes out the entire three-level while the 3♣ opening leaves the opponents room to play a three-level contract. Therefore, a 3♠ opening bid is more likely to buy the hand than a 3♣ opener, so you must be a bit more prepared to play it there.

A good rule of thumb is: Count the number of cards in your suit, subtract four, and preempt at that level. We can see how this works by looking at some model preempts. In each case South deals, none vul.

♠6, ♡KQJ842, ◇1065, ♣1086.   A model weak 2♡ bid
♠6, ♡KQJ10842, ◇65, ♣1086.   A model 3♡ preempt
♠6, ♡KQJ108432, ◇65, ♣86.   A model 4♡ opening bid.

Naturally this rule shouldn't be followed blindly; it is just a guideline. Other factors such as vulnerability, strength of suit, rank of suit, etc. play an important part when considering how high to go.

E-W vul., South holds: ♠7, ♡83, ◇KQ10975, ♣10975

NORTH	EAST	SOUTH	WEST
—	—	?	

Even if you are playing weak 2 ◇ bids, it would be cowardly not to open 3 ◇ on this hand. A 2 ◇ bid just doesn't do enough damage, and with this hand which is perfect for preempting, South should open 3 ◇ even though he has only a six-card suit. Look at it using the law of total tricks. North's average number of diamonds is two, giving the partnership eight diamonds. If E-W have an eight or nine card major suit fit, as is likely, N-S want to compete to 3 ◇ anyway, so why not bid it now. However, with ♠KQ10975, ♡83, ◇7, ♣10975 I would settle for a weak 2 ♠ bid. The problem with opening 3 ♠ is that it may be too effective. The opponents have no bidding room left at all, so they are quite likely to drop you in 3 ♠. With only a six-card suit, you can't be very confident that this is a good result. If partner has two spades and it is a part-score competitive hand, the law of total tricks indicates that you probably shouldn't be competing to 3 ♠ over their three-level contract. If I were in third seat, however, I would open 3 ♠. There would be so many plus factors that the high preempt would figure to gain most of the time.

Both vul., South holds: ♠AQ1085432, ♡8, ◇92, ♣95

NORTH	EAST	SOUTH	WEST
—	1 ◇	?	

I would bid only 3 ♠ despite having an eight-card suit. The hand is otherwise featureless, and it does contain the ace of spades—a definite liability for a high preempt since you are quite likely to buy it for 4 ♠ doubled if you bid it. The problem with 4 ♠ is that it doesn't give the opponents much choice. They pretty well have to double or pass, and this could easily turn out badly for N-S. A 3 ♠ bid will do plenty of damage, and there is much less risk of being stuck with the contract and being wrong. However, with ♠8, ♡AQ1085432, ◇92, ♣95 I would bid 4 ♡ over 1 ◇. Now the opponents may miss a spade fit or bid 4 ♠ when partner has a spade stack. A mere 3 ♡ call makes it a bit too easy for them to discover their spade fit or lack of it.

RESPONDING TO PREEMPTS

When your partner preempts, you are in complete control of the auction. You know approximately what he has, and can accurately assess both the offensive and defensive potential of the combined hands. Consequently, it is up to you to make the decision for the team. Partner will not bid again. Only in special situations (such as the one-under auctions discussed earlier) will the preemptor even consider taking action, so it is up to you to place the contract.

The most important principle to follow is: Be direct. Decide where and how high you wish to go, and bid it immediately. The opponents can't always tell if you are bidding for a make or an advance save if you go right to game. With E-W vul., the auction:

NORTH	EAST	SOUTH	WEST
2 ♠*	Double	4 ♠	

*weak two-bid

Would be correct with either ♠A92, ♡K9, ◇KQ92, ♣AJ98 or ♠A1086, ♡5, ◇10872, ♣K762 and if the opponents misjudge which hand you have they will be headed for a very bad result, for they will either let you take an undoubled save or go for a telephone number. You don't have to worry about fooling partner, for he has no further say in the proceedings.

It usually does not pay to be tricky with psyches, false no-trump bids, or the wait in the bushes approach opposite a preempt. These tactics usually help the opponents. To see this, consider the following example:

N-S vul., South holds: ♠KQ62, ♡AJ75, ◇3, ♣J1063

NORTH	EAST	SOUTH	WEST
—	—	—	3 ◇
Double	4 NT	?	

Obviously East is fooling around with his 4NT bid, and you

should be grateful to him for doing so. Now you can double, showing strength. When the bidding continues pass-pass-5 ◇ as it almost certainly will, you can now pass. After your double of 4NT this pass is forcing, so partner will place you with some high cards and an offensively oriented hand but no good suit to bid, which is exactly what you have. With this knowledge he has a good chance of making the right decision, whether it be to double, bid five of a major, or bid a slam. However, suppose the bidding had instead gone:

NORTH	EAST	SOUTH	WEST
—	—	—	3 ◇
Double	5 ◇	?	

Suddenly a nice descriptive sequence is no longer available. There is no logical reason why a pass by you would be forcing, for East might be bidding to make and you could hold a yarborough. You are definitely too strong to sell out, so what should you do? A bid of five of a major is a shot in the dark. It could be right, but you have no reason to be confident of making eleven tricks in your best trump suit and, more important, no way to find your best trump suit. Consequently, you are pretty well forced to double. Partner will have to pass on most hands, including many which will produce eleven or twelve tricks in a major, and the penalty against 5 ◇ will probably not be sufficient compensation. This example shows how much easier it is to bid over fool-around bids than over direct no-nonsense bids in this situation.

If you choose to raise partner's preempt, how high should you go? This was discussed in the chapter on the last guess. You should go to the level where you don't know what the correct action for the opponents is. For example:

E-W vul., South holds: ♠93, ♡K543, ◇AJ10, ♣9875

NORTH	EAST	SOUTH	WEST
3 ♡	3 ♠	?	

E-W are almost certainly cold for at least ten tricks in spades.

You could conceivably go for 700 in 5 ♡, but it will be a good save far more often. While there are E-W hands that will produce a slam, the odds seem to be against it; in fact 5 ♠ just might be going down if your side can score one heart trick and two diamond tricks. So what should you do? If you bid 4 ♡ you know it is correct for E-W to bid 4 ♠. They will undoubtedly do so, and you haven't accomplished a thing except to give them a chance to exchange some information to make a later decision easier. If you bid 5 ♡ you don't really know what E-W should be doing. If 5 ♠ is down or if 5 ♡ is −700 they should double, but there is certainly a good chance that 5 ♠ will make and 5 ♡ will cost 500. If you bid 6 ♡ you know that it is correct for E-W to double. 6 ♠ is probably down, and 6 ♡ could easily be set four tricks. Consequently, it is correct to bid 5 ♡. Since you don't know what they should do neither will they, so their next bid will be the last guess which is what you want.

None vul., South holds: ♠A103, ♡K54, ◇Q54, ♣K763

NORTH	EAST	SOUTH	WEST
2 ♡*	Double	?	

*weak two-bid

Bid 3 ♡. Not only is this bid indicated by total tricks, but it puts the most pressure on the opponents without sticking your neck out too far. You don't know whether you are rooting for them to bid, pass, or double, so how can they know what to do. If you bid 4 ♡ it is too easy for them just to say double for lack of anything better to do, and you probably won't like it. Conversely, if you pass the opponents will probably subside in 2 ♠ or three of a minor. Now you will be compelled either to sell out, which is probably wrong on trick total, or to bid 3 ♡ after the opponents have exchanged more information and increased the risk of a double.

There is one type of hand on which a wait and see approach is correct. If you know that you have a good sacrifice at any level, it may be a good idea to let the opponents bid to what they think they can make unimpeded, and then save over that. For example:

E-W vul., South holds: ♠K954, ♡A, ◇975432, ♣96

NORTH	EAST	SOUTH	WEST
—	—	—	1 ♡
3 ♠	4 ♣	?	

You figure to be safe at the five-level, if necessary. The problem with bidding any number of spades at this point is that the opponents just might bash into a slam. Then what would you do? If you save you might find that the slam is off two cashing aces, while if you don't save the slam could well be cold. You will have to make the last guess, which is what you are trying to avoid. Your best bet is to pass and let the opponents find out what they can make in peace. They will not leap to a slam trying to stampede you into a save, for they have no way to know that you have any interest in saving. Consequently they will bid the hand as accurately as they can, so you can trust their bidding and eventually take a save over whatever contract they reach.

PENALTY DOUBLES

The hand clearly belongs to the opponents and they have arrived in their contract, but you have reason to believe they will go down. Should you double? This is often a very difficult problem. There is more involved than just the probability of setting the contract, although that is obviously the number one consideration. As always, we are concerned about the potential matchpoint gain if the double is successful vs. the potential matchpoint loss if it fails.

The double can affect the probability of the contract's success. The contract may be more likely to make because of the double, more likely to go down because of the double, or the double might not make any difference.

N-S vul., South holds: ♠953, ♡A875, ◇—, ♣987653

NORTH	EAST	SOUTH	WEST
—	—	—	1 ♠
Pass	3 ♠*	Pass	4 NT
Pass	5 ♡	Pass	6 ♠
Pass	Pass	?	

*lmit raise

If South doubles, it is a Lightner double calling for an unusual lead. On this auction the double should show a void, so North will lead his longest side suit. That suit is likely to be diamonds, so the double improves South's chances of beating the contract.

E-W vul., South holds: ♠QJ109, ♡982, ◇A8, ♣5432

NORTH	EAST	SOUTH	WEST
—	1 ♠	Pass	2 ♠
Pass	4 ♠	?	

A double by South will not affect the chances of 4 ♠ making. If partner has a trick it will go down; if not, it will make.

None vul., South holds: ♠72, ♡QJ97, ◇52, ♣Q9753

NORTH	EAST	SOUTH	WEST
—	1 ♡	Pass	3 ◇
Pass	3 ♡	Pass	4 ♡
Pass	6 ♡	?	

On this hand, a double could improve the chances of the contract making. Without the double declarer would undoubtedly lose two trump tricks. If South doubles, however, declarer will know about the heart stack, and if he can now play the hearts so as to lose only one trick he will make an otherwise unmakeable contract.

There is another way for a double to affect the outcome. If the opponents have a possible alternative contract the double may warn them of a bad trump split and drive them to the other contract. For example:

Both vul., South holds: ♠62, ♡J10985, ◇Q98, ♣642

NORTH	EAST	SOUTH	WEST
—	—	—	2 NT
Pass	3 ◇*	Pass	3 ♡
Pass	4 NT	Pass	6 ♡
Pass	Pass	?	

*transfer

South can certainly defeat 6♡, but it is possible that 6NT will make. South must take into account both the probability of 6NT making and the likelihood of the opponents running to 6NT when he considers doubling.

It is also possible for a speculative double to drive the opponents to a worse contract. For example:

Both vul., South holds: ♠QJ103, ♡65, ◇A73, ♣KJ42

NORTH	EAST	SOUTH	WEST
—	1 ♡	Pass	1 ♠
Pass	2 ♠	Pass	3 ♡
Pass	4 ♡	?	

If South chooses to double 4♡, E-W may think that it is the hearts which are breaking badly and run to 4♠, which South would enjoy.

If you are considering doubling a voluntarily bid game or slam, it is important to determine if the contract is likely to be reached at other tables. If the contract figures to be a normal one, then you have even-money odds on your double—you simply gain one-half matchpoint from every other table if you are right and lose one-half matchpoint to every other table if you are wrong. Consequently, all that is needed is that you be a favorite to defeat the contract after the double. This means that you can risk helping declarer play the hand if the contract is still more likely than not to go down after declarer has this help.

None vul., South holds: ♠A6, ♡Q108, ◇10963, ♣9764

NORTH	EAST	SOUTH	WEST
—	1 ♡	Pass	3 ♡*
Pass	4 NT	Pass	5 ◇
Pass	6 ♡	?	

*limit raise

Should South double? If he doesn't double he is almost sure to defeat the slam; declarer probably won't pick up the trump suit even if he can. If South does double, however, he will tell declarer how to make the contract if dummy has AJxx or KJxx in trumps. Declarer is more likely to have the trump strength, so the slam will still go down more often than not. Let's suppose that the slam will go down all the time if not doubled, 70% of the time if doubled. On this strong auction, it seems clear that the slam is easy to bid and the field will be there. Assume that the slam isn't doubled at other tables. If you don't double, you will get an average for +50. If you double, 70% of the time you get a top for +100, and 30% of the time you get a bottom for −1210. Double is obviously the percentage action, even though it may get you a very bad board. When this hand came up, the slam was bid at twelve out of thirteen tables. The two enterprising players who doubled collected +100 and 11½ matchpoints on a 12 top, while the remaining ten who didn't double had to settle for 5½ matchpoints, not realizing that they had passed up a golden opportunity.

If the contract may not be reached at other tables, the odds on information giving doubles change radically. On the previous hand, suppose the auction had instead been:

NORTH	EAST	SOUTH	WEST
—	1 ♡	Pass	3 ♡*
Pass	4 ♣	Pass	4 ◇
Pass	4 ♡	Pass	5 ♣
Pass	5 ◇	Pass	5 ♡
Pass	6 ♡	?	

*limit raise

They finally got there, but what a struggle! Since each opponent signed off at some point in the auction, this is a marginal slam at best. It seems reasonable to assume that at least half the other pairs won't bid the slam. Let's look at the matchpoint cost analysis of the double under this new assumption. If we double and are right (i.e. we beat the slam anyway), the double gains one-half matchpoint from other tables in the slam. It gains nothing against tables in game, for they were beaten regardless. If we double and are wrong (i.e. the double tells declarer how to make the slam which he otherwise would not have done), we lose one-half matchpoint to other tables in slam. In addition, we now lose a full matchpoint to other tables in game, for we would have beaten them had we kept quiet. Consequently, if we assume that half the field will bid the slam we must set them at least 75% of the time for the double to be correct, because the double gives up three to one matchpoint odds. Not doubling gets us nine on a twelve top, while doubling gets us either a zero or a twelve, so we are risking nine matchpoints to gain three.

Under these assumptions, the double is no longer a percentage bid. It should be noted that the double would be a terrible bid at IMPs or rubber bridge regardless of the auction. When it is right it gains 50 points or two IMPs, but when it is wrong it costs 1260 points (from +50 to −1210) for a fifteen IMP loss. At matchpoints this type of double can be quite correct since frequency rather than size of the swing is what matters.

If the opponents are in a normal contract, it is necessary to be a favorite to defeat them before you double. Even if the double improves the defense's chances, it is not a good double unless those defensive chances go over the 50% mark.

None vul., South holds: ♠72, ♡AQ1098, ♢732, ♣K72

NORTH	EAST	SOUTH	WEST
—	—	—	1 ♣
Pass	1 ♡	Pass	1 NT
Pass	3 NT	?	

South obviously wants a heart lead, and there doesn't appear to be much hope for the defense without one. Unfortunately, South has no reason to be confident that a heart lead will set the contract, although it will certainly improve the chances of a set. The auction is strong, 3NT is probably an easy contract to bid, and it will be reached at just about every table. If South doubles he gains one-half matchpoint from every table if he is right, and loses one-half matchpoint to every table if he is wrong, so it's a fifty-fifty proposition. Since South can't expect to be a favorite to defeat 3NT even with the heart lead, the double is incorrect. Note that at IMPs the double would be much better, for it loses 150 points or four IMPs (−400 to −550) when wrong, but gains 500 points or eleven IMPs (−400 to +100) when right. These figures have to be shaded due to the possibility of a redouble and/or overtricks, but the odds on the double are still much better than at matchpoints.

Make the auction on the last hand a bit slower:

NORTH	EAST	SOUTH	WEST
—	—	—	1 ♣
Pass	1 ♡	Pass	1 NT
Pass	2 NT	Pass	3 NT
Pass	Pass	?	

Now the odds on the double are much better. In the first place, the opponents do not have excess strength since East only invited, so the chances of beating the contract are better than before. More important from a matchpoint angle, E-W may have stretched to a thin game which will not be bid at some tables. If South doubles and is wrong he loses one-half matchpoint only to those tables in game, as the hand was already lost to those not in game. If South doubles and is right (the heart lead is necessary to defeat 3NT), he gains one-half matchpoint from other tables in game and also gains one full matchpoint from each table not in game. In this case if the double improves South's chances of beating the contract by 25 or 30% the double is correct, even if South is still a slight underdog to defeat 3NT.

If the opponents have more than one possible game or slam contract available, it is important to decide if there are other higher scoring contracts. You will get a bottom regardless if you double and are wrong, but the double will not be too costly if the opponents are in their highest scoring contract, for you will lose one-half matchpoint only to other tables in the same contract. As an extreme example, suppose you double 7NT. This is a top scoring contract, so you only gain or lose one-half matchpoint against other tables in 7NT; therefore it is an even money proposition assuming the double will not affect the play. However if you double 7 ♠ there is more to lose when wrong. If both 7 ♠ and 7NT make you lose a full matchpoint to other tables in 7NT as well as the half matchpoint to tables in 7 ♠. This is because 7 ♠ is not a top scoring contract. A more practical example:

E-W vul., South holds: ♠A6542, ♡9753, ◇KQ10, ♣9

NORTH	EAST	SOUTH	WEST
—	—	—	1 ♠
3 ♣*	3 ◇	Pass	4 ◇
Pass	5 ◇	?	

*preemptive

South is certainly a favorite to defeat 5 ◇. He has excellent chances of socring one spade trick and two diamond tricks, and even if one of these tricks evaporates partner may produce a trick. Nevertheless, South should refrain from doubling. Either E-W have gone completely off the walls, in which case it won't matter much what South does since an undoubled penalty will defeat N-S scores at other tables, or E-W have most of the outstanding high card strength. If the latter is the case, it would be hard to imagine E-W not having a good play for nine or ten tricks at notrump, which is likely to be a more popular contract than 5 ◇. Consequently, it would be very costly to double, be wrong, and lose a full matchpoint to every −630. This is one double which has far more to lose than to gain.

Both vul., South holds: ♠K6, ♡QJ109, ◇KJ8, ♣7652

NORTH	EAST	SOUTH	WEST
—	1 ◇	Pass	1 ♡
Pass	1 NT	Pass	2 ♣*
Pass	2 ♡	Pass	2 ♠
Pass	2 NT	Pass	3 ♡
Pass	4 ♡	?	

*forcing

Normally this is a good situation for doubling a voluntarily bid game. The opponents staggered into game, they are getting a bad trump split, and South's kings lie over the opening bidder. While 4 ♡ is a favorite to go down in my opinion, a double is still not recommended. The reason is that the opponents have an alternative possible contract, 3NT, which may be found at other tables, and it is probably a higher scoring contract on this hand. It would be a matchpoint catastrophe to double 4 ♡, have them make it for −790, and then find you could have had a very good board by passing because the field was in 3NT making four. If the auction had instead gone:

NORTH	EAST	SOUTH	WEST
—	1 ◊	Pass	1 ♡
Pass	2 ♡	Pass	3 ♡
Pass	4 ♡	?	

The double would be substantially better. The chances of beating 4 ♡ are about the same, but the cost of being wrong by doubling has decreased. If E-W had a reasonable auction it is clear that the field will be in hearts, so if you think they are more likely than not to go down you should double. It should be noted that it does not matter what percentage of the field bids the game on this hand, for the double will not affect the comparison with tables not in game. The double simply gains one-half matchpoint from other tables in 4 ♡ if right, and loses one-half matchpoint to them if wrong. If the double might help declarer in the play this analysis wouldn't be so simple as we have seen, but on this hand declarer can do nothing about the bad heart split so the double is unlikely to affect his chances of making 4 ♡.

Conversely, if the opponents are in a top-scoring contract, a double may be correct even if they are slight favorites to make. The reason is that you get a very bad board if they make it anyway, so you might as well assume that they are going down and collect as big a number as possible. This type of double should only be made when you have reason to believe that the alternative contract will also go down; otherwise the double doesn't stand to gain when it is right.

Both vul., South holds: ♠QJ92, ♡A8, ◇962, ♣K732

NORTH	EAST	SOUTH	WEST
—	1 NT	Pass	2 ♣
Pass	2 ♠	Pass	3 ♠
Pass	3 NT	?	

Just your luck! The opponents looked like they were headed for 4♠, and all of a sudden they stopped off in 3NT. This is very likely to be the best scoring contract if it makes, as it is hard to imagine spades taking one more trick than notrump considering your spade holding. In addition 4♠ is quite likely to go down, for you are looking at at least three tricks and partner is marked with about five or six points by West's non-forcing 3♠ call. Consequently, you figure to lose to other tables in 4♠ or in a part-score if 3NT makes, and the double if wrong will cost one-half matchpoint to only those few pairs who also reject the four-four spade fit. Now let's look at the bright side. Suppose the double is right; 3NT is going down. If this is the case you will gain at least one-half matchpoint from all other tables in game, whether it be 3NT or 4♠. 4♠ contracts will probably escape un-doubled because defenders won't risk telling declarer about the spade stack. As an added bonus, the double might scare some unsophisticated players back into 4♠, which you would love. Since this double has so much more to gain than to lose, I think it is correct, even though I rate 3NT a slight favorite to make on the given information.

On occasion, your opponents will have a seemingly absurd auction or land in a contract that appears ridiculously high from looking at your hand. Should you double? Many people say no. Their reasoning is: If the contract is that absurd nobody else will be there, so the double has nothing to gain. This appears to make sense, but the argument can be put the other way: If nobody else is there the double has nothing to lose, so why not double? The important question is: What makes the contract absurd? If you conclude that if they are going down then nobody else will be there while if they are making they will have some company, then it is correct to refrain from doubling. For example:

E-W vul., South holds: ♠9542, ♡A8, ♢A84, ♣8764

NORTH	EAST	SOUTH	WEST
—	—	—	1 ♣
2 ♢	2 ♡	5 ♢	6 ♡
Pass	Pass	?	

South's 5 ♢ call was quite enterprising, but it certainly seems to have paid off. West was deprived of room to investigate slam possibilities, so he bashed into a slam which is probably off two cashing aces. The question is: Should South rub salt into the wound with a double? Either the ace of diamonds cashes or it doesn't, so the play will not be affected by a double. What about other tables? They are not likely to face such fierce competition, and so they should be able to find out if they are off two cashing aces and stop short of slam. Therefore if the ace of diamonds cashes doubling won't gain anything because nobody else will be in slam. However, if the ace of diamonds doesn't cash there may well be some other pairs finding their way to slam on this hand. The double can never gain anything if it is right, but it will cost one-half matchpoint to other pairs in slam if it is wrong. Consequently, South should pass, even though 6 ♡ is a big favorite to go down.

Don't get into the habit of not doubling when you think the opponents have gone crazy. If they got so high it may be a trouble hand, and others may have problems also. If this is the case, it is important to collect as big a number as you possibly can. Keep in mind that if the opponents land in a crazy contract and make it your double will only make your zero a little rounder. Be sure that they don't have a likely runout that can make and that there is no great risk of your double telling them how to make the hand, but for the most part it is quite correct to double what is under your nose.

N-S vul., South holds: ♠ 10942, ♡ AQ102, ◇ K4, ♣ 652

NORTH	EAST	SOUTH	WEST
—	—	—	1 ♡
Pass	2 ◇	Pass	3 ♡
Pass	4 NT	Pass	5 ◇
Pass	6 ♡	?	

Double away. Sure, they might make it if East has three hearts and enough entries to take three heart finesses and doesn't have a diamond loser, but all this is extremely unlikely. It is important to double, for many pairs holding the E-W cards will be going minus due to the bad heart split, and you must collect as big a number as possible.

Both vul., South holds: ♠ A8, ♡ 73, ◇ KQJ6, ♣ J10432

NORTH	EAST	SOUTH	WEST
—	—	—	1 ♡
Pass	1 ♠	Pass	3 ♡
Pass	4 NT	Pass	5 ♡
Pass	6 NT	?	

What are you doing with all these cards? Don't worry about it—just double and lead the king of diamonds. If you are an extremely unlucky bridge player, the full hand will be:

```
                    NORTH
                    ♠ J 5 4 2
                    ♡ 9 6 5
                    ◊ 9 8 4 3
                    ♣ 9 6
    WEST                        EAST
    ♠ 10 7                      ♠ K Q 9 6 3
    ♡ A K Q J 10 8 4            ♡ 2
    ◊ 10 2                      ◊ A 7 5
    ♣ A 5                       ♣ K Q 8 7
                    SOUTH
                    ♠ A 8
                    ♡ 7 3
                    ◊ K Q J 6
                    ♣ J 10 4 3 2
```

East wins the opening diamond lead and runs his hearts, keeping KQxx of clubs and a spade honor. You are squeezed in three
suits, and must give declarer his twelfth trick. Unlucky, but
don't blame the double—blame West for holding seven hearts
and the ten of diamonds, or East for holding a four-card club
suit, or perhaps the gods of bridge for dealing you this hand in
the first place. On this hand 6NT will make whether you double
or not, so the cost of doubling is relatively small since the opponents are certainly in the top scoring contract. It is far more
likely that 6NT will go down, so you must collect the most you
can to guard against all the other E-W pairs who may be finding
their way into trouble.

If partner doubles the opponents at a game contract, it is
almost never right to pull unless you think you have some
chance of making what you bid. Even if you have stretched considerably for a previous bid and he may be basing his double
partly on values you have shown and don't have, you are better
off passing and taking your lumps. The only exception occurs
when you were planning on taking a sacrifice and he doubled
before you had a chance to save. Even then, think twice before
pulling. It is just possible that partner knows what he is doing.
If you were not planning on taking a sacrifice then the reason
must be that the save figures to go down too much, and this

estimate hasn't been changed by partner's double. Avoid traps such as the following:

E-W vul., South holds: ♠QJ1095, ♡6, ◇K83, ♣J954

NORTH	EAST	SOUTH	WEST
—	1 ♣	1 ♠	2 ♡
2 ♠	3 ♡	Pass	4 ♡
Double	Pass	?	

Many players will make the mistake of bidding 4 ♠ here. They would not have taken the save if partner hadn't doubled simply because 4 ♠ is too likely to be − 700. Once partner doubles, they say to themselves "I don't have the values for my overcall and partner had only a 2 ♠ bid, so how can we beat them? I must pull to protect partner, who is playing me for more than I have." This is faulty reasoning. Perhaps South should have passed or made a weak jump overcall rather than overcalling 1 ♠, but that is water over the dam. If South felt that 4 ♠ would be set four tricks before the double, prospects are even worse now that partner presumably has values in hearts. Bidding 4 ♠ even if it is "right" (i.e. − 700 instead of − 790) won't salvage many matchpoints, but if 4 ♡ happens to be going down the 4 ♠ bid will be a complete top to bottom swing. Partner is allowed to know what he is doing. The full hand:

```
                    NORTH
                    ♠ K 8 3
                    ♡ K Q 10
                    ◇ 10 9 7 2
                    ♣ 10 3 2
    WEST                          EAST
    ♠ A 2                         ♠ 7 6 4
    ♡ A 9 7 4 2                   ♡ J 8 5 3
    ◇ J 5 4                       ◇ A Q 6
    ♣ K 8 7                       ♣ A Q 6
                    SOUTH
                    ♠ Q J 10 9 5
                    ♡ 6
                    ◇ K 8 3
                    ♣ J 9 5 4
```

As you can see, everybody has their bids except South, and 4 ♡
is a normal contract. Partner was simply betting that 4 ♡ would
go down, and he was right. If you bid 4 ♠ you will be −700
against a game that isn't making—not a very impressive result.
To make matters worse you would probably have had a top, for
not many will be doubling 4 ♡. This sort of error is one of the
most costly mistakes one can make at matchpoints.

SACRIFICE BIDDING

The goal on most bridge hands is to achieve the greatest possible plus score. There are, however, some hands on which a plus score is very unlikely. On these hands the goal may change to getting the smallest possible minus score. One way to do this can be to take a successful sacrifice against the enemy game or slam.

Sacrifices are very dangerous bids to make. For a sacrifice to be successful, three conditions must be met:

1. The enemy contract must make.
2. The sacrifice must not be too expensive.
3. The field must get to the game or slam against which you are sacrificing.

This is quite a parlay. All through this book we have been searching for bids that have more than one way to win, and a sacrifice has three ways to lose! If any part of the parlay fails your sacrifice will net a very poor matchpoint score, although the cost of being wrong may vary. If the field fails to get to the contract your sacrifice costs nothing (if anything it gains a bit), but you remain with a poor matchpoint score and lose out on any possible chance of declarer going down in his contract. If the sacrifice is too expensive you lose one-half matchpoint to every other table, assuming you would have tied the normal result of game bid and made had you not saved. The most serious error occurs when the enemy contract isn't making, which means you have taken a phantom sacrifice. This not only costs one-half matchpoint to other tables at which the same contract is reached, but also a full matchpoint to those tables where the pairs holding your opponents' cards stop short of game. To put it another way, you turn a well above average score into a bottom.

There is a good general rule about sacrifices that will avoid the parlay problem. You should never sacrifice unless you are virtually 100% sure of two of the three necessary conditions. In other words, if you think (but are not sure) that the enemy contract will make and you think (but are not sure) that your save will not be too expensive, then you should not take a sacrifice. The problem is that the conditions are not necessarily independent. The onside finesse that allows the opponents to make their contract just might be the offside finesse that defeats your save one trick too many.

None vul., South holds: ♠A843, ♡43, ♢QJ98, ♣KQ9

NORTH	EAST	SOUTH	WEST
—	—	—	1 ♡
2 ♠*	4 ♡	?	

*preemptive

Should South save? It is probable that 4 ♡ is making, but by no means certain. It would not be unreasonable to score one spade, one diamond, and two clubs on defense. It is also probable that N-S can score eight tricks in spades, but this is also nowhere near certain. N-S could easily lose two tricks in each side suit if North doesn't have a singleton. South can't even be all that sure that the game will be bid at all the other tables, but this isn't quite so important—on a distributional fitting hand you can assume that other tables will get to game even without twenty-six high card points. A look at all four hands shows the dangers involved in taking a sacrifice which bets on a parlay.

```
                    NORTH
                    ♠ K Q J 7 5 2
                    ♡ 9 5
                    ◇ 10 6
                    ♣ 10 4 2
      WEST                        EAST
      ♠ 10 9                      ♠ 6
      ♡ A Q 10 8 6                ♡ K J 7 2
      ◇ K 7 3                     ◇ A 5 4 2
      ♣ A J 5                     ♣ 8 7 6 3
                    SOUTH
                    ♠ A 8 4 3
                    ♡ 4 3
                    ◇ Q J 9 8
                    ♣ K Q 9
```

4♡ makes, but 4♠ goes down three for −500 if the defenders attack clubs in time, which shouldn't be too hard. Suppose the E-W minor suit aces were interchanged. Now 4♠ goes down two, but 4♡ also may go down.

A slight change in the hand or the conditions would make the sacrifice a reasonable bid. If N-S were at favorable vulnerability or if South were a bit more distributional, say ♠A843, ♡4, ◇QJ983, ♣KQ9 South could be quite confident that 4♠ would not be too expensive a save, although 4♡ still might go down. Take away South's diamond holding leaving him: ♠A843, ♡43, ◇9842, ♣KQ9 and now South can be virtually sure that the 4♠ sacrifice won't be a phantom, even though it might be too expensive. The idea is to have all but one of the conditions nailed down tight. Then you can examine the one condition in question, and if you think the odds are right go ahead and save.

Sacrificing against slams is a very tricky proposition. Usually the save won't be too expensive, or you wouldn't be thinking about saving in the first place. The big problem is that many other pairs may not bid the slam, so that even if the save is a success you won't get many matchpoints. If there is any kind of chance that the slam can be beaten it is better to defend unless you are quite sure that the field will bid the slam. Incidentally, potential slam sacrifices are often an exception to the double or save principle. You don't double because you think slam is a favorite to make. However, you don't save even though you think the save will be right more often than not because the gain when the save is right is small if most of the field doesn't bid the slam, while the cost of saving if the slam is going down is huge.

Many players will take a marginal save against a slam if they think their save will go down less than the value of an enemy game. This approach has some validity for the save now has a second way to win—some pairs may sell out to the game. However, in a good field this is a losing approach. The danger is that other pairs holding your cards may buy the contract one level lower, in which case the save gains nothing when it is right (since you will go for an extra trick) but loses a full matchpoint to these pairs when it is wrong.

E-W vul., South holds: ♠108763, ♡9, ◇QJ32, ♣A97

NORTH	EAST	SOUTH	WEST
—	—	—	1 ♡
3 ♠	4 ♡	4 ♠	6 ♡
Pass	Pass	?	

South has reasonable defensive prospects against the slam. North might have a singleton club, or E-W may have a third round diamond loser which can't be disposed of. Some players will take the save anyway, figuring that there might be nine tricks available in spades so the save would go down − 500, less than the value of game. However, had the auction gone:

NORTH	EAST	SOUTH	WEST
—	—	—	1 ♡
3 ♠	4 ♡	4 ♠	5 ♡
Pass	Pass	?	

These same players will pass even though they know they almost certainly have a good save available at 5 ♠. Their reasoning would be that they don't want to push the opponents to slam. Personally, I think this is exactly backward. South should take the 5 ♠ save which he knows is correct, but if the opponents bid

284

$6 \heartsuit$ South should take his chances on defense. The $6 \spadesuit$ save just has too many ways to lose, particularly since South has good defensive prospects against $6 \heartsuit$. The slam might go down, other N-S pairs may buy the hand for $5 \spadesuit$ doubled, and the $6 \spadesuit$ save might still be -700. The $5 \spadesuit$ save on the other hand is a definite improvement over defending $5 \heartsuit$, and if it pushes the opponents to slam, which probably won't happen, they haven't made it yet.

There are some added bonuses which can make sacrificing more profitable. They are:

1. The opponents might take the push and bid one more. You know you have done well with your sacrifice when this happens, for you now have a free shot at a plus score. This is another reason why the most important consideration when pondering a sacrifice is whether or not it is a phantom. If you are absolutely sure that the opponents are making, it may be worth risking a save being too expensive if you think there is a chance of pushing them higher.

E-W vul., South holds: $\spadesuit 103$, $\heartsuit KJ108$, $\diamondsuit A43$, $\clubsuit 8753$

NORTH	EAST	SOUTH	WEST
—	—	—	1 $\spadesuit$
3 $\diamondsuit$*	4 $\spadesuit$	?	

*preemptive

South cannot be sure of making eight tricks in diamonds. It looks as though $4 \spadesuit$ is cold, South may have some chance against $5 \spadesuit$, and he will welcome a $6 \spadesuit$ bid. Consequently, $5 \diamondsuit$ is a reasonable call. If South were sure that $5 \diamondsuit$ would be doubled he might not bid it, for it could easily go for -700 if partner has the wrong hand. However, the extra way to win—the opponents take the push to $5 \spadesuit$ and go down—makes the $5 \diamondsuit$ sacrifice a worthwhile gamble.

2. The opponents may not double. It can happen that you know you are taking a sacrifice, but E-W don't know enough about the hand to be sure of this. If this is the case, you may

escape undoubled for a very good board.

E-W vul., South holds: ♠QJ4, ♡86, ◇KQ32, ♣QJ82

NORTH	EAST	SOUTH	WEST
2 ♠*	3 ♡	?	

*weak two-bid

4♠ will certainly be a good save against 4♡, but it is not clear that 4♡ will make. South could try to buy the hand for 3♠, but this may goad West into a marginal 4♡ call and then South would have no idea what to do. A better idea is to bid 4♠ at once. South knows that he is taking a save, but E-W may not know this. If neither of them has extra strength it will be very difficult for them to double, for South could easily be bidding to make. The full hand:

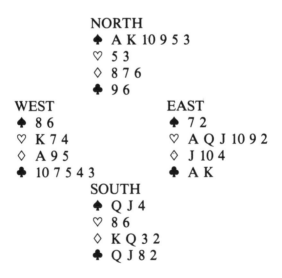

NORTH
♠ A K 10 9 5 3
♡ 5 3
◇ 8 7 6
♣ 9 6

WEST
♠ 8 6
♡ K 7 4
◇ A 9 5
♣ 10 7 5 4 3

EAST
♠ 7 2
♡ A Q J 10 9 2
◇ J 10 4
♣ A K

SOUTH
♠ Q J 4
♡ 8 6
◇ K Q 3 2
♣ Q J 8 2

If South passes West might or might not bid game, while if South bids 3♠ West will be more inclined to try 4♡. It turns out that 4♡ makes because of West's nine of diamonds, and 4♠ goes down three because of that same card. However, if South jumps to 4♠ it is very hard for either East or West to double, for they have no reason to think that South isn't bidding to make. If South slips it by 4♠ undoubled will be −150, which even beats those defending a heart partial for −170.

3. The save might make. This, of course is the best kind of sacrifice to take. The extra way to win, the possibility of making, radically improves the odds on the sacrifice. For example:

None vul., South holds: ♠AJ6, ♡K2, ◇J1087, ♣KQ82

NORTH	EAST	SOUTH	WEST
3 ♠	4 ♡	?	

South has pretty good defensive prospects against 4♡, so the save is not at all clear. If South chooses not to save, he should of course double, for this is a perfect double or save situation. The deciding factor in favor of the save is that 4♠ just could be a make if North has a singleton diamond. This possibility, coupled with the chance that 4♡ makes and 4♠ is a good save, tips the balance in favor of the 4♠ call. If South's save had no chance to make, then it would be better to defend.

These factors can give extra incentive toward sacrificing. However, most of the time your sacrifice will simply be doubled and you will get a minus score. A successful sacrifice usually nets only a slightly above average matchpoint score, while an unsuccessful one virtually always gets a bottom. The dice are loaded against the saver, because he is betting on a parlay. Consequently it is generally best to avoid marginal sacrifices; stick to those which are clearly correct. A bad sacrifice, particularly if it is a phantom, is one of the most costly bids at matchpoints. The saver voluntarily takes the last guess upon himself, so he better be right.

REVIEW PROBLEMS

1. None vul., South holds: ♠K, ♡QJ10983, ◊754, ♣AKJ

NORTH	EAST	SOUTH	WEST
—	—	—	1 ♠
Pass	2 ◊	?	

2. None vul., South holds: ♠3, ♡63, ◊A732, ♣KQ10432

NORTH	EAST	SOUTH	WEST
Pass	1 ◊	?	

3. E-W vul., South holds: ♠KQ109432, ♡J87, ◊752, ♣—

NORTH	EAST	SOUTH	WEST
—	—	—	1 ♡
Pass	2 ♣	3 ♠	4 NT
Pass	5 ♡	Pass	5 NT
Pass	6 ◊	Pass	6 ♡
Pass	Pass	?	

4. E-W vul., South holds: ♠4, ♡K96, ◊AQ10532, ♣Q105

NORTH	EAST	SOUTH	WEST
—	1 ♠	2 ◊	2 ♠
3 ◊	4 ♠	?	

5. N-S vul., South holds: ♠KQ9, ♡J10753, ◊A, ♣AQ52

NORTH	EAST	SOUTH	WEST
—	1 ◊	?	

6. E-W vul., South holds: ♠2, ♡95, ◊KJ9532, ♣A763

NORTH	EAST	SOUTH	WEST
3 ♣	3 ♠	?	

7. Both vul., South holds: ♠62, ♡5, ◇K98, ♣AQ109643

NORTH	EAST	SOUTH	WEST
—	—	—	1 ◇
Pass	1 NT	?	

8. N-S vul., South holds: ♠102, ♡J954, ◇32, ♣AKQJ7

NORTH	EAST	SOUTH	WEST
—	—	—	1 ◇
Pass	2 ◇*	Pass	2 ♠
Pass	2 NT	Pass	3 NT
Pass	Pass	?	

*10+ points

9. N-S vul., South holds: ♠AQJ965, ♡7, ◇KJ2, ♣QJ6

NORTH	EAST	SOUTH	WEST
—	—	1 ♠	2 ♡
2 ♠	4 ♡	?	

10. N-S vul., South holds: ♠KJ85, ♡A74, ◇A5, ♣8642

NORTH	EAST	SOUTH	WEST
—	1 ♠	Pass	2 ♠
Pass	4 ♠	?	

SOLUTIONS

1. Pass. A 2 ♡ overcall is safe enough, but what does it accomplish? No space is consumed, N-S are unlikely to buy the contract, and South is not interested in a sacrifice. As for lead-direction the overcall has negative value, for South wants a club lead against a spade contract.

2. 3 ♣. With partner a passed hand and none vul., this preempt is worth the gamble. It could go for a number, of course, but if E-W have to search for their best contract the difference in space consumption between 2 ♣ and 3 ♣ is enormous. A 2 ♣ overcall may be no more than a mild annoyance, while the 3 ♣ bid will make accurate exploration very difficult for the opponents.

3. Pass. This is not the time for a Lightner double. The opponents may well have a successful runout to 6NT. Even if they stay in 6 ♡ South can't be sure of beating the slam with a club lead. If the slam still makes after the ruff and the same number of tricks were available in notrump, then the double becomes very costly, because the opponents are not in the top-scoring contract. Lastly, South can't even be positive that he wants a club lead (imagine North with Qx of hearts, short spades, and a natural club trick, for example).

4. Pass. South probably can take eight tricks in diamonds, and E-W probably can make 4 ♠, but South is far from certain about either of these conditions. There are unlikely to be any of the bonus factors for saving (5 ◇ can't be making and E-W will almost certainly double), so the sacrifice doesn't figure to be the percentage bid.

5. 1 ♡. This will make future bidding easier than if South starts with a takeout double. If the opponents are in 3 ◇ by the time it comes around to South, as they often will be, South will be better placed after having overcalled as he can then double and keep all his options open. Interestingly enough, if we take

away one of South's aces the double becomes a better bid. South is only planning to take one bid on the hand, and with a weak heart suit and good support for all other suits the double is more descriptive.

6. 6♣. E-W can certainly make at least 5♠, and it is hard to imagine that South can buy the hand for 5♣. Furthermore N-S can probably take nine tricks in clubs, so 6♣ figures to be a good save. South doesn't know what E-W should do over 6♣, so he should bid it planning to sell out if E-W bid the slam. This approach will make the E-W slam decision most difficult. In addition, if E-W happen to have enough distribution to make a grand then this 6♣ bid makes it virtually impossible for them to get there.

7. 2♣. There just is no good reason to preempt. East has described his hand and E-W have already determined that they don't have a major suit fit, so the preempt accomplishes little and risks going for a number. The 2♣ overcall probably won't do much good in the auction, but it's pretty safe and will get partner off to the right lead if West declares a diamond partial, as is likely.

8. Pass. South knows that E-W have a runout, and East is likely to diagnose the weakness and run to 4♢ if South doubles. The opponents have apparently bid a marginal game from the wrong side, so South should take his profit. However if South weren't on lead (say West had rebid 2NT), then the double would be correct. The odds shift completely. While E-W might still run, the double which alerts North to make an unusual lead greatly increases South's chances of defeating the contract.

9. 4♠. It looks like a pretty marginal sacrifice. South has plenty of defense so he can't be sure that 4♡ is making, and 4♠ could easily go down two if things lie badly. Nevertheless, 4♠ is the percentage bid because it has all the plus factors in its favor. First of all, it is not out of the question that 4♠ will make. Secondly, even if 4♠ is going down E-W may not be sure of this and may fail to double or better yet take a 5♡ save themselves.

There are so many ways for the 4 ♠ bid to work out well that it must be made.

10. Double. This sounds like a standard auction to get to a normal contract, and South figures to beat 4 ♠ more often than not even after he tips off his trump holding. If dummy puts down Q9x of spades and declarer picks up the trump suit for one loser which he wouldn't have done without the double, that is just too bad. The double will be right more often than not, and that is all that counts if the field figures to be in the same contract.

THE PLAY

THE PLAY

OPENING LEADS

Opening lead strategy is not much different at matchpoints than at IMPs. The opening leader has little enough information to go on, so he usually just takes his best shot. There are certain situations which do call for special tactics at matchpoints, and the winning player learns to recognize them and act accordingly.

The primary difference in the play between matchpoints and IMPs is the importance of overtricks. Overtricks are relatively unimportant at IMPs, so you go all out to beat the contract. At matchpoints, this isn't the case. Allowing declarer to make an overtrick by your opening lead can be just as costly as allowing him to make the contract. The trick is to determine which hands call for the all out effort and which hands require caution to hold in the overtricks.

There are three types of contracts the opponents might arrive at. First, there are normal contracts, likely to be reached at most tables. Against this sort of contract overtricks are just as important as setting the contract. Second, there are abnormal contracts, such as a marginal slam or a doubled contract. Against these setting the contract has the highest priority, so you should make what you think is the best lead to defeat the contract without regard to possible overtricks. Third, there are alternative contracts. These are contracts which may not be popular, but which can compete with other possible contracts. A four-three major suit game or 3NT when a good major suit fit is availble are examples of alternative contracts. Another is a contract that is likely to be played from the other side at most tables. These are the trickiest of all. It may be necessary to defeat the contract to get any matchpoints. On the other hand, an overtrick can swing a full matchpoint against other tables;

for example, it might take you from −630 to −660 when others your way are −650. It is important to try to judge from the auction which type of contract you are up against.

A normal contract is one which figures to be reached at most tables. It can usually be recognized by the simplicity and directness of the auction. If the bidding is something like:

NORTH	EAST	SOUTH	WEST
—	—	1 NT	Pass
3 NT	Pass	Pass	Pass

or:

NORTH	EAST	SOUTH	WEST
—	—	1 ♠	Pass
2 ♠	Pass	4 ♠	Pass
Pass	Pass		

you can be pretty confident that the auction will be echoed around the room. More complex auctions can also lead to obviously normal contracts. For example:

NORTH	EAST	SOUTH	WEST
—	—	1 ♡	Pass
2 ♣	Pass	2 ♢	Pass
2 ♠	Pass	2 NT	Pass
3 NT	Pass	Pass	Pass

The auction may be different at other tables, but the final contract is likely to be the same simply because the opponents don't have any place else to go. Of course it might be played from the other side, which can make a difference, but 3NT it will be around the room.

If the contract is the same at other tables you gain one-half matchpoint against every table for each trick your opening lead gains, and lose one-half matchpoint for each trick your opening lead loses, assuming that the other table results are within one trick of yours. This is true whether the contract or an overtrick is at stake. Consequently, your goal on opening lead is not necessarily to set the contract, but to take as many tricks as you can. This often means a more passive lead than usual. For example:

None vul., West holds: ♠KJ8, ♡1092, ◊A63, ♣9543

NORTH	EAST	SOUTH	WEST
—	—	1 NT	Pass
3 NT	Pass	Pass	Pass

At IMPs you might get brilliant and try the jack of spades. The best chance to beat the contract appears to be to find partner with length and strength in spades, and overtricks are relatively unimportant. At matchpoints you can't afford this luxury. A spade lead is more likely to cost a trick than to gain one, and each overtrick will swing several matchpoints. A passive heart or club lead is recommended.

Both vul., West holds: ♠Q83, ♡J107, ◊J109, ♣KJ72

NORTH	EAST	SOUTH	WEST
—	—	1 ♡	Pass
3 ♡*	Pass	4 ◊	Pass
4 ♡	Pass	Pass	Pass

*limit raise

At IMPs a good case can be made for leading a low club. The idea is to hope to cash three club tricks and get an uppercut on the fourth round. With the opponents trying for slam it will take a lot of luck to beat 4♡, but the possibility exists. This may be a winner at IMPs, but at matchpoints forget the brilliance and lead the normal jack of diamonds. It is extremely improbable that you can set 4♡ whatever you lead, and the club lead is much more likely to cost the defense a trick than to gain one, for partner can't hold much in high cards. Note that even though 4♡ might not be a universal contract since some pairs may reach slam, you should defend as though it is a normal contract. Your opening lead won't affect the pairs in slam. They will beat you or lose to you at their table whatever you do. Con-

297

sequently, your only real competitors are those defending the same 4 ♡ contract, so lead accordingly.

It is not always correct to make a passive lead against a normal contract at matchpoints. If the bidding indicates that an aggressive lead is called for, go ahead and make it.

E-W vul., West holds: ♠1087, ♡A53, ◊10983, ♣KJ3

NORTH	EAST	SOUTH	WEST
—	—	1 ♠	Pass
2 ♡	Pass	2 ♠	Pass
4 ♠	Pass	Pass	Pass

It appears as though the major suits lie favorably for declarer, and dummy's hearts will soon be established for minor suit discards. This is not the time to be passive. A club lead is correct both at IMPs and matchpoints. In addition to being the best lead to set the contract, it is also the best lead to hold down the overtricks by establishing club tricks before West's ace of hearts is knocked out. If the club lead blows a club trick there is a good chance that declarer would have been able to discard the potential club loser on dummy's hearts anyway, so the lead might not cost even if it gives declarer a free finesse.

Another type of lead that is common at matchpoints is laying down an ace for a possible cashout. Often the cashout will merely hold in the overtricks, unimportant at IMPs but critical at matchpoints. For example:

N-S vul., West holds: ♠AQ10, ♡932, ◊J108, ♣9743

NORTH	EAST	SOUTH	WEST
—	—	1 ♡	Pass
3 ♣	Pass	3 ♡	Pass
4 ♡	Pass	Pass	Pass

With this strong auction and West's weakness in hearts and clubs, it is likely that the only tricks for the defense will be in diamonds and spades. At IMPs the jack of diamonds lead is clear. It is hard to imagine beating the contract if partner doesn't own the ace of diamonds, so this lead gives the defense the option of cashing diamond or spade tricks, whichever are available. At matchpoints, however, the ace of spades is a better shot. East is just as likely to hold the king of spades as the ace of diamonds, and if he does, failing to cash the spades will cost several overtricks. Even if East doesn't hold the king of spades the cashout could well be right. Dummy may have the spade king in which case no harm and possibly some good is done by the lead, and if East has no entry at all (perhaps his high card is the onside king of hearts), then the spade lead may be necessary to hold declarer to six, which is quite important since many other N-S pairs also figure to arrive in 4 ♡. The spade lead costs only when South owns the king of spades and East has an entry. In all other cases the lead either gains or breaks even. Consequently, the spade lead will be right more often than not, even though it virtually gives up on setting the contract.

When the opponents arrive in an abnormal contract, it is usually right to go all out to beat them. Overtricks are relatively unimportant, for there won't be many others in the same contract. The exception to this is the major vs. notrump decisions, where overtricks are extremely important.

Both vul., West holds: ♠A975, ♡J103, ♢9865, ♣KJ

NORTH	EAST	SOUTH	WEST
1 ♣	Pass	1 ♢	Pass
3 ♣	Pass	3 ♢	Pass
3 ♠	Pass	4 NT	Pass
5 ♡	Pass	6 NT	Pass
Pass	Pass		

Not a very impressive auction, but it is likely that they have hit the jackpot. Your club holding is a complete disaster for the defense. At IMPs I would try a low spade lead, as this seems to be the best shot if not the only one. The opponents' contract appears unusual enough that the same lead should be made at matchpoints. The overtrick probably won't matter much, but setting the contract will be a full board swing if the field stays out of slam or plays 6 ♢.

Often it is a good idea to determine why the opponents have reached the unusual contract when a better alternative contract seems more likely. You can base your opening lead on the assumption that the opponents are right, for if they are wrong your opening lead won't matter. For example:

Both vul., West holds: ♠AQ96, ♡9654, ♢52, ♣QJ9

NORTH	EAST	SOUTH	WEST
—	—	1 ♢	Pass
1 ♡	Pass	3 ♢	Pass
4 ♢	Pass	5 ♢	Pass
Pass	Pass		

Not a particularly scientific auction. You would think they would try a little harder to get to 3NT. Perhaps they know what they are doing, perhaps not, but it is clear that if N-S hold the king of spades 3NT is likely to score well above 5 ♢, and the field will be there. Therefore, you should base your opening lead on the assumption that E-W don't hold the king of spades, for if they do you will probably get a good board regardless of what you lead. The ace of spades is the best lead, with the idea of cashing as many spade tricks as possible. If the lead blows a trick, it won't cost many matchpoints.

The most difficult contracts to lead against are those which may not be normal but are competitive with other contracts. The most common of these is 3NT when the field figures to be in four of a major, or vice versa. Every trick can swing a full matchpoint against another table, and you don't really know what your goal is. What you must do is look at your hand, try to determine if the opponents have done well or not in their choice of contracts, and choose your opening lead accordingly.

E-W vul., West holds: ♠QJ97, ♡1094, ◊KJ43, ♣85

NORTH	EAST	SOUTH	WEST
—	—	1 NT	Pass
2 ◊*	Pass	2 ♠	Pass
3 ♠	Pass	3 NT	Pass
Pass	Pass		

*Forcing Stayman

Just as the opponents were headed for your spade suit, they both guessed to play notrump. From your point of view it looks like they guessed right. To make matters worse, most of the field will probably go with the four-four major suit fit. Notrump will have to take one trick less than spades for spades to be the right contract for N-S, which seems unlikely. However, you must base your opening lead on the assumption that this is the case, for you will be headed for a bad result regardless of your lead if notrump always scores at least as many tricks as spades. How can spades be better? Only if the opponents have a weak side suit, and you can see that the most likely weak suit is diamonds. Consequently, you should make the aggressive lead of a diamond. If partner doesn't have a diamond card the lead may cost a trick, but if this is the case you are probably headed for a bad score whatever you lead. If partner does have a diamond card it may be necessary to lead a diamond now, and the lead may be the difference between getting one more trick on defense than those defending spades and getting the same number of tricks, so the diamond lead could swing the full board. Of course, if the opponents had landed in 4 ♠ you wouldn't touch a diamond lead with a ten foot pole. Then you are happy with their contract, so you avoid blowing a trick.

Both vul., West holds: ♠Q3, ♡A98, ◊QJ754, ♣754

NORTH	EAST	SOUTH	WEST
—	—	1 NT	Pass
2 ◊*	Pass	2 ♡	Pass
2 NT	Pass	3 ♡	Pass
4 ♡	Pass	Pass	Pass

*Forcing Stayman

In spite of the opening 1NT bid, the opponents had the tools to find a five-three heart fit. At many other tables N-S pairs will be playing standard Stayman or transfer bids, and the auction is likely to go 1NT-2♣-2♡-3NT. Against 3NT, other Wests will lead a diamond. If East has a diamond honor this lead will be a success, and you will not do well defending 4♡ regardless of what you lead, for 3NT is likely to go down or be held to nine tricks if declarer doesn't have time to use his heart suit. You must assume that the diamond lead against 3NT will not be successful in order for you to have a chance. Therefore, stay away from the diamond lead against 4♡, because by the necessary assumption it will not work well. Instead lead a passive club, wait for your tricks, and hope that the notrumpers will be able to score the same number of tricks as your opponents take in hearts.

None vul., West holds: ♠KJ954, ♡962, ◊K2, ♣A73

NORTH	EAST	SOUTH	WEST
—	—	1 NT*	Pass
2 ◊**	Pass	2 ♡	Pass
3 ◊	Pass	3 ♡	Pass
4 ♡	Pass	Pass	Pass

*12-14
**transfer

Normally you might be inclined to lead a spade on this kind of auction. If you don't establish a spade trick fast it may go away on a minor suit winner in dummy, so even if the spade lead rides to the AQ it may not cost a trick. The problem with a spade lead on this hand is that you may have been fixed by the bidding. At most tables South will open one of a minor, West will overcall in spades, and North will be declarer in 4 ♡ with a spade lead from the other side. Consequently, if you lead a spade you get an average when it is right and a bottom when it is wrong, as you are competing with spade leads from your partner's hand. It makes more sense to assume that the spade lead is not necessary, so lead a trump. This could conceivably do some good if South has to ruff diamonds in the short hand, and at least you get away from the average or worse position you would be in if you tried to compete with the other spade leaders.

E-W vul., West holds: ♠62, ♡K10653, ♦Q2, ♣K1085

NORTH	EAST	SOUTH	WEST
—	—	1 ♦	Pass
1 ♡	Pass	1 NT*	Pass
3 NT	Pass	Pass	Pass

*15-17

Your opponents are playing weak notrumps, which accounts for the auction. The contract appears normal, but the information available to the opening leader is not. It is easy to project the likely auction at other tables: 1NT-2♣-2♦-3NT. On this auction most Wests will lead a heart. You know that dummy will show up with four hearts, so a heart lead will probably be bad for the defense. Having been warned off the heart lead, should you try a club or a spade? I think you should lead a spade. The important point is that you are already ahead of the field by not blowing a trick with a heart lead, so you should play completely safe rather than go for the killer. If the club lead is right you will probably still do well for having avoided the heart lead, but if the club lead gives up a trick you are back down to average.

Both vul., West holds: ♠54, ♡8762, ◇KQ8, ♣A742

NORTH	EAST	SOUTH	WEST
—	—	1 ♡	Pass
2 ♠	Pass	3 ♣	Pass
4 ♠	Pass	4 NT	Pass
5 ♡	Pass	6 NT	Pass
Pass	Pass		

This is a very unusual problem. How could you not lead the king of diamonds? A little thought will show that the lead might be very costly. North has shown a long solid spade suit, and South's hearts are likely to run considering your anemic heart holding. It is not hard to imagine that N-S have seven spades, five hearts, and a diamond off the top, so it may be essential to cash the ace of clubs. An important consideration is that a popular contract is likely to be 6♠ by the North hand, and other Easts won't know which minor to lead. Consequently there may be several − 1460's your way, so there will be a big swing between − 1440 and − 1470. It is not often that you virtually give up on trying to beat a slam even at matchpoints, but this is one time when the overtrick and the alternative possible contract really make a big difference. The full hand:

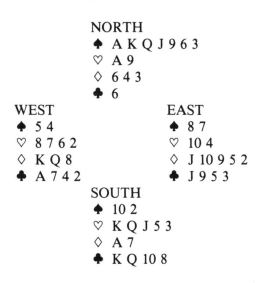

```
                    NORTH
                    ♠ A K Q J 9 6 3
                    ♡ A 9
                    ◇ 6 4 3
                    ♣ 6
    WEST                            EAST
    ♠ 5 4                           ♠ 8 7
    ♡ 8 7 6 2                       ♡ 10 4
    ◇ K Q 8                         ◇ J 10 9 5 2
    ♣ A 7 4 2                       ♣ J 9 5 3
                    SOUTH
                    ♠ 10 2
                    ♡ K Q J 5 3
                    ◇ A 7
                    ♣ K Q 10 8
```

304

The slam is easy to reach, and many pairs played 6♠ making seven after East's natural jack of diamonds lead. The swing between cashing the ace of clubs and losing it against 6NT was from a well above average score to a tie for bottom.

DECLARER PLAY

In my younger days I once asked an expert how a hand should be played at matchpoints. His simple but illuminating answer was: "For all the tricks you can take." This is not always correct, but it is not far from the truth. It is often even correct to risk your contract for the possibility of extra overtricks.

When the dummy comes down the first thing a declarer should do at matchpoints is assess his contract and the effect the opening lead has on his chances. If he is in a routine contract with a normal opening lead, he naturally plays to maximize his expected number of tricks taken. If the lead was unusually favorable, he will play conservatively to attempt to retain his advantage. If the lead was unusually devastating, he may make very daring plays to get back even with the field. If there are alternative possible contracts, he should estimate the likely results in those contracts and take whatever action is necessary to beat those results if possible.

NORTH
♠ A Q 6 4
♡ A J 10 9
◇ 8 7 4
♣ Q 2

SOUTH
♠ K J 10 8 2
♡ 4 3
◇ A K 5
♣ K 9 8

Both vulnerable.

NORTH	EAST	SOUTH	WEST
—	—	1 ♠	Pass
3 NT*	Pass	4 ♠	Pass
Pass	Pass		

*forcing raise

Opening Lead: Queen of diamonds

You win the queen of diamonds lead, draw two rounds of trumps ending in your hand (they split two-two), and lead a heart to the jack which loses. East returns a diamond, you win, and West plays the ten. Now what?

Let's assess your position. The 4 ♠ contract was easy to bid, and the field should all get there from the South side one way or another. Furthermore, it appears as though West started with QJ10 of diamonds, so the lead was normal as was the diamond continuation. Therefore, every other South player will face this exact problem.

There are two possible lines of play. One is to play West for the missing heart honor and take another finesse. If the finesse succeeds South will make five, but if it loses he will go down unless East has no more diamonds and the ace of clubs. The alternative line is to play East for the missing heart honor by leading a heart to the ace and taking a ruffing finesse. This will make five if East started with both honors, and guarantees the contract because even if the ruffing finesse loses South will have pitched his diamond. The second line of play is obviously best at IMPs, but what about at matchpoints?

Restricted choice tells us that West is a two to one favorite to have the missing heart honor. If you don't understand restricted choice, look at it in the following way: Initially, there was a 25% chance that West had both honors, a 25% chance that East had both honors, and a 50% chance that the honors were split. In other words, it was initially twice as likely that the honors were split as that East had both honors. The fact that we have lost to an honor in the East hand (it doesn't matter which one) doesn't change this figure. All we know is that West didn't start with both honors.

Now, let's look at the matchpoint cost analysis. Whichever line of play we take, if it is wrong we will cost ourselves one-half matchpoint to every other table regardless of what they do. If the other table goes right we get a loss instead of a tie, while if the other table is wrong we get a tie instead of a win. Consequently, it is correct to make the play which is most likely to be right. In this case this means taking the second heart finesse, despite the risk to the contract.

Even if you are faced with a mildly unfriendly lead, it is usually correct to make the percentage play for as many tricks as possible if you are in a normal contract. On the previous hand, suppose the opening lead had been the two of diamonds to East's queen, and East had returned the ten of diamonds. This is not good for South. West has apparently found the killing lead from Jxxx, and the lead certainly will not be found at every other table. If a diamond is not led, South can take both heart finesses without risking his contract. It might seem as though you should therefore take the anti-percentage ruffing finesse and go for a top or a bottom, since you can at best tie those tables which don't get a diamond lead if you play the same way they do and the second finesse wins, while you will lose to them (down one while they make four), if the second finesse loses. Let's analyze it:

We already know that the double finesse is best against other tables which receive the diamond lead. Against tables which don't get the diamond lead you lose one-half matchpoint if you take the ruffing finesse and are wrong (from a tie to a loss), while you gain a full matchpoint if the ruffing finesse is right (you make five instead of going down one, while they make exactly four). So you are getting a two to one matchpoint payoff against tables not getting the diamond lead if you take the ruffing finesse, but giving two to one odds by making the anti-percentage play, so it's exactly break-even. One-third of the time you gain one matchpoint, two-thirds of the time you lose one-half matchpoint. Consequently, the double finesse is still the best play at matchpoints, because some other tables will receive the same diamond lead.

Let's change the hand slightly, sticking with the same theme:

NORTH
- ♠ A Q 6 4
- ♡ A Q 10 2
- ◊ 8 7 4
- ♣ Q 2

SOUTH
- ♠ K J 10 8 2
- ♡ 4 3
- ◊ A K 5
- ♣ K 9 8

Again, you are in 4♠ with the queen of diamonds lead. You win, draw trumps in two rounds and lead a heart to the ten which loses to the jack. Back comes a diamond. Do you take another heart finesse or play to ruff out king-third of hearts? Restricted choice is not applicable here—East would always play the jack from the king-jack, so the king is equally likely to be with either defender. If you take the finesse, a 50% play, you will lose one-half matchpoint to every other table when it fails. If it wins you will not necessarily gain one-half matchpoint, since if West has Kxx the play of ace and ruff a heart works as well as the finesse. Suppose you play the ace of hearts and ruff a small one. You will surely gain one-half matchpoint from every other table when the king is offside, and if it is onside you will still not lose if West has Kxx. Thus the finesse costs half the time, while the rest of the time it either gains or breaks even, while rejecting the finesse gains half the time, and either costs or breaks even the other half. So the ace is the better play.

How about with the two of diamonds lead? Now the lead is not necessarily normal. Those declarers not receiving a diamond lead will certainly take two heart finesses, the percentage play in hearts, as they are still safe even if both finesses lose. What should you do when your ten of hearts loses to the jack and the ten of diamonds comes back? If you finesse you will tie declarers who did not get a diamond lead half the time and lose to them half the time. Suppose you play a heart to the ace and ruff a heart instead. You will then tie or beat those other declarers more than half the time—whenever East has the king

309

of hearts or West has Kxx—and lose to them only if West has Kxxx(x) of hearts. Thus ace and ruff a heart is the better play.

The preceding analysis is quite complex, and it would be difficult to go through all these possibilities at the table. Still, this hand does shed some light on when declarer should make his best play for the most tricks and when he should hedge and play moderately safely. In general you should look for the play that has the highest matchpoint expectation, even though this isn't necessarily the best play for the most tricks. For example, in the hand where dummy had AQ10x of hearts, the second finesse was the best play for the most tricks, but playing for the drop was the best matchpoint play.

Should you ever take an anti-percentage play in a normal contract? Usually not, but occasionally it may be necessary if you are badly fixed by the opening lead. For example:

NORTH
♠ K Q 8 2
♡ A 8 6
◇ K J 9
♣ J 10 4

SOUTH
♠ A J 10 9 4
♡ K 3
◇ A 5 4
♣ Q 5 3

E-W vulnerable.

NORTH	EAST	SOUTH	WEST
—	—	1 ♠	Pass
3 NT*	Pass	4 ♠	Pass
Pass	Pass		

*forcing raise

Opening Lead: King of clubs

West leads king of clubs, club to East's ace, and ruffs the third round. He now exits with a trump. How should you handle the diamond suit? The normal play is to lead a diamond to the jack, which wins whenever West has the queen. The other possibility is the "backward finesse" of swinging the jack off the dummy, planning on then finessing the nine if East covers the jack. This requires both East to hold the queen and West to hold the ten to be successful, hence it will work only half as often as the straightforward finesse.

Now for the matchpoint cost analysis. Against other tables where the king of clubs was led the backward finesse gains one-half matchpoint 25% of the time and loses one-half matchpoint 50% of the time, for an average loss of one-half matchpoint 25% of the time. When East holds both the queen and ten of diamonds, 25% of the time, the play breaks even. What about tables which receive another lead? These tables don't lose the club ruff, so the backward finesse costs nothing to these tables when it is wrong since they will make five (via the straightforward finesse which they certainly will take), and this is out of your reach. However, the backward finesse does gain one-half matchpoint the 25% of the time it works, for they now lose a diamond trick and you don't, so you go from a loss to a tie. Consequently, if you think that the majority of Souths will not get the killing club lead, a very reasonable assumption, then the backward finesse is the best play. The idea is that if an unusual lead has definitely cost you a trick it may be correct to take an anti-percentage play to try to get that trick back, for taking the same play as the rest of the field will leave you one trick behind them whether the play works or not.

Safety plays have their place in matchpoints, but it is at the bottom of the totem pole. Some safety plays can only gain, and these should be made routinely. For example:

North: Axxx
South: KQ9xx

If there are no entry problems, the ace should be played first at any form of scoring to guard against J10xx in the East hand. However, most safety plays involve losing a trick that might not have to be lost in order to insure the contract against a very bad

311

split. This is fine for IMPs, where making the contract has the highest priority, but at matchpoints these plays will result in far more bottoms than tops in normal contracts. For example:

NORTH
♠ 9 8 3
♡ 9 3
◊ 3 2
♣ A K Q 6 5 4

SOUTH
♠ A K 4
♡ A K 4
◊ Q J 8 5 4
♣ 7 3

N-S vulnerable.

NORTH	EAST	SOUTH	WEST
—	—	1 NT	Pass
3 NT	Pass	Pass	Pass

Opening Lead: Queen of hearts

At IMPs it would be a routine safety play to duck the first round of clubs. This assures the contract aginst against a four-one club split. Playing matchpoints, this safety play would be the height of folly. The contract is trivial to reach, and the opening lead appears normal. Ducking a club will cost a trick when the clubs split three-two, and gain at least one trick when they split four-one. Since a three-two split is far more likely than a four-one split, ducking will be wrong more often than it will be right, so you should ignore the safety play and try to take as many tricks as possible in this normal contract.

In abnormal contracts, where just making the contract is important, safety plays can be correct. If you are doubled, overtricks are virtually inconsequential because making any doubled contract usually guarantees a top or near top. The same is true about a hard to bid slam. For example:

NORTH
- ♠ A K 6
- ♡ K 4 3 2
- ◇ A 9 6 5
- ♣ 7 5

SOUTH
- ♠ 9 4 3
- ♡ A Q J
- ◇ K J 7 4
- ♣ A Q 6

E-W vulnerable.

NORTH	EAST	SOUTH	WEST
—	—	1 ◇	Pass
1 ♡	Pass	1 NT*	Pass
2 ♣**	Pass	3 ♡	Pass
3 ♠	Pass	4 ♣	Pass
4 ◇	Pass	4 ♡	Pass
4 ♠	Pass	5 ♣	Pass
6 ◇	Pass	Pass	Pass

*15-17
**forcing

Opening Lead: Jack of clubs

You went through a rather involved sequence to get to a marginal slam, which looks a lot better after the jack of clubs opening lead. You can be pretty sure that most of the field won't be anywhere near this contract after a strong notrump opening, and the overbidders probably won't find their diamond fit and will get to 6NT which you can't outscore if it makes. Therefore, you should take the standard safety play in the trump suit of king of diamonds and then low to the nine (unless West shows out). The potential lost overtrick is virtually meaningless, while the whole board could ride on making this contract, and this safety play guarantees the contract against all but the worst of splits.

Another type of hand which calls for a safety play to insure the contract for an entirely different reason is one where you have arrived at an abnormal low-scoring contract. Since you can't compete with the normal higher-scoring contracts if they make, you have to assume that they will go down, so you must attempt to insure your contract to avoid tying other tables at down one. For example:

NORTH
♠ A 2
♡ K Q 9
♢ A 8 4 3
♣ A 9 4 3

SOUTH
♠ 9 8 7
♡ A J 7
♢ K 7
♣ K 10 7 6 2

N-S vulnerable.

NORTH	EAST	SOUTH	WEST
1 ♢	1 ♠	2 ♣	Pass
3 ♣	Pass	3 ♡	Pass
3 ♠	Pass	4 ♣	Pass
5 ♣	Pass	Pass	Pass

Opening Lead: Two of spades

Don't ask me what partner has against notrump, but here you are in 5 ♣. 6 ♣ makes on a club pickup, and 3NT will make many overtricks if the club suit comes in. Both of these contracts will be down one if the clubs don't behave, since the spades appear to be five-three on the bidding and opening lead. Most of the field will play 3NT, and those that don't will probably get to 6 ♣. You can't compete with either of these contracts if they make, so you must assume that they don't. Therefore, it is important to insure making 5 ♣, so take the safe-

314

ty play of a low club to the ten at trick two to guard against a four-zero club split. A lost overtrick figures to cost almost nothing, but going down instead of making can cost one-half matchpoint compared to other tables which are down one in the more normal contracts.

Sacrifices can lead to interesting play decisions. Obviously your target is to go down less than the value of the contract against which you are sacrificing. You can assume that the field won't all take the sacrifice, and it is important to get that full matchpoint swing against tables at which the save isn't taken.

NORTH
♠ 5 3
♡ A J 10 6
◇ K 10 9 5
♣ 9 8 2

SOUTH
♠ 2
♡ 5 2
◇ Q J 8 7 4 3 2
♣ A 6 3

E-W vulnerable.

NORTH	EAST	SOUTH	WEST
—	1 ♠	3 ◇	4 ♠
5 ◇	Double	Pass	Pass
Pass			

Opening Lead: King of spades

West leads the king of spades, and continues spades which you ruff. You try a heart to the jack and East's king, and East returns a club. Even though the second heart finesse is a two to one favorite, it would be silly to try it. You figure to get a good board for − 500, since not everybody will take the save and E-W may be able to make 5 ♠ anyway. It would not be a good idea to risk a full matchpoint against tables where E-W are playing and

315

making a game in spades in order to perhaps gain one-half matchpoint against tables where the contract is the same as yours. With neither vulnerable, however, the second heart finesse would be clear-cut. Now your target is nine tricks, not eight, so you must try it. Even though it requires two defensive errors on West's part (not shifting to clubs and not playing the queen on the first heart lead), you must assume that these errors have been made. With neither vulnerable there won't be much matchpoint difference between -500 and -700, but there will be a huge difference between -300 and -500.

When you take a sacrifice, you will always get a bad result if your save is a phantom. Consequently, it is necessary to assume that the opponents' contract is making when you are trying to go for less than the value of their game. It makes no sense to play for a lie of the cards on which the enemy contract would not have made. For example:

NORTH
♠ K J 5 2
♡ 9 2
◇ 6 5 4 2
♣ 9 3 2

SOUTH
♠ A 7 6 4 3
♡ 7 4
◇ A 9 3
♣ A 6 5

E-W vulnerable.

NORTH	EAST	SOUTH	WEST
—	1 ♡	1 ♠	4 ♡
4 ♠	Double	Pass	Pass
Pass			

Opening Lead: Queen of hearts

Neither you nor your partner took a totally unreasonable action, yet the final contract doesn't look too good. The defense takes the first two rounds of hearts and shifts to a club. You have six losers outside of trumps, so you must avoid losing a trump trick to get out for less than the value of their potential game. Both follow when you lead the ace of trumps, and West follows small on the second round. Do you finesse or play for the drop? On the bidding the drop seems better, since East doubled. However, if the queen drops you will still get a very bad board. The opponents will have four losers in 4 ♡ if the spades are two-two, so you must hope that they are three-one. If the finesse works you will be − 500 with 4 ♡ making for a good sacrifice, while if the finesse loses your − 700 will only be a slightly rounder zero than − 500 since the save was a phantom. Therefore, the finesse is clearly correct.

The most difficult contracts to play at matchpoints are those which may be in competition with alternative contracts. If there is another likely contract which may or may not beat yours, it is very important to assess the likely results of the other contract depending on the lie of the defenders' cards, and to plan your play accordingly.

NORTH
♠ A J 10 4 3
♡ A 6 5
◊ 5 2
♣ A 6 2

SOUTH
♠ K 7
♡ K Q 9 3 2
◊ A 4 3
♣ K 10 5

None vulnerable.

NORTH	EAST	SOUTH	WEST
—	—	1 ♡	Pass
1 ♠	Pass	1 NT	Pass
2 ♣*	Pass	2 ♡	Pass
4 ♡	Pass	Pass	Pass

*artificial and forcing

Opening Lead: Queen of diamonds

West leads the queen of diamonds, which you duck. He continues with a diamond to the king and ace, and you ruff the third round of diamonds low in dummy, East following. You draw trumps pitching a club from dummy; East follows three times while West pitches a diamond on the third trump. Now, how do you tackle the spades?

At this point, you might be wishing you were in 6♡. That contract is not relevant to you. Either it makes or it doesn't, but those in slam will decide their fate at their table and nothing you can do will affect your result against them, so you might as well assume anybody in slam is playing in another event. How about 3NT? This may well be a popular contract. Many Souths will open 1NT on your cards, after which the five-three heart fit probably won't be found. How will 3NT fare after the natural diamond lead? Eventually, declarer will have to take a spade finesse. If it loses the notrumpers won't take more than ten tricks, while if it wins they will take at least eleven. This is the clue for how to play the spades in 4♡. If the spades are three-three with the queen offside South won't mind too much losing a spade trick, for he will still score eleven tricks to beat the notrumpers. The danger situation is when West has Qxxx of spades (if he has Qxx all plays work). Now the notrumpers will take exactly eleven tricks, so it is essential to make twelve tricks in hearts. Another way to look at this situation is to realize that South is a trick ahead of the notrumpers due to the diamond ruff in dummy. Consequently, if South plays the spades the same way they will be played in 3NT he will remain a trick ahead regardless of whether the spade finesse wins or loses. Therefore,

South should play king of spades and a spade to the jack.

The play of this hand in 3NT is also interesting. How many times should South hold up in diamonds? There is a strong argument for not holding up at all, and hoping both major suits behave for thirteen tricks. As long as South doesn't know how the diamonds are splitting he might as well go whole hog and assume the best. If it works he is at least sure of beating 4 ♡ contracts regardless of how many tricks they make.

NORTH
- ♠ 7 4 2
- ♡ K J 6 2
- ◇ K 10 6 3
- ♣ 3 2

SOUTH
- ♠ A 10 8
- ♡ A 7
- ◇ Q J 8 5 2
- ♣ Q 10 8

E-W vulnerable.

NORTH	EAST	SOUTH	WEST
—	—	1 ◇	Pass
1 ♡	Pass	1 NT	Pass
2 ◇	Pass	Pass	Pass

Opening Lead: Queen of spades

What a nice comfortable contract. It seems as though only a madman would take the heart finesse for an overtrick and risk going down. Yet, careful analysis shows that at matchpoints playing for the overtrick is the only sensible line of play.

What are some other possible results? Your opponents were silent, but not all E-W pairs figure to keep quiet holding half the deck. How they will fare depends a lot on where the jack of clubs and queen of hearts are, but it is not difficult to envision some N-S pairs collecting +100 against 2 ♠ or 3 ♣. If this is the case, there will be a big difference between +90 and +110, for you will swing a full matchpoint against every N-S pair who is +100. N-S pairs who are pushed to 3 ◇ will be forced to play to make it, so by taking the heart finesse you tie them if it wins and beat them if it loses, as you will be −50 to their −100. N-S pairs playing notrump will either make one or go down a bundle, depending on where the jack of clubs is. If they go down you will beat them regardless, while if they make one you are as likely to gain as to lose to them by taking the heart finesse. The point is that there is much more activity between +90 and +110 on this hand than there is between −50 and +90. No conceivable score falls completely inside the latter range, so the finesse can cost at most one-half matchpoint to any table if it is wrong, while it can gain a full matchpoint against +100 if it is right. If E-W were not vulnerable, it would be correct to play safe for the contract. Now +50 falls between −50 and +90, so the finesse will gain less if it is right and lose far more if it is wrong.

NORTH
♠ A 8 6
♡ K Q 8 6 5
◇ J 6 3
♣ Q 9

SOUTH
♠ K Q J 9
♡ A 7 4
◇ A 5
♣ K 8 4 2

N-S vulnerable.

NORTH	EAST	SOUTH	WEST
—	—	1 NT	Pass
2 ♣	Pass	2 ♠	Pass
3 NT	Pass	Pass	Pass

Opening Lead: Two of diamonds

One can sympathize with North's decision not to search for a five-three heart fit since he holds extra strength and values in every suit, but it doesn't appear to be right on this hand. You try the jack of diamonds at trick one, but East covers with the king and you win the ace. On the ace of hearts West plays small and East plays the nine, and West plays another small heart when you continue the suit. Now what?

Playing for the three-two split is the percentage play in the heart suit. The finesse of the eight wins only when East started with the stiff nine, while going up wins when East started with J9, 109, or J109. Admittedly the last two holdings are less likely because East might have played a different card than the nine (restricted choice again), but the drop is still the percentage play in the suit. However, at matchpoints the finesse is the percentage play on the hand!

When partner bid 3NT, he was betting that you could take the same number of tricks in notrump as in a possible five-three heart fit. You must try to live up to his expectation despite the unfavorable lead. At hearts N-S can easily take eleven tricks if the hearts split, for they have time to set up the club trick while you don't. Consequently you should go ahead and take the double heart finesse, even though you will be down in a cold contract (if the diamonds are four-four) if it fails. If the hearts actually are four-one you will now come to ten tricks, which is all those playing in 4♡ will take since they will play the hearts normally. Besides, what about those in 3NT who don't get a diamond lead? If the hearts split three-two they have time to set up a club trick and make eleven tricks, while on a four-one heart split they may be held to nine tricks if they play the hearts normally. Therefore the double heart finesse gains a full matchpoint against both 4♡ and 3NT without a diamond lead if it is right, and loses nothing to these contracts if it is wrong. This analysis shows that the finesse has so much more to gain than to lose that it is clearly the best play even though it is very anti-percentage for the heart suit in isolation.

Incidentally, against weak opposition it might be a good idea to try to steal a club at trick two on this hand. If you get away with this you will beat the 4♡ players if the hearts split. Against good opponents this should not work. If West has, say, Q9xx of diamonds he will be able to deduce from your play of the jack at trick one that you don't have the ten, for if you did you would have played low to insure two diamond tricks. With a good player in the West seat, the straightforward approach is best.

DEFENSE

Defense is difficult enough at any form of scoring, but at matchpoints there are even more problems than usual. The difficulty is that you don't always know what your goal is. At IMPs you know your goal is to set the contract, so you just assume that declarer has whatever hand he needs for the contract to be defeated, almost regardless of how unlikely that hand actually is and defend accordingly. If you are wrong the cost will only be an unimportant overtrick or two. At matchpoints you can't afford to take this reckless sort of approach. Those overtricks can be very important. On the other hand, it is a catastrophe to let declarer make a contract you could have beaten because you were trying to hold in the overtricks. It is often quite a dilemma.

```
                    NORTH
                    ♠ A Q 10 9
                    ♡ Q 10 9
                    ◇ 8 7 6 5 3
                    ♣ 5

        WEST
        ♠ 8 6 4 3
        ♡ J 7
        ◇ K Q
        ♣ A 10 8 4 2
```

N-S vulnerable.

NORTH	EAST	SOUTH	WEST
—	—	1 NT*	Pass
2 ♣	Pass	2 ◇	Pass
2 NT	Pass	3 NT	Pass
Pass	Pass		

*15-17

Opening Lead: Four of clubs

Your club lead goes to partner's queen and declarer's king. He leads the jack of spades to dummy's queen, partner playing the two. Now declarer plays a small diamond from dummy, partner plays the jack, declarer plays small, and you are in. Now what?

It is pretty easy to reconstruct most of declarer's hand. We know from trick one that he has the jack of clubs, and partner's play of the two of spades (showing an odd number) marks declarer with the KJ doubleton. Declarer must have started with A109xx of diamonds for the diamond plays to make sense; he obviously went to dummy to try to duck a diamond trick safely to your hand. Therefore, declarer either has ♠KJ, ♡Kxx, ◇A109xx, ♣KJx or ♠KJ, ♡Axx, ◇A109xx, ♣KJx, but which one? If East has the ace of hearts, a heart switch will garner in a two-trick set while after a passive return declarer has nine tricks. On the other hand, if declarer has the ace of hearts a heart shift will allow him to take the rest of the tricks (four diamonds, three hearts, four spades, and one club), while a passive return holds him to ten tricks. It seems sensible to reason as follows: If declarer has the hand with the ace of hearts he has a good sixteen points and a fairly clear 3NT bid, but if he has the hand with the king of hearts he has only fifteen points and might not have bid 3NT despite his good five-card suit. Therefore, it is better to play safe and avoid giving up overtricks.

Let's try a matchpoint cost analysis on this one. If we go for the set and are wrong it costs one-half matchpoint against other tables in 3NT, as they will presumably be faced with the same problem, but nothing to tables in any other contract since we were beaten by these tables in the bidding. Since N-S have only twenty-four high card points and a five-five diamond fit with North having some distribution, there will be many pairs not in 3NT. Let's say that half the field reaches 3NT. Then we lose one-half matchpoint to half the tables, for an average cost of one-quarter matchpoint per table.

Suppose we defend passively and are wrong. This means that South has the weaker hand, which makes 3NT a very unlikely contract at most other tables. If we fail to set 3NT when we could have we will lose one-half matchpoint to other tables in 3NT and a full matchpoint to tables in any other reasonable

324

contract. Consequently, our average cost per table will be almost one full matchpoint. In other words, failing to set a super-thin game which could have been beaten and will not be bid at other tables is a full top to bottom swing. Therefore we are giving about four to one matchpoint odds if we don't try for the set, so we would have to be very sure that South wouldn't have bid 3NT on the hand with the king of hearts before we take this position.

The moral of this hand is: When there is a reasonable lie of the cards which allows the contract to be set and the contract is not a normal one if that lie of the cards exists, then you should play for the set. If you fail to defeat such a contract it will be very costly, while if you give away an overtrick or two it might not cost very much particularly if the contract is not normal. This approach must not be overdone. There must be a reasonable chance for the set, not an extremely unlikely one. On the previous hand if North had owned the jack of spades, then South would have to have a fourteen-count for the hand to be defeated. This would not be reasonable at all if the opponents were playing strong notrumps, so it would be better to go passive and hold in the overtricks rather than play for the impossible.

When you know you are defending against a normal contract, it is a different story altogether. Now giving up an overtrick is just as expensive as letting declarer make the contract, so you should simply make the play which maximizes your probable tricks.

NORTH
♠ 4 3
♡ A Q 8 5
♢ A Q J 2
♣ 10 9 5

EAST
♠ A 8 5 2
♡ 7 2
♢ 7 5 4 3
♣ A K 2

N-S vulnerable.

NORTH	EAST	SOUTH	WEST
—	—	1 ♡	Pass
3 NT*	Pass	4 ♡	Pass
Pass	Pass		

*forcing raise

Opening Lead: Queen of spades

It is clearly right to win and shift to clubs, but which club? If partner has the queen of clubs it doesn't matter, but if declarer has it the choice will make a difference. At IMPs there is no problem. The defense must take three club tricks if the hand is to be defeated, so East should shift to a low club and hope that declarer has Qxx, with which he will certainly misguess. At matchpoints it is another story. The contract is normal, and the opening lead is probably fairly standard. Leading a low club gains only when declarer has specifically Qxx or Qxxx of clubs. It loses whenever declarer has the jack of clubs with the queen or when he holds a singleton or doubleton queen (assuming he remembers to put up the queen), for declarer will then score at least one extra trick by discarding clubs on dummy's diamonds. There are more holdings on which the low club play loses, so East should just cash his AK of clubs even though this is not his best play to set the contract. On this hand the overtrick is at least as important as the setting trick, perhaps even more so. The full hand is:

NORTH
♠ 4 3
♡ A Q 8 5
♢ A Q J 2
♣ 10 9 5

WEST
♠ Q J 7 6
♡ 10 9
♢ 10 9 8
♣ 8 7 4 3

EAST
♠ A 8 5 2
♡ 7 2
♢ 7 5 4 3
♣ A K 2

SOUTH
♠ K 10 9
♡ K J 6 4 3
♢ K 6
♣ Q J 6

Your partner did well to lead a spade. At many other tables a red suit was led, and declarer easily took eleven tricks by pitching two clubs on dummy's diamonds. If you try for the set declarer will make twelve tricks instead of ten, so you will lose a full matchpoint to tables which didn't get a spade lead. Even if going for the set had worked it would have gained one-half matchpoint only against other tables where a spade was led, since simply cashing out beats tables receiving a red suit lead.

As with declarer play, the most difficult defensive problems at matchpoints occur when there are possible alternative contracts which are in competition with the one you are defending. These can be very hard to analyze, but the effort must be made. If you can determine the likely fate of the alternative contract, this will help you decide on your trick-taking goal.

NORTH
- ♠ 10 4 3
- ♡ A Q 10 7 2
- ◇ A Q 10
- ♣ 6 3

EAST
- ♠ A J 9 5
- ♡ 9 8
- ◇ 9 4 3 2
- ♣ A 5 2

Both vulnerable.

NORTH	EAST	SOUTH	WEST
—	—	1 ◇	Pass
1 ♡	Pass	2 ♡	Pass
2 ♠	Pass	3 ◇	Pass
3 ♡	Pass	3 NT	Pass
Pass	Pass		

Opening Lead: Queen of clubs

North has taken quite a position by choosing 3NT rather than 4♡. It is apparent that many other pairs will play 4♡, and you are in competition with those defending the heart game. On the bidding South seems to have five diamonds and three hearts, and the red suits will certainly run once declarer gets in. So how should you defend after winning the ace of clubs at trick one?

The way to beat 3NT, of course, is to shift to the jack of spades, playing declarer for ♠Qxx, ♡KJx, ◇KJxxx, ♣Kx. This is by no means an unreasonable construction, and the jack of spades shift would certainly be correct at IMPs. The problem with the play is that it gives declarer his twelfth trick whenever he holds the king of spades, assuming he has five diamonds. A club return doesn't set up anything for declarer, but will be wrong when partner holds the king of spades. How about ace and a spade? This gives up on some legitimate chances of beating the hand, but at least allows us to score three tricks when West holds the king of spades and two tricks when he doesn't. Let's look at some hands declarer might hold and see what is likely to happen in 4♡. Keep in mind that East is not likely to lay down an ace against 4♡, since he doesn't know about the diamond threat.

a. ♠Qxx, ♡KJx, ◇KJ10xx, ♣Kx. 4♡ will make five after a red suit lead (declarer pitches two spades on the diamonds and eventually leads to the king of clubs). The jack of spades is the killing shift, but ace and a spade, holding declarer to four, will probably get a good board. A club continuation, allowing declarer to make five, would be very costly.

b. ♠Kxx, ♡KJx, ◇KJ10xx, ♣Kx. Again, 4♡ will make five. Either the ace of spades or a club continuation holds declarer to five, while the jack of spades shift allows six to make. Whatever we do will probably result in a bad score, but the jack of spades shift is worst of all.

c. ♠KQx, ♡Jxx, ◇KJ10xx, ♣Kx. Now 4♡ will make six on a red suit lead (declarer can pitch his losing clubs and establish two spade tricks). This time the jack of spades shift is really bad, as it costs a full matchpoint to most tables in 4♡.

This analysis shows that ace and a spade, while never correct in an absolute sense, is the only play which is not very costly when it is wrong, so it is the best defense. It may seem odd to take this sort of a compromise, but it is the best play.

On the same hand, suppose East had diamonds stopped, giving him ♠AJ95, ♡98, ◇J982, ♣A52. Now the club continuation is best, for this will hold declarer to nine tricks (he won't duck since he has no reason to expect the diamonds not to split). If West chooses instead to attack spades it is now correct to lead the jack of spades, going for the set, since declarer can't run the rest of the tricks even if the play doesn't work. Ace and a spade now becomes the worst of the three possible plays.

NORTH
- ♠ 6 2
- ♡ Q 10 9 6 5 3
- ◇ 4
- ♣ Q 8 5 3

WEST
- ♠ A J 5
- ♡ A 8 4
- ◇ A Q 10 8 5
- ♣ 7 4

None vulnerable.

NORTH	EAST	SOUTH	WEST
—	—	1 ♠	1 NT
2 ♡	Double	2 ♠	Pass
Pass	Double	Pass	Pass
Pass			

Opening Lead: Seven of clubs

Dummy wins the opening lead with the queen of clubs, partner playing the jack. A diamond is led from dummy, partner plays the two, declarer the jack, and you win the queen. What now?

The bidding and the carding on the first two tricks indicate that declarer's distribution is 6-0-4-3. It is clear to shift to a trump, for any trump tricks that may be lost by the trump shift will come back in the diamond suit. But which trump should West shift to? If East has Qx of trumps, then ace and a trump is necessary to defeat the contract; the defense would score two spade tricks and four diamond tricks. A low trump shift would allow the contract to be made, for declarer would score four trump winners in his hand, a ruff in dummy, and three club tricks. On the other hand, if East has Kx of trumps a low trump shift will defeat the contract two tricks, while ace and a trump will allow declarer to escape for down one. Declarer apparently has either ♠K109xxx, ♡—, ◇KJxx, ♣AKx or ♠Q109xxx, ♡—, ◇KJxx, ♣AKx.

330

Let's see what is likely to happen at other tables. Other N-S pairs may not be so frisky or other E-W pairs may pass up the penalty and play a notrump game or partial. It is clear that the cards lie very favorably for E-W, and they can take at least two spades, three hearts, and four diamonds at notrump. You can't compete with the tables at which 3NT is bid, since they will outscore you whatever you do. To beat tables which stop at a notrump part-score it is essential to collect + 300, for + 100 will lose to them anyway. Consequently you should play a low spade, even though this risks allowing declarer to make 2♠ doubled when you had a sure set. The difference in matchpoints between + 100 and + 300 on this hand figures to be far greater than the difference between + 100 and − 470.

Vulnerability is the key to hands such as this one. If it had been E-W vul., a low spade would be correct for the same reasons, but with both vul., ace and a spade would be clear-cut. Again you can't compete against the 3NT bidders, and your + 200 will outscore the part-score bidders, so you play for the set. At this vulnerability there is little difference between + 200 and + 500. If it were N-S vul., you could have a serious problem. Failing to collect + 500 when available will cost a full matchpoint to tables at which 3NT is bid, for their + 400 now beats your + 200 instead of losing to your + 500. On the other hand, leading a low spade and being wrong costs a full matchpoint to tables which stop in a part-score, for you now get − 670 instead of + 200 while they are scoring + 150. This is a close decision, but it is probably correct to play for the sure set. Even if East has the Kx of spades it will only give him eight points, so many E-W pairs won't bid the game anyway. Therefore, being wrong will not lose to every table. On the other hand, if East has Qx of spades he has only seven points, so game doesn't figure to be bid very often. If this is the case, failing to beat the contract will be almost a complete top to bottom swing.

NORTH
♠ K 9
♡ J 10 6 5
◇ A 10 9
♣ J 5 3 2

WEST
♠ A Q J 10 8 5 2
♡ K
◇ K J 6
♣ A Q

None vulnerable.

NORTH	EAST	SOUTH	WEST
Pass	Pass	3 ♡	4 ♠
5 ♡	Double	Pass	Pass
Pass			

Opening Lead: Ace of spades

You lead ace and a spade, everybody following, and dummy's jack of hearts rides to your stiff king. How do you exit?

So far, things have gone well. You have a chance of scoring +500 to beat your potential +420 at 4♠. If partner has both the king of clubs and the queen of diamonds it won't matter what you do, but if declarer has one of these cards a shift to the wrong minor will blow a trick. If declarer's hand is ♠xx, ♡AQ10xxxx, ◇Qx, ♣xx a rather neat defense is necessary to collect +500. You must shift to the queen of clubs, and partner must overtake and put a diamond through. This spectacular defense would occur to some players holding the West hand and they might try it, but the practical matchpoint player would reject it and shift to a diamond. The reason that the diamond shift is correct is that if declarer has the queen of diamonds you cannot make 4♠, for there would be no way to avoid losing one spade, one heart, and two diamonds against competent defense. Therefore, if the diamond shift costs a trick the 5♡ sacrifice is a phantom, and you will still get an excellent result for +300.

However, if declarer holds the king of clubs and partner the queen of diamonds then 4♠ will make, so it is important to get +500 if this is the case. The full hand:

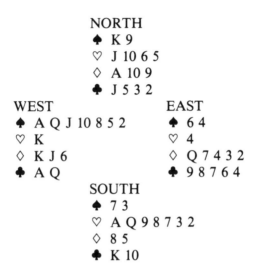

```
                    NORTH
                    ♠ K 9
                    ♡ J 10 6 5
                    ◊ A 10 9
                    ♣ J 5 3 2
       WEST                      EAST
       ♠ A Q J 10 8 5 2          ♠ 6 4
       ♡ K                       ♡ 4
       ◊ K J 6                   ◊ Q 7 4 3 2
       ♣ A Q                     ♣ 9 8 7 6 4
                    SOUTH
                    ♠ 7 3
                    ♡ A Q 9 8 7 3 2
                    ◊ 8 5
                    ♣ K 10
```

4♠ is cold, and the diamond shift collects the necessary +500. The "brilliant" queen of clubs shift would actually allow declarer to get out for down one, for he not only loses only one club trick but also gets to pitch his losing diamond on dummy's jack of clubs. This would be catastrophic, for you would score only +100, losing not only to the game bidders but to the part-score bidders as well. It would be a complete top to bottom swing.

Incidentally, what about declarer's line of play—finessing the heart instead of playing for the split? It didn't work on this hand, but it is the correct play. Declarer has no reason to think that you don't have a club loser in 4♠, so from his point of view if the hearts are one-one his 5♡ save is likely to be a phantom. Consequently, he played the hand on the assumption that 4♠ would make, and the most likely way for this to happen is for hearts to be two-zero.

NORTH
♠ 9 8 7
♡ K 5
◇ A K Q 10
♣ 7 5 4 2

WEST
♠ K Q 5
♡ Q J 10 8
◇ J 5 2
♣ A J 9

E-W vulnerable.

NORTH	EAST	SOUTH	WEST
—	—	1 ♠	Pass
2 ◇	Pass	2 ♠	Pass
3 ♠	Pass	Pass	Pass

Opening Lead: Queen of hearts

Dummy wins the king of hearts, and passes the nine of spades to your queen. If declarer happens to have Qxx of clubs, a low club shift will defeat 3 ♠. This would give declarer ♠AJ10xx, ♡Ax, ◇xxx, ♣Qxx, a minimal opening bid. In the more likely case where South holds the king of clubs, a club shift may give away an overtrick. What is likely to be happening at other tables? At your table North took a very conservative position. Most other Norths will drive to game opposite an opening 1 ♠ bid. If game makes it won't matter what you do, for you will beat these tables anyway. However, if 4 ♠ is down one, it is important to try to tie this result by defeating 3 ♠. Overtricks won't matter, but beating 3 ♠, a trick will turn a loss into a tie against 4 ♠ down one, so West should go for the set by under-leading his ace of clubs. A further consideration is that if South has the super-light hand not all Souths will open. If South passes N-S are likely to be in 2 ♠ for +110, so there will be a big difference between +50 and −140 for E-W.

REVIEW PROBLEMS

1. E-W vul., West holds: ♠ J5, ♡ 106, ◊ 1098, ♣ K108764

NORTH	EAST	SOUTH	WEST
—	Pass	1 NT	Pass
3 NT	Pass	Pass	Pass

Opening lead?

2. N-S vul., West holds: ♠ 9653, ♡ 842, ◊ QJ7, ♣ AQ8

NORTH	EAST	SOUTH	WEST
—	—	1 ♡	Pass
1 ♠	Pass	3 ♡	Pass
3 ♠	Pass	4 ♡	Pass
Pass	Pass		

Opening lead?

3. Both vul., West holds: ♠ J107, ♡ 6432, ◊ 965, ♣ KJ6

NORTH	EAST	SOUTH	WEST
—	—	1 ◊	Pass
1 ♡	Pass	1 NT	Pass
3 ◊	Pass	4 ◊	Pass
5 ◊	Pass	Pass	Pass

Opening lead?

4. Both vul., West holds: ♠Q52, ♡QJ83, ◊QJ97, ♣104

NORTH	EAST	SOUTH	WEST
—	—	1 ♣	Pass
1 ♡	Pass	1 ♠	Pass
1 NT	Pass	2 ♡	Pass
2 ♠	Pass	Pass	Pass

Opening lead?

5.

NORTH
♠ K 10 9 6 4
♡ K Q J 9
◊ 8 5 4
♣ A

SOUTH
♠ Q 5 3
♡ A 5 2
◊ A Q 10
♣ K 7 6 5

None vulnerable.

NORTH	EAST	SOUTH	WEST
1 ♠	Pass	2 NT	Pass
3 ♡	Pass	3 ♠	Pass
3 NT	Pass	Pass	Pass

Opening Lead: Three of diamonds

The three of diamonds lead goes to East's king and South's ace. Plan the play.

6.   NORTH
                            ♠ J 7
                            ♡ 3 2
                            ◇ A K 10 9 8 5 4
                            ♣ 6 3

                            SOUTH
                            ♠ A 10 6 4
                            ♡ A Q 10 5
                            ◇ 6 3
                            ♣ A K 7

N-S vulnerable

NORTH	EAST	SOUTH	WEST
—	—	1 NT	Pass
3 NT	Pass	Pass	Pass

Opening Lead: Two of clubs

West leads the two of clubs, and East plays the queen. Plan the play.

7.   NORTH
                            ♠ A J 10
                            ♡ A K J 5 4
                            ◇ 7 3 2
                            ♣ Q 3

                            SOUTH
                            ♠ 8 7
                            ♡ 8 6
                            ◇ A K 10
                            ♣ K J 10 9 8 6

Both vulnerable.

NORTH	EAST	SOUTH	WEST
—	—	1 ♣	Pass
1 ♡	Pass	2 ♣	Pass
2 ♠	Pass	2 NT	Pass
3 ♣	Pass	3 ◊	Pass
4 NT	Pass	5 ◊	Pass
6 ♣	Pass	Pass	Pass

Opening Lead: Two of spades

West leads the two of spades. Plan the play.

8.

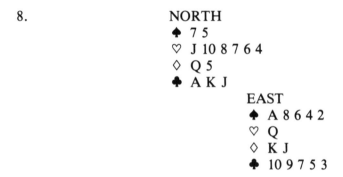

NORTH
♠ 7 5
♡ J 10 8 7 6 4
◊ Q 5
♣ A K J

EAST
♠ A 8 6 4 2
♡ Q
◊ K J
♣ 10 9 7 5 3

E-W vulnerable.

NORTH	EAST	SOUTH	WEST
—	—	1 ♡	Pass
4 ♡	Pass	Pass	Pass

Opening Lead: Queen of spades

West leads the queen of spades, and you win the ace as declarer follows small. How do you continue?

9.

NORTH
♠ K 8 7 2
♡ K 5
◇ Q J 8 2
♣ 9 4 3

WEST
♠ A Q
♡ Q J 7 6 3
◇ 7 4
♣ A J 6 5

E-W vulnerable.

NORTH	EAST	SOUTH	WEST
—	—	1 ♠	Pass
3 ♠*	Pass	4 ♠	Pass
Pass	Pass		

*limit raise

Opening Lead: Queen of hearts

Declarer wins your queen of hearts lead in his hand with the ace, and leads the jack of spades to your ace. Plan the defense.

10.

	NORTH	
	♠ A Q J	
	♡ K Q J 9 5 4 3	
	◊ K	
	♣ K 7	

WEST
♠ 7 6 5 4
♡ A
◊ Q J 9 5
♣ A 8 6 3

E-W vulnerable.

NORTH	EAST	SOUTH	WEST
1 ♡	Pass	1 NT	Pass
3 ♡	Pass	3 NT	Pass
Pass	Pass		

Opening Lead: Queen of diamonds

Partner plays the two of diamonds on the opening lead as dummy's king wins. Declarer leads a low heart to the eight-spot, partner playing the two. What now?

SOLUTIONS

1. Ten of diamonds. This is not an attempt to defeat the contract by hitting partner's suit; it is merely the safest lead on a hand on which you have little chance of a set. The best lead to beat 3NT is a club, but the bidding indicates likely minor suit length in dummy since North didn't use Stayman, so the club lead is more likely to cost a trick than to gain one. Partner doesn't figure to have substantial strength in either major since he passed as dealer, so the safest lead is best.

2. Ace of clubs. The bidding and your major suit holdings indicate that both major suits may run, so this lead is best. Partner may have the king of clubs, and even if he doesn't the cash may save an overtrick.

3. Six of clubs. If the opponents have clubs stopped they will do well in notrump at other tables, so you assume that they do not have club strength. Partner can't have a good spade suit since he failed to overcall.

4. Two of spades. The opponents apparently are playing a four-three fit, and their extra trick, if any, over notrump figures to come from ruffs since you have the red suits bottled up. Consequently, it is correct to lead a trump, even away from the queen.

5. Most of the other tables figure to be in 4 ♠. This will make eleven or twelve tricks depending on the spade suit. You can make the same number of tricks as they do if you play the spades the same way, so lead a heart to dummy and play a spade to the queen, planning to finesse for the jack. If the finesse loses and East returns a diamond you must go up and hope that East started with AJx of spades and a doubleton diamond, in which case you will take the same eleven tricks as the spade players. Suppose East had played the jack of diamonds at trick one. Now you would know that the spade players could make at most eleven tricks, since the diamond finesse would lose for

them, so if you could guarantee eleven tricks you would beat them even if you were to lose an extra spade trick. Therefore, you would go to dummy with a heart and ride the ten of spades. Even if this lost to West's jack you would be assured of eleven tricks and a very good board, while if East had the jack of spades you have a super-top. It would be important not to lose the first spade trick to East, for a diamond return would put your eleven tricks in jeopardy.

6. This is a normal contract, and the lead is moderately unfavorable. You can guarantee ten tricks by ducking a diamond, but this does not figure to be a very good result. The best line is to go whole hog by winning the opening lead, playing a diamond to the ace, heart to the ten, and hoping for a two-two diamond split (but finessing if East drops an honor on the first round). This will produce thirteen tricks if everything works, and will get the maximum out of the hand provided the diamond suit comes in. If the diamonds don't behave—unlucky. Had you gotten a more favorable lead such as a heart away from the KJ, you would be more inclined to duck a round of diamonds so as to not blow your good start.

7. Partner obviously got carried away. The rest of the room figures to be in 3NT which is cold, so you must go all out to make 6♣ regardless of possible extra undertricks. It is inconceivable that West would underlead a KQ against a slam, so you must go up ace of spades, play a diamond to the ten, heart to the jack and cash the AK of hearts before playing trumps. If everything works it is your lucky day; if not, you can't get worse than a bottom.

8. 4♡ can be beaten by leading the king of diamonds if West has the ace of diamonds and South has a minimum opening such as ♠Kxx, ♡AKxxx, ◊xxx, ♣Qx. It is far more likely that South has the ace of diamonds, in which case the diamond shift will cost a trick. Since everybody figures to get to 4♡, it is better to exit passively and accept −450.

9. If East has the king of clubs, 4♠ may be beaten by a low

club shift. This would leave South with a minimum opener such as ♠ J109xx, ♡ Ax, ◊ AKx, ♣ Qxx, which is not out of the question. Is it worth risking a possible overtrick to play for the set? I think it is. Not many Norths will consider their hand worth more than a 2 ♠ bid, which means that game will not be bid at many tables. Consequently, it is worth going all out for the set, since it is a reasonable possibility and you will be headed for a bad result if they make the contract with or without overtricks. A further consideration is that a club shift probably won't cost a trick if South has both the king and queen of clubs.

10. Partner's two of diamonds warns you away from a diamond continuation, but should you shift to a club or a spade? If partner has the king of spades it makes little difference what you do. Declarer has ten tricks if you shift to a spade, and even if you play a club into declarer's strong club holding you can win the club return and shift to a spade, tangling declarer's entries sufficiently so that he can't take the rest of the tricks. What if declarer owns the king of spades? Now a low club return will hold declarer to four if he has the jack of clubs and misguesses, but allows him to make six if anything else happens. The pairs in the more normal 4 ♡ contract will always make five if South has the king of spades. Consequently, there is little difference between − 460 and − 490, but a great difference between − 430 and − 460, so the risky underlead is correct even though it will be wrong more often than not.

50 HIGHLY-RECOMMENDED TITLES

**CALL TOLL FREE 1-800-274-2221
IN THE U.S. & CANADA TO ORDER ANY OF
THEM OR TO REQUEST OUR
FULL-COLOR 64 PAGE CATALOG OF
ALL BRIDGE BOOKS IN PRINT,
SUPPLIES AND GIFTS.**

FOR BEGINNERS
#0300 Future Champions' Bridge Series 9.95
#2130 Kantar-Introduction to Declarer's Play 10.00
#2135 Kantar-Introduction to Defender's Play 10.00
#0101 Stewart-Baron-The Bridge Book 1 .... 9.95
#1121 Silverman-Elementary Bridge
       Five Card Major Student Text 4.95
#0660 Penick-Beginning Bridge Complete 9.95
#0661 Penick-Beginning Bridge Quizzes 6.95
#3230 Lampert-Fun Way to Serious Bridge 10.00

FOR ADVANCED PLAYERS
#2250 Reese-Master Play 5.95
#1420 Klinger-Modern Losing Trick Count 14.95
#2240 Love-Bridge Squeezes Complete 7.95
#0103 Stewart-Baron-The Bridge Book 3 .... 9.95
#0740 Woolsey-Matchpoints 14.95
#0741 Woolsey-Partnership Defense 12.95
#1702 Bergen-Competitive Auctions 9.95
#0636 Lawrence-Falsecards 9.95

BIDDING — 2 OVER 1 GAME FORCE
#4750 Bruno & Hardy-Two-Over-One Game Force:
       An Introduction 9.95
#1750 Hardy-Two-Over-One Game Force 14.95
#1790 Lawrence-Workbook on the Two Over One System 11.95
#4525 Lawrence-Bidding Quizzes Book 1 .... 13.95

Prices subject to change without notice.

DEFENSE
#0520 Blackwood-Complete Book of Opening Leads 17.95
#3030 Ewen-Opening Leads 15.95
#0104 Stewart-Baron-The Bridge Book 4 .... 7.95
#0631 Lawrence-Dynamic Defense 11.95
#1200 Woolsey-Modern Defensive Signalling 4.95

FOR   INTERMEDIATE   PLAYERS
#2120 Kantar-Complete Defensive Bridge 20.00
#3015 Root-Commonsense Bidding 15.00
#0630 Lawrence-Card Combinations 12.95
#0102 Stewart-Baron-The Bridge Book 2 .... 9.95
#1122 Silverman-Intermediate Bridge Five
      Card Major Student Text 4.95
#0575 Lampert-The Fun Way to Advanced Bridge 11.95
#0633 Lawrence-How to Read Your Opponents' Cards 11.95
#3672 Truscott-Bid Better, Play Better 12.95
#1765 Lawrence-Judgment at Bridge 9.95

PLAY OF THE HAND
#2150 Kantar-Test your Bridge Play, Vol. 1 .... 10.00
#3675 Watson-Watson's Classic Book on
      the Play of the Hand 15.00
#1932 Mollo-Gardener-Card Play Technique 12.95
#3009 Root-How to Play a Bridge Hand 15.00
#1124 Silverman-Play of the Hand as
      Declarer and Defender 4.95
#2175 Truscott-Winning Declarer Play 10.00
#3803 Sydnor-Bridge Made Easy Book 3 .... 8.00

CONVENTIONS
#2115 Kantar-Bridge Conventions 10.00
#0610 Kearse-Bridge Conventions Complete 29.95
#3011 Root-Pavlicek-Modern Bridge Conventions 15.00
#0240 Championship Bridge Series (All 36) 25.95

DUPLICATE STRATEGY
#1600 Klinger-50 Winning Duplicate Tips 12.95
#2260 Sheinwold-Duplicate Bridge 4.95

FOR ALL PLAYERS
#3889 Darvas & de V. Hart-Right Through The Pack 14.95
#0790 Simon: Why You Lose at Bridge 11.95
#4850 Encyclopedia of Bridge, Official (ACBL) 39.95

Andersen THE LEBENSOHL CONVENTION COMPLETE .... $ 6.95
Baron THE BRIDGE PLAYER'S DICTIONARY $19.95
Bergen BETTER BIDDING WITH BERGEN,
      Vol. I, Uncontested Auctions $11.95
Bergen BETTER BIDDING WITH BERGEN,
      Vol. II, Competitive Auctions .... $ 9.95
Blackwood COMPLETE BOOK OF OPENING LEADS $17.95
Blackwood-Hanson PLAY FUNDAMENTALS .... $ 6.95
Boeder THINKING ABOUT IMPS $12.95
Bruno-Hardy 2 OVER 1 GAME FORCE: AN INTRODUCTION .... $ 9.95
Darvas & De V. Hart RIGHT THROUGH THE PACK $14.95
DeSerpa THE MEXICAN CONTRACT .... $ 5.95
Eber & Freeman HAVE I GOT A STORY FOR YOU .... $ 7.95
Feldheim FIVE CARD MAJOR BIDDING IN
      CONTRACT BRIDGE $12.95
Flannery THE FLANNERY 2 DIAMOND OPENING .... $ 7.95
Goldman ACES SCIENTIFIC .... $ 9.95
Goldman WINNERS AND LOSERS AT THE
      BRIDGE TABLE .... $ 3.95
Groner DUPLICATE BRIDGE DIRECTION $14.95
Hardy
      COMPETITIVE BIDDING WITH 2-SUITED HANDS .... $ 9.95
      TWO-OVER-ONE GAME FORCE $14.95
      TWO-OVER-ONE GAME FORCE QUIZ BOOK $11.95
Harris BRIDGE DIRECTOR'S COMPANION (3rd Edition) $19.95
Kay COMPLETE BOOK OF DUPLICATE BRIDGE $14.95
Kearse BRIDGE CONVENTIONS COMPLETE $29.95
Kelsey THE TRICKY GAME $11.95
Lampert THE FUN WAY TO ADVANCED BRIDGE $11.95
Lawrence
      CARD COMBINATIONS $12.95
      COMPLETE BOOK ON BALANCING $11.95
      COMPLETE BOOK ON OVERCALLS $11.95
      DYNAMIC DEFENSE $11.95
      FALSECARDS .... $ 9.95
      HAND EVALUATION $11.95
      HOW TO READ YOUR OPPONENTS' CARDS $11.95
      JUDGMENT AT BRIDGE .... $ 9.95
      PARTNERSHIP UNDERSTANDINGS .... $ 5.95
      PLAY BRIDGE WITH MIKE LAWRENCE $11.95
      PLAY SWISS TEAMS WITH MIKE LAWRENCE .... $ 9.95
      WORKBOOK ON THE TWO OVER ONE SYSTEM $11.95

Lawrence & Hanson WINNING BRIDGE INTANGIBLES .... $ 4.95
Lipkin INVITATION TO ANNIHILATION .... $ 8.95
Michaels & Cohen 4-3-2-1 MANUAL .... $ 4.95
Penick BEGINNING BRIDGE COMPLETE .... $ 9.95
Penick BEGINNING BRIDGE QUIZZES .... $ 6.95
Robinson WASHINGTON STANDARD $19.95
Rosenkranz
       BRIDGE: THE BIDDER'S GAME $12.95
       TIPS FOR TOPS .... $ 9.95
       MORE TIPS FOR TOPS .... $ 9.95
       TRUMP LEADS .... $ 7.95
       OUR MAN GODFREY $10.95
Rosenkranz & Alder BID TO WIN, PLAY FOR PLEASURE $11.95
Rosenkranz & Truscott BIDDING ON TARGET $10.95
Silverman
       ELEMENTARY BRIDGE FIVE CARD MAJOR STUDENT TEXT .... $ 4.95
       INTERMEDIATE BRIDGE FIVE CARD MAJOR STUDENT TEXT .... $ 4.95
       ADVANCED & DUPLICATE BRIDGE STUDENT TEXT .... $ 4.95
       PLAY OF THE HAND AS DECLARER
         & DEFENDER STUDENT TEXT .... $ 4.95
Simon
       CUT FOR PARTNERS .... $ 9.95
       WHY YOU LOSE AT BRIDGE $11.95
Stewart & Baron
       THE BRIDGE BOOK, Vol. 1, Beginning .... $ 9.95
       THE BRIDGE BOOK, Vol. 2, Intermediate .... $ 9.95
       THE BRIDGE BOOK, Vol. 3, Advanced .... $ 9.95
       THE BRIDGE BOOK, Vol. 4, Defense .... $ 7.95
Truscott BID BETTER, PLAY BETTER $12.95
Von Elsner
       EVERYTHING'S JAKE WITH ME .... $ 5.95
       THE BEST OF JAKE WINKMAN .... $ 5.95
Wei PRECISION BIDDING SYSTEM .... $ 7.95
Woolsey
       MATCHPOINTS $14.95
       MODERN DEFENSIVE SIGNALLING .... $ 4.95
       PARTNERSHIP DEFENSE $12.95
World Bridge Federation APPEALS COMMITTEE DECISIONS
       from the 1994 NEC WORLD CHAMPIONSHIPS .... $ 9.95